The Best Possible Way to Live:
A Journey Through God's Word

Marianne J. Grano

Parson's Porch Books
www.parsonsporchbooks.com

The Best Possible Way to Live: A Journey Through God's Word
ISBN: Softcover 978-1-949888-70-6
Copyright © 2019 by Marianne J. Grano

All rights reserved. No part of this book may be reproduced or transmitted in any form or by any means, electronic or mechanical, including photocopying, recording, or by any information storage and retrieval system, without permission in writing from the publisher.

The Best Possible Way to Live

Contents

Introduction 9
Week One: Who and Why 11
   Genesis 1
Week Two: God Is Calling 16
   Genesis 12
Week Three: Committed 21
   Genesis 22
Week Four: Miracles Aren't Easy 25
   Exodus 12
Week Five: In the Wilderness 30
   Exodus 17
Week Six: God's Backside 34
   Exodus 33
Week Seven: The Best Way to Live 38
   Leviticus 23
Week Eight: Fight Snakes with…Snakes? 44
   Numbers 21
Week Nine: Because I Said So 49
   Deuteronomy 11
Week Ten: God Wins 54
   Joshua 6
Week Eleven: Mighty Warrior 58
   Judges 6
Week Twelve: Seeds in Winter 62
   Ruth 4
Week Thirteen: Leadership 67
   1 Samuel 16
Week Fourteen: Courage 73
   2 Samuel 12
Week Fifteen: Jerusalem 77
   1 Kings 5:1-13
Week Sixteen: Resurrection 82
   2 Kings
Week Seventeen: Dynasty 85
   1 Chronicles
Week Eighteen: Posers 92
   2 Chronicles

Week Nineteen: Rebuilding 97
   Nehemiah 8
Week Twenty: Woman of Wisdom 101
   Esther 4
Week Twenty-one: A Weathered Faith 105
   Job 2
Week Twenty-two: Where is God in Suffering? 109
   Job 19
Week Twenty-three: Advocate 112
   Job 38
Week Twenty-four: Before and After 115
   Psalm 30
Week Twenty-five: What is Justice? 120
   Psalm 72
Week Twenty-six: Orientation 125
   Psalm 119
Week Twenty-seven: Pledge 129
   Psalm 146
Week Twenty-eight: Cricket's the Name 132
   Proverbs 1
Week Twenty-nine: Hobbits, Dogs, and the Meaning of Time 135
   Ecclesiastes 3
Week Thirty: Who You Gonna Call? 141
   Isaiah 7
Week Thirty-one: The Suffering Servant 145
   Isaiah 53
Week Thirty-two: Lighthouse 149
   Isaiah 60
Week Thirty-three: Written On Your Heart 152
   Jeremiah 31
Week Thirty-four: A Strange God 156
   Ezekiel 1
Week Thirty-five: The Good Shepherd and Good Sheep 161
   Ezekiel 34
Week Thirty-six: Kings of Industry 165
   Daniel 7
Week Thirty-seven: Brokenhearted God 168
   Hosea 11
Week Thirty-eight: Ice Princess 172
   Obadiah

Week Thirty-nine: Glory 176
    Haggai
Week Forty: Company's Coming.. 180
    Malachi
Week Forty-one: God Gives Handouts... 184
    Matthew 5
Week Forty-two: Jump 188
    Mark 9
Week Forty-three: Finding Nemo 192
    Luke 15
Week Forty-four: Born Again 196
    John 3
Week Forty-five: Church Potluck 201
    Acts 2
Week Forty-six: Have it Your Way.. 206
    Acts 17
Week Forty-seven: Attitude of Gratitude.. 211
    Romans 5
Week Forty-eight: Harmony in The Church.. 216
    1 Corinthians 12
Week Forty-nine: Garbage... 220
    Philippians 4
Week Fifty: A Man of Business... 224
    2 Timothy 2
Week Fifty-one: Entertaining Angels... 229
    Hebrews 12
Week Fifty-two: Wrapped.. 232
    Revelation 22
In Gratitude.. 235

Bible Reading Schedule... 237

Introduction

"How sweet your words taste to me; they are sweeter than honey."
Psalm 119:103

If the average preacher cited Hezekiah 3:16 in a sermon, the average churchgoer wouldn't blink an eye. The Bible is still the world's best-selling book, but few people have actually bothered to read it. Even those who consider themselves Bible-literate are often surprised to discover new truths from Scripture.

Reading through the Bible in a year is highly valuable for the Christian life. Spending fifteen to twenty minutes in dedicated Bible study daily has been shown to have a greater impact on spiritual growth than any other factor. Seriously studying the Bible gives the Christian greater knowledge about what the Bible says (and doesn't say), leads the Christian to ask difficult questions about the nature of God and this life, and helps the Christian to apply the teachings of Scripture to the world around him or her.

For a church, reading through the Bible in a year together is even more valuable. The congregation comes together in a project. Members encourage one another in their commitment. The church is encouraged to discuss and ask questions about what they have read in small groups and Bible studies.

For our church, reading the Bible in a year lead to spiritual renewal and personal growth for many of our members. Several of our members were inspired to start all over the next year, and the year after that! The weekly preaching helped the congregation to understand and digest what they had read.

What follows is a collection of messages based on a fifty-two week walk through the Bible. It is my earnest hope and fervent prayer that these messages will inspire you and your community to greater faith, hope, and love. These messages may be helpful for your devotional life, or if you are in a preaching ministry, you are encouraged to use them to begin your own sermon-writing process; so far as I know, no text exists to help preachers in the task of preaching through the Scriptures cover-to-cover in one year. The quotations are generally from the New Living Translation of the Bible, and the Bible reading plan is that used in the Daily Walk Bible (dailywalk.org).

May the Lord add his blessing to your reading of his Holy Word. "For the word of God is alive and powerful. It is sharper than the sharpest two-edged sword, cutting between soul and spirit, between joint and marrow. It exposes our innermost thoughts and desires." Hebrews 4:12.

Week One: Who and Why
Genesis 1

Our church has felt called this year to walk through the Bible, chapter by chapter, verse by verse, as one community. We believe that this journey will deepen our faith and trust in God personally and as a community. We believe that walking through the Bible together will offer us new challenges and opportunities. We believe that we will be changed.

I would like to caution you, and me, all of us as we begin this journey to take it seriously. To pray today for strength to begin and continue this journey. For those of you who have a daily devotional practice, this will be easier. For those that do not have a daily practice, I would like to encourage you to set a time and make this reading a part of your routine. Early in the morning is the best time for most people and helps to set the tone for the day. But for others of us who are barely able to function in the morning, let alone discover eternal truths, take a few minutes at lunch to do your reading and reflection.

I would like to encourage you as well to take some time with the reading. Ask yourself, what is God's message to me through this reading? Take notes! Ask questions! Email them to me and I will see what insight I can bring.

Like all journeys, there will be beautiful vistas and moments of breathtaking wonder—and there will be times when you have to wade your way through the mud. I believe Scripture is God-breathed, divinely inspired. But I will admit to you that God's message is harder to discern in certain passages of Leviticus and Obadiah than in, say, the Sermon on the Mount.

But don't give up! Whether you label it Satan, or your own sinful nature, there will be forces working very hard to get you to quit this journey. But every time your mind wanders, every time you get off track, that is an opportunity to return to God, to resist the temptation to quit and continue the journey. Because if you keep going, you will gain spiritually. If you take this journey seriously, when you look back at your journal entries, when you talk to your family and spouse, you will see personal growth, and spiritual growth. And I ask you: what could be more important than that? So we begin our walk through the Bible in the only place we can begin: in the beginning.

Why are we here? What is the meaning of life? These are the fundamental questions of human existence. Philosophers and thinkers have pondered these questions through the ages.

The Bible's answers are already here, clear and concise. In the first words of Genesis, hear two fundamental truths: first, who created the universe; and second, why.

The Bible starts out with the amazing words: "In the beginning God created the heavens and the earth." These words are amazing because, unlike all other creation stories, it is God who creates, and he creates "in the beginning;" before God creates, there is effectively nothing. "Creatio ex nihilo," or creating something out of nothing, is the technical term for this. And creating something out of nothing is the unique role of the God of the Bible.

In other Near Eastern creation stories from about this time, a god would generally take on a horrible monster, such as the Babylonian mythical beast Tiamat, and slay her. Then, the god would create the earth from the body of the dead beast.

Look how different this story is from the story of other gods: first, God is not warring with some beast or force in order to create. How does God create? Not through violence, but through communication. God speaks, and it happens. There is no battle to be won; God has unchallenged power to speak the world into being.

This God is fundamentally different from other gods in that he is almighty, all-powerful; he is the Creator of all things, from the beginning of time.

Look at another important difference: the earth is not created from the decaying body of an evil beast but through the life-giving purpose of a good God, and as such, the earth, the light, the waters, the dry land, the plants and animals are all by their nature good. We are not created evil.

In this way the Biblical story is different not only from the Near Eastern creation stories, but also from Greco-Roman philosophy which tended to view the body as dirty and bad, a corrupt vessel from which humanity needs to escape. God created everything that is, and over and over said, "it is good. It is good. It is good." Except when God creates humanity, the crown of creation, made in the image and likeness of God.

When God creates us, He says, "It is *very* good."

And from the goodness of creation, we learn more about who God is. God is the author and definer of Goodness. The world is good because God says so, and because God says so, it is good.

That is: goodness, the sense of truth and righteousness and justice and what love is meant to be, was baked into us, so to speak, from the very beginning, by God himself. We were created good, and we were created to know the good when we see it. That is how God made us, because God is Goodness, by His very nature.

So the first great question: Who created us? An all-powerful, perfectly good God.

And the second: Why?

This answer is not stated in a word or two; Genesis does not come right out and say something like "God created the humankind to glorify God and enjoy Him forever." And indeed, we can't completely fathom the billions of reasons God had for creating all that is. We can't peer into the mind of God. But Genesis gives us a glimpse.

Here's something you may not have noticed in this first chapter of Genesis: God is not just working on creation, God is working *with* creation.

God calls the waters to come into one place, and the land to sprout forth vegetation, and the skies to teem with birds. God calls the animals and people to be fruitful and multiply and help Him with the work of filling the earth. This, by the way, is the one commandment humanity has actually followed pretty well; with about eight billion people now on earth, we've been fruitful and multiplied. God calls the creation to work with him in creating!

God is not just working on creation but with creation. God is, from the beginning, in a relationship with his world. And did you catch how God is doing his work? Again, not by violence, but by communication. By relationship. And this relationship is most fully realized in the crown of God's creation; humankind, created in God's image and likeness.

The image of God in humankind is not clearly defined; it is clear that, like God, we are to have dominion, that is, power and authority, over creation. We are to rule over the earth and take care of it. A great power, and a great responsibility. Yet the image of God, I believe, is more than that. God created someone He could relate to and with.

This was not because God was lonely. Theologically there are two reasons God could not be lonely. First, God cannot be in need of anything. He is perfection in himself. Second, God already had community inside himself, in the Holy Trinity.

Yet although God was not lonely, God did desire us and pursue us in relationship. We were created for relationship with God, with humanity, and with creation. How do we know this? The litany of Genesis 1 is, it is good, it is good, it is very good. In Genesis 2:18, for the first time, God says something is *not* good. And what is it? "It is not good for the man to be alone."

Who created us? A good and sovereign God. Why were we created? For relationship. More specifically: for love. To glorify God and enjoy Him and His creation forever. These are the answers Genesis gives to the great questions of life. From these answers, everything else stems. These answers in Genesis best explain our nature, our desires, our thirst for love and goodness and our need to know we are not alone.

But they aren't everyone's answers. Our current societal creation story is that of evolution. I believe Christians can also believe in evolution. I think it's important that we as Christians study and understand science to better understand how God is working. We need people of faith to engage with science and add morality and perspective to the scientific conversation. As people of faith we should encourage scientists to keep an open mind. I'm a child of the nineties, and I think Phoebe said it best, on the show *Friends*:

PHOEBE: Uh-oh. It's Scary Scientist Man.

ROSS: Ok, Phoebe, this is it. In this briefcase I carry actual scientific facts. A briefcase of facts, if you will. Some of these fossils are over 200 million years old.

PHOEBE: Ok, look, before you even start, I'm not denying evolution, ok, I'm just saying that it's one of the possibilities.

ROSS: It's the only possibility, Phoebe.

PHOEBE: Ok, Ross, could you just open your mind like this much, ok? Wasn't there a time when the brightest minds in the world believed that the world was flat? And, up until like what, 50 years ago, you all thought the atom was the smallest thing, until you split it open, and this like, whole mess of crap came out. Now, are you telling me that you are so unbelievably arrogant that you can't admit that there's a teeny tiny possibility that you could be wrong about this?

ROSS: There might be, a teeny, tiny, possibility.

PHOEBE: I can't believe you caved.

ROSS: What?

PHOEBE: You just abandoned your whole belief system. I mean, before, I didn't agree with you, but at least I respected you. How, how, how are you going to go into work tomorrow? How, how are you going to face the other science guys? How, how are you going to face yourself? Oh! That was fun. So who's hungry?

Why do I like what Phoebe said? Because when evolution becomes a religion, people start to believe that we can and should manipulate evolution, help people evolve, get rid of genetically undesirable traits and, ultimately, genetically undesirable people. Science is giving us great advances in medicine and technology that are improving the quantity and quality of our physical lives. But science has no morality, and cannot answer the great questions that consume the human soul: Why am I here? Am I alone? Does anyone hear me? Does anyone care?

Science can't answer those questions, but Scripture can. And the answer is this: you are not alone.

There is a God who loves you, who made you with care, with a purpose and with power to do great things. He has been with you all along and he is with you still. He did not leave you alone, but surrounded you, as he did the very first person, with those to love and support you. And he made you very, very good. You are not a mistake. You were made in the image and likeness of God, and you are beautiful.

God spoke to us then. God speaks to us now. God created all that is by communication. And God is creating still. God is speaking still. He has a lot to say.

Come. Join us on the journey. Listen for what he will speak next.

In the name of the Father, and the Son, and the Holy Spirit, Amen.

Week Two: God Is Calling
Genesis 12

As we journey through Genesis, we have seen that God created us for relationship. God created by communication—by speaking—and he created us in his image and likeness; he created us good, and he created us in community, never to be alone.

But in these first chapters of Genesis, we see how humankind abuses that relationship. The disobedience of the snake, the woman, and the man ruptures the relationship between men and women, between people and the earth, between humanity and God, and because of this rupture, pain and death enter into the world.

Then with the first two siblings, brother murders brother, and Cain is forced into exile, forced into the state of aloneness that God has already told us is not good for humankind.

The story of Noah begins with the wickedness of humankind, who have intermarried with fallen angels or evil spirits; God breaks the relationship with humankind and with creation in a dramatic way—by destroying nearly everything that is, sparing only two of each kind of animal, and one faithful family.

Finally, in the Tower of Babel, humanity comes up with its own solution to fixing things—building a tower to heaven. My interpretation is this: God sees that humanity will be able to do big things, and so far, all the big things we've been doing on our own are big, bad things. So God scatters humankind and confuses language so that humans won't be able to do even more damage to the world. By Genesis 11, human language is confused, creation has been washed out, our relationships with God, one another, and creation, have all been twisted and abused; it's not looking good. God created us for relationship, and now all our relationships are very, very broken.

Why? Very simply, because God created us free. A relationship that is compelled is no relationship at all. If I took a gun and put it to my wonderful husband Dan's head and said, hey, let's go to the church, you're marrying me, well, he probably wouldn't still be around after ten years, let alone helping at church here today—because that's not a real relationship, that's not real love. Real love, real relationship, has to allow the possibility of rejection. And God consistently allows us to reject, to break the relationship. And that freedom is why things don't look at all like they did back in Genesis 1, when God pronounced, "it is very good."

We have broken the relationship that God intended. So here in Genesis 12, God, not humankind, initiates restoration. How will God work restoration of this relationship? Personally. Intimately. God's focus shifts from the whole earth to one man: Abraham.

God begins to work not on the earth, but on the particular, singular hearts of individual people. God enters the life of this man and his family, into their problems and struggles, and through them God intends to bless not only this little family, but all families of the earth.

I've noticed something since starting ministry: bulletin announcements, newsletter posts, advertisements on social media—they don't usually work. They don't get people, in general, to come to church, or to help with this event or that project, or to get more involved.

Do you know what works? A personal phone call. A text message. Going out for coffee. Not the general invitation to the whole world, but the personal invitation: I see you. I'm thinking of you. God is thinking of you. God has a calling that's just for you.

When we first hear about Abraham, he's no one special in particular; just another guy, tucked among the descendants of Shem, one of three sons of Terah. There's no hint that this guy is going to be the founder of the three great monotheistic religions. Abraham was not a particularly saintly man. He was a guy who, in more than one instance, passed off his wife as his sister! That act left Sarah vulnerable to rape! Abraham also failed to trust God, and entered into a relationship with Hagar, his wife's servant.

What is important about Abraham is not that he was perfect, but that Abraham was the guy who was willing to go out for coffee with God, so to speak. He was, first, listening to hear what God had to say—and second, he was willing to trust.

God's particular call on Abraham doesn't mean that God is no longer in communication with the rest of the world. Note that in Genesis 15:16, God says that he will not yet give over the Amorites' land, because they have not yet sinned so badly that God must take away their possessions. God has not given up on the nations of the world! Or consider God's relationship with Hagar, Sarah's servant, mother of Ishmael. Even though her relationship with Abraham was undertaken because Abraham distrusted God, God doesn't give up on Hagar or her child. Rather, God has called Abraham for this particular relationship so that the story begun in him will eventually bless all people of every nation.

One interesting thing about the call of Abraham is that God never identifies himself. God doesn't say, Hey Abram, God here. In many of the messages of the Old Testament and indeed the new, there is some kind of divine self-identification. To Moses God says, "I am the God of your father, the God of Abraham, the God of Isaac, and the God of Jacob." To Paul the Lord says, "I am Jesus, whom you are persecuting." But to Abram, who will later be called Abraham, the first word of the Lord is, Go. The imperative masculine singular of the Hebrew Halak, to go, or walk.

God's message starts with a command. And Abraham trusted God and answered the call. He picked up and left everything behind. He never saw all that God had promised. In his lifetime, Abraham was an itinerant herdsman; the only property he ever bought was a little piece of land to bury Sarah on. When he died, his only offspring by Sarah were Isaac, and the teenage boys Esau and Jacob. Not exactly a great nation. But he trusted in the promises of God. God said, go; Abraham listened, and Abraham went. You don't always have to know where you're going, if you know who you're following.

We the readers have no idea how Abraham heard this command, whether it was an actual voice that he heard or a sense of calling that deepened over time. How do we know that it was God calling at all and not the hallucination of an uneducated backwater herdsman who had spent too much time in the Mediterranean sun? As I have said before, you know God's call because it is trustworthy, tenacious, and tricky.

First, is the call trustworthy? God won't give you a command that goes against Scripture or against what you know is right. 1 John 4:1 says to test the spirits to see if they come from God. How do we do that? As Christians, we must look to the teaching and example of Jesus as our test: is this something Jesus would do? Is this an act of loving my neighbor as myself? These tests help us to determine whether we are being called by God or by a spirit of evil. Is the call trustworthy?

Second, is the call tenacious? Does God keep after us until we do what He wants? I have a rule that if three people tell me the same thing in the same day, that's probably not just people talking. If you have an idea you can't shake—that might be God, because he's not too shakable.

Third, is the call tricky? God doesn't tend to step in unless it's something really hard, something we don't want to do. God doesn't have to ask us to binge-watch Netflix, because, well, we're going to do that anyway. God calls us to do hard things, like leave our friends and family behind and go to Canaan, or build an ark, or fight the giants, or die on a cross.

I still don't understand why, exactly, I am in law school right now. For a long time, I resisted; but God kept closing other doors, and after a lot of prayer, and encouragement from others, I decided to apply. I just felt like I was called to move forward in this way, for a new adventure. I applied late, after the deadline. I took the LSAT late, after the deadline. I was physically late to the test; I got lost and had to run through Detroit, pregnant, to make it to the exam. I had no idea what I was doing. But then, in mid-July, I not only got accepted but got a full scholarship. I prayed about it and decided to go. But Dan and I had to be on the same page, and he felt it was too much while we were expecting a baby. So, I was about to reject the scholarship.

On the day the deadline approached, I went into the church as usual and went about my morning. On the other side of town, my husband Dan mentioned casually to his interns at work that I had been awarded a full scholarship but was turning it down. They were flabbergasted. Do you realize that's thousands of dollars of free education? Dan said, yeah, I do, but it's not a good time right now. But he began to mull over it in his head. Then, sitting at his desk, he got a call on his cell phone. It was from the dean of the law school. Mind you, the dean never called me, just Dan. He said "Dan, I'm calling to ask you to tell your wife to take the scholarship." Dan said we were really honored, but he was unsure how it would work with final exams and my due date. The dean assured him that we could figure out the exams if need be. Dan said he would think about it and went out to lunch.

At the restaurant, he saw a woman he hadn't seen in a long time. She walked up to his table; she was an associate dean from the law school, and she said, "Dan, you need to tell your wife to take the scholarship." So, Dan just gave up and said, "OK God, you win."

I took the offer. Two weeks later, after several years of looking for a church to pastor, I received a call from the church I now serve as pastor, Starr Presbyterian Church. It was to me, as though when I finally gave God what he wanted, God gave me what I wanted! I still don't know exactly where I'm going. But you know what? Even though I'm this naturally anxious person, I'm the kind of person who always wants a twenty-year plan, and this, none of this, was in the plan—even though I don't know where in the world I'm going— I know who I'm following. And that's enough for today.

Today, you will be bombarded by messages from hundreds of people in hundreds of ways: the inbox chain letters, the mailbox catalogs, the people from Colorado who want to give me a loan for my small business. Among all those voices, will you be ready to hear the still, small voice of God, calling: *go?* To hear, and to trust? If Abraham hadn't been listening, if Abraham hadn't been trusting, where would we be?

Think of all the billions of people, Jewish, Christian, Muslim, who have come to know God through that one act of openness, trust, and obedience. We have seen in the first chapters of Genesis humankind keeps twisting and breaking relationships with God, with creation, with one another. Abraham wasn't a perfect man; but his one act of personal faith changes the course of not just of the book of Genesis, but of all of human history.

Is God calling one act of personal faith out of you? Does God intend to bless others, others you have never met, across the world, across the generations, through your faith? I believe he does. I can't tell you how, and I can't promise you that you will see the fruits of your decision to trust God. But I can tell you this: in my experience, God isn't so much working in rand, sweeping gestures, as in those tiny moments, when we decide to stop trying to be in charge and build our towers and execute our twenty-year plans and instead, just say, "OK God, you win." It's through those moments of faith and trust that God is ultimately restoring the world.

In the name of the Father, and the Son, and the Holy Spirit, Amen.

Week Three: Committed
Genesis 22

What was the most disturbing Bible story you read this week? Was it the story of Lot offering up his daughters to be raped? Or Abraham casting out the mother of his child, leaving the woman and child to die in the desert? Or Jacob tricking his brother out of his inheritance? Joseph's brothers selling him into slavery? Or Simon and Levi using their sister's rape as an excuse for mass murder, and some rape and pillaging of their own?

The family of Abraham ranges from ordinary dysfunctionality to all-out criminality. These great fathers of the faith are also, in many cases, pretty bad fathers, and husbands, and people. And the women aren't much better as they catfight among themselves. This is the family God has singled out for their great faith, to bless all families of the earth?

But among all the disturbing stories of Genesis, the one story that is hardest for me is Genesis 22: the near-sacrifice of Isaac. This story is told in terrifying detail, as though to show us how terrible this act must be. The sharp knife, the fire, blazing on its torch. The wood. All the steps detailed as though in slow motion. The Bible tells us that Abraham rises early in the morning, which makes sense. Would you have slept that night?

They come to the mountain. It stands tall and terrible before them, unmoving and impossible as God's command. And from here, Abraham and Isaac must go on alone. He makes Isaac carry the wood. And Isaac's question that wrenches the heart, "father, where is the ram for the sacrifice?" The father answers, "God will provide the ram."

They reach the top of the mountain, and Abraham take his son Isaac, binds him with rope to the rock, straps him down and raises the knife over his own child. How can we read this story and simply accept it? How can we accept as Holy Scripture a text that I feel uncomfortable reading when children are in the sanctuary? How can we just say, "The Word of the Lord," to this? Can you imagine your own child? A child you love? God says, Abraham, take your son, your only son, whom you love, as though to torture this father.

Isaac is not just a child. Isaac is the long-awaited promise of the future. Isaac is the fulfillment of years of hope deferred. Isaac is the hope of any couple who have experienced infertility: a miracle baby. God has ordered Abraham to kill that miracle. And there's even more here. As we have seen, people at that time and in that region were obsessed with their descendants. Why?

Because they were consumed with what, remember, was God's first commandment: be fruitful and multiply, fill the earth. Abraham and his descendants have a strong desire to see their children's children flourish. And that desire is still so very deep in human nature. Today, in American culture, the idolatry of family, and particularly of children and grandchildren, is very strong. Putting your children first is a strong societal value. It's difficult for us to think of putting anything before your children, even God.

When my daughter was born, I had never known such a visceral love. I began to have irrational fears of all the things that could happen to her. I could leave her car seat behind my car, forget and run her over. What if she rolled over in the night and was smothered in her bed? Shouldn't I watch her all night long? I imagined my daughter's death and I imagined how I would kill myself. Because there seemed to me no other choice. And when I heard myself have that thought, I prayed. I prayed, "God, do not let my daughter become an idol." I prayed to love God more than I loved my daughter, knowing that by putting God first I would be a better mother. And in that moment my whole perspective changed. I confess that I worry about my kids, but I don't fear for them. Because God loves them more than I do.

Part of what God is doing here is asking Abraham to demonstrate that Abraham loves God more than he loves his child; to put God first. Because until Abraham can put God first and family second, the dysfunction will only get worse. The dysfunction, sinfulness, competitiveness, and violence in Genesis shows us where we end up on our own, with our natural, selfish desires to advance our own interests and those of our family. Remember, in Genesis the people have not yet received the law of God. God is just beginning his relationship with these people. And he doesn't begin by issuing a series of commands. God begins by issuing a promise: you will become a great nation. In order for God to continue the work of restoration, Abraham must trust God fully. God wants to know his investment in this family is not in vain.

But does Abraham's trust in God lead him to murder? In this age when so much violence has been done in the name of God, we in the church must say emphatically, no! My reading of this text is different from many preachers and theologians and biblical scholars I have heard and read. I was struck by the commentary of a South African professor, Juliana Claasens: "The true act of faith on the part of Abraham thus is not the blind faith that often has been the dominant message emerging from this text, but rather the ability to recognize God's provision in the ordinary, especially in those circumstances when everything appears to be futile."

I believe Abraham's faith was not an unquestioning obeisance of whatever command he believed he heard from on high. I believe Abraham's faith was such that *he trusted that God would show mercy*. And Scripture supports my belief. Abraham said to his two assistants in verse 5 that he would come back down the mountain *with Isaac*. He believed that was what would happen. And that when Abraham told Isaac God would provide the ram in verse 14, *that is exactly and literally what he believed*. That Abraham held within him *both the faith to take every step leading up to the altar, and the faith that God was a merciful God*.

I believe this story is included in Scripture not to tell us to sacrifice to our children, but the exact opposite: to teach God's people not to kill children, to not follow the popular religion of Molech at that time an in that area, which Scripture records had drawn away the Israelites from the worship of the one true God, or the many ancient religions that practiced child sacrifice. In many places in Scripture God condemns child sacrifice, and God would not contradict God.

Indeed, as God's message to humankind is unfolding, one of God's first messages to us is to protect children. Listen to God's repeated cry in verse 11: "Abraham! Abraham!" God cries out urgently, you can hear the desperation as God breaks into the violence, and dysfunction, and fear of Genesis, and says, "don't you lay a hand on that boy!" God shows humanity a better way; God makes a provision, God provides a sacrifice, God shows grace to humankind.

This is a story fundamentally about grace. Christians believe this story does not stand on its own. Abraham finds a ram in the bushes, but in verse 8, Abraham does not say, "God will provide a ram." He says, "God himself will provide the lamb." The Hebrew word Seh is also the word used in Isaiah 53:7, which we read on Good Friday: "He was oppressed, and he was afflicted, yet he did not open his mouth; like a lamb that is led to the slaughter." The lamb foreshadows the Lamb: Christ. I believe this story points us to another son, who carried wood up another hill, Who let himself be bound, Who gave himself as a sacrifice.

The grace of Jesus Christ did not come for you and for me amidst perfect, Christmas-card families, where everyone gets along, and no one hurts one another. Who here has a perfect family? Or, is there more of us in the families of Genesis than we'd like to admit? The grace of Jesus Christ came to us amid dysfunction and chaos, amid selfishness and idolatry, in our petty desires to see our own children advance. The grace of Jesus Christ didn't come to perfect people but to criminals, like the one hanging next to him on the cross. In Christ, God hung among murderers and rapists, God stood with prostitutes and sinners—God breaks into the pain and violence of our human condition, and God offers himself.

While this story is so often put forward as an example of Abraham's commitment to God, his great faith, it is truly the story of God's commitment to us, to God's faithfulness. Over, and over, and over, God takes the first step of repairing our brokenness, of redeeming our pain, of restoring our lives. God provides, over and over, mercy upon mercy, grace upon grace, more than we can receive or deserve. So why look to anyone else? What can you trust God for today?

In the name of the Father, the Son, and the Holy Spirit, Amen.

Week Four: Miracles Aren't Easy
Exodus 12

As I've considered miracles this week, reading the book of Exodus, my working definition of a miracle is: a miracle is when God demonstrates who He is.

Up until now, we have seen God doing amazing things—creating the world, the great flood, the destruction of Sodom and Gomorrah, the birth of Isaac—but we haven't seen the dramatic miracles, the demonstrations of who God is that we see now, in the plagues of Exodus, the parting of the Red Sea. Why does God work in such a dramatic way in this story?

In Genesis, God first revealed his nature as Creator; then, as someone who will keep his promises. But in Exodus, God reveals His nature as our Savior. The miracles in Exodus are so dramatic because God wants to demonstrate that He will go to amazing lengths to help lead us out of trouble and strife.

But why does God wait four hundred years? The Israelites were enslaved for generations, and God did nothing. But it's not until this time, when life became so difficult, so oppressive, when they had become enslaved to oppressive and cruel powers, that Israel cried out to God.

Israel slips into slavery without even seeming to realize it. We don't hear a lot about the four hundred years between Joseph and Moses, but it feels like, for a period of years, Israel wasn't aware of what was happening, or wasn't worried about it. One day, they're herding sheep; then, they just start making bricks. And more bricks. And then some more. And before they know it, they've gone from sheep-herders to brick-makers. They've become enslaved to brick-making. It's become their way of life. They've developed a new way of being, a new life path: we make bricks. We live in slavery. This is how it is. And it goes on like this for some time—and Israel just manages.

So often in life, you and I try to manage on our own. I know I'm deep it debt. I can handle it. I know my drinking has become a problem. I've got it covered. And God allows us the freedom to do that, to try to handle it on our own. It's when we have become so desperate that we cry out to God for help, when we admit we can't handle it, that we need God's help, that God will step in. And this is what he does in Exodus, in 3:7. He will only step in, can only work miracles, when we are in so much pain that we cry out to him for help.

Each of God's miracles has deep meaning. In the ten plagues of Egypt, God's miracles symbolize the subversion of creation as he intended it in Genesis 1. God made the light good: now light turns to darkness. God created humans with dominion over the animal kingdom: now the Egyptians have frogs in their beds. God created rivers of life to water the garden: now the seas turn to blood.

God needs to show us that the slavery and the oppression of the Egyptians is uncreating creation. Sin, slavery, oppression anger God! Salvation miracles aren't easy because God has to destroy in order to save. Here, he is upending creation, he is wreaking havoc on Egypt, he is allowing children to die because in order to save His people.

How can we reconcile a loving God with what happens to the Egyptians? Perhaps there are no easy answers here. Miracles aren't always easy. But does something have to be good for us in order for it to be a miracle? When God parted the Red Sea, we consider it a miracle, because he saved His people, the Jews. But for the Egyptians, that same miracle brought death. So, was it a miracle for the Egyptians?

Here's something about miracles that you might never have considered before: Miracles come through pain. Miracles of healing, for example come only when a person is sick.

Part of this is because who we are is so at odds with who God is. Miracles are a demonstration of who God is—and sometimes, that's at odds with what humanity is doing. God uses miracles to help us grow in our relationship with Him. And growth can be painful. Miracles come through pain—but what happens to the Egyptian boys, and their animals, is still disturbing.

I have three thoughts to offer you: first, God doesn't just punish Pharaoh for oppressing the people, he punishes the Egyptians for going along with it. The Egyptians didn't step up and say anything when the Hebrew boys were being slaughtered. In our own era, Dr. King said, "Our lives begin to end the day we become silent about things that matter." For the African American church of Dr. King, the Exodus story has special meaning, and in his words, I hear the echoes of that story. The Egyptians, through their silence, were already living in a culture of death. This is an important warning to you and me who live in a world still plagued with injustice: silence in the face of oppression incurs the wrath of God.

The second thought I have to offer to help us reconcile this painful miracle is that life and death belong to God. Either everything is a miracle, or nothing is; either the life and death of a two-year-old is a tragedy, or it is a gift. The lives and deaths of the Egyptians and their animals were in God's hands, and in this case, those lives became part of God's great message.

And the third thought I have for you is this: the plague on the firstborn was necessary for God to show us an amazing message, which was that God would go to great lengths in order to save us. God wanted, needed to show us that salvation always involves sacrifice. That miracles so often come only through pain, only through death.

If you've suffered from addiction, if you've been trapped in an abusive relationship, if you've experienced depression, then you know that in order for your new life to start your old life has to end. That in order for you to live, something must die. If you've experienced salvation, you know that miracles come through pain. These miracles aren't easy for the Egyptians, and they aren't easy for the Israelites either. Look at all the detailed instructions God gives His people concerning the Passover. God does not do the work of salvation on His own.

God gives them these specific instructions, and tells them every year, they must repeat this ritual, must teach it to their children in order that all may know about the great and amazing lengths God went to save His people.

The bitter herbs: reminding the people of the bitterness of oppression so they will never want to go back. The roasted lamb, that could not be boiled: reminding the people that water became the instrument of death, and God used fire to lead them through the desert. The unleavened bread: reminding the people that they can't waste any time in leaving the old life behind. Girding their loins: this language is so old fashioned, we've lost its meaning, but it meant winding a piece of cloth to strengthen you when you had something heavy to carry, hard work to do. Think of an athlete taping up before a big event, or a weightlifter using a belt. Their salvation would be an athletic event. It would be work! They couldn't sit down and relax to eat this meal; they had to stand up and eat quickly. And finally, the lamb. A perfect lamb, that they had cared for, they would have to kill. And smear the blood on the doorposts. The same doorposts they were about to pass through to leave everything behind.

In order for new life to begin, the old life must die. Miracles come through pain; salvation comes through sacrifice. This Passover would restart time; from this moment, the Israelites would have a new calendar, a new agenda, a new life. But the miracle would come through pain. The new life would come through death. Is there an old life you need to let die?

Are there unhealthy patterns that have crept into your life, in your work, in your diet, in your finances, in your relationships that are holding you back, that have you feeling trapped, even enslaved? Many of us today are experiencing, or have experienced, being trapped in addiction, or abusive relationships, or crippling depression.

But sometimes the things that hold us captive aren't so glaring. It's the patterns of bickering and sarcasm in our relationships; the patterns of overspending and under-saving in our finances; the patterns of unhealthy living that we keep treading over, and over, and over. You know what that is. What door do you need to walk out of today?

We get trapped into oppressive ways of life such that we don't really know an alternative. We make bricks. That's what we do. We don't know how to raise sheep anymore. The pathways are ingrained in the chemical structures of our brains, so well-traveled that we don't know a way out. We become hesitant to leave Egypt, hesitant to walk out, because we know that the doorposts will be, must be, stained with blood. We know that something must die in order for us to truly live. We've got to make the sacrifice. We've got to stand up, gird our loins, and walk through the door.

I heard an interview with Danny Gokey on the radio; he's a Christian singer, and his story just stuck with me. Danny Gokey lost his first wife, his high school sweetheart. He got through it; he even remarried. But three years later, he was struck with a depression that would not let go. He went through days in bed. He was literally trapped in his bed, waiting for God to heal him, waiting for a miracle. But God doesn't always work that way. Sometimes God needs us to sacrifice, to gird our loins, to walk through the door. Sometimes the miracle comes through pain. The old life has to die. Danny read Isaiah 60:1: "Arise from your spiritual depression." And he got up. He got up, and he started to write. The album he eventually wrote was picked up by a secular label; it was the first Christian music they had ever put out, and they took a huge chance. The sales of his first album doubled their sales projections. The title track, called "Rise," contains these words: "You hear the call of your Creator: 'I made you for more. I unlocked the door. I want to restore your glory.'"

I have been there; I have been in that place of depression, where in order for God's miracles to happen, I had to cry out to God, to stop managing and handling it and keeping it under control and let God be in control instead.

Getting out of depression, or out of addiction, or out of abuse isn't like stepping out of a puddle, it's like pulling yourself out of quicksand. And you know what? You can't pull yourself out of quicksand. You have to grab a rope. You need help. I had to accept help. I had to trust. And when I did that, I started to see all the miracles. Miracles of people who cared for me; miracles of angels I didn't even know who lifted me up.

Miracles come through pain. Salvation comes through sacrifice. The old life has to die for a new life to begin. But God loves us enough that he will stop at nothing to save us. If the gnats don't work, he'll send the locusts. If the boils won't work, he'll send a plague. If the prophets don't work, he'll send his Son.

Because for us as Christians, this passage does not stand on its own. We know that it is not just the Israelites who sacrifice a lamb; the Lamb of God laid down his life for us. The Egyptians sacrificed their firstborn; but God gave his firstborn Son for our sake. Christ's blood is the doorway to new life. Step through.

And once you step through, don't stop. Don't stop until you've passed through the waters and walked through the desert and crossed the Jordan and entered into the promised land. Remember where you've been and remember who brought you out. He never stopped loving you; he gave everything to rescue you. And he won't stop now.

In the name of the Father, and the Son, and the Holy Spirit, Amen.

Week Five: In the Wilderness
Exodus 17

Some passages of Scripture are very hard to read. For instance, as we read through Exodus, we read at several points that God hardened Pharaoh's heart. How do we take this? Did God cause Pharaoh to turn away from him, leading to the deaths of thousands of Egyptian boys? That's a difficult concept for us to accept.

Like many things we read, understanding this text takes a combination of study and faith. One thing we can know from study is that, in these passages, it's unclear where God's will ends and Pharaoh's begins; several passages say Pharaoh hardened his own heart, so it wasn't all on God. 8:15, 8:32, 9:34. In other words, it's not all God's fault. Additionally, where the Scriptures say God hardened Pharaoh's heart, it can be kind of like a figure of speech. For example, when we say to someone "you make me feel so mad." Anyone who's had a millisecond of therapy knows you have a choice whether to get mad when someone says something of an inflammatory nature. So they didn't "make you mad." But on the other hand, their words or actions contributed to your experience. It's the nature of relationship that we influence each other. Here, God allowed Pharaoh's heart to be hardened, and Pharaoh let his heart get hardened, and Moses spoke the words that triggered Pharaoh's stubbornness.

But we can't ignore God's part in all this. God did mastermind what happened, in order to perform miracles that showed the people the depth of God's love, lead to the Ten Commandments, bring faith to millions of people, and in our own national history, inspire the abolition movement, the Civil Rights movement, and the history and theology of the Black church, one of the pillars of the African American community. There's also nothing in the text to suggest 1) that the Egyptian boys who died were not ultimately saved by God or 2) that God did not make some provision for Egyptians who had come to the aid of the Israelites; the Egyptian Underground Railroad, so to speak. Perhaps some of those faithful Egyptians even joined the escaping Hebrew people (by the way, there is some evidence that the word Hebrew comes from the ancient Egyptian word Habiru, meaning slaves, so it is possible some of the Egyptians went with the people of Israel). Perhaps it is not for us to say whether God's action upon Pharaoh's heart was improper in the great scheme of things.

So coming now to our text for today, we meet Moses and the people in a desert place. Have you ever been really thirsty? Have you ever run a race in the hot sun, or eaten a whole bowlful of pretzels? Have you ever been to a movie theater and just ordered the popcorn, bravely declining the soft drink; and then you're sitting there in the theater staring lustily at your neighbor's straw, your tongue scraping across the roof of your mouth, with all that fake buttery powder stuff rolling around in your mouth? I mean, have you ever been really thirsty?

When I was about eight my family went to the Sleeping Bear Dunes and we were going to walk across them to Lake Michigan, only I think we went in the wrong entrance, and we got lost in the dunes. It's funny how all memories are distorted by childhood, because I know logically, we must have only been out there a few hours, but in my mind, it might as well have been forty years. And I'm sure I complained as much as the Israelites, whining to my parents, "I'm tired! I'm hot! I'm thirsty! Have you taken me here to kill me with thirst?"

The Israelites must have been even thirstier than that. Yet I can't feel too sorry for them, because the Israelites are suffering from something else too; a confounding case of amnesia. When I read about their latest problem of not having any water and I hear the Israelites saying, God has forgotten us! God has taken us out here to kill us! --I have to do this: Remember that plague of frogs people? The hail falling from the sky? The river turning to blood? The hot boils on Pharaoh's nose? The let my people go, the Red Sea parting in two, the manna that came from heaven in the last chapter?

The Israelites demonstrate an absolutely remarkable lack of faith that after all this, God is going to, yeah, allow them to die of thirst. Kind of like a whiny eight-year-old overdramatic, accusing her parents, who have loved her and cared for her whole life, "You brought me out here because you want me to die!"

Why is it that the people of God are always experiencing amnesia? When it comes to the stories of our own lives, why do we forget what happened in the last chapter, or even the last verse? Why do we so easily forget that the God who rained down manna in our wildernesses last week will pull water out of our rocks this week? Could it be because deliverance is so often followed by wandering?

That sometimes, maybe most of the time, there's a gap between Egypt and the Promised Land. There's a halfway house, so to speak, between rehab and getting back home. There's a dry spell, so to speak, between the abusive relationship and Mr. Right. There's a season of sitting on the couch between the bad job and the good one.

Sometimes God makes us leap before we can see the other side. And that's what the Israelites did. But the desert time is important, because this is where God teaches us. Sometimes you need the halfway house; sometimes you need to sit on the couch. Sometimes need to learn what went wrong with Mr. Wrong before you are ready for Mr. Right.

That doesn't mean you do nothing in the wilderness. Rather, while you are waiting for the next phase in your life, you are actively learning spiritual, emotional, physical truths. Indeed, the wilderness is the best place for learning, because there are no distractions. The wilderness is the blank chalkboard, the bare cubicle, where learning can begin. It's manna and quail every day. There's no milk and honey to distract you from the hard work of becoming a new person, a new nation. It's in the wilderness where God teaches his Law, delivers the Ten Commandments. It's in the wilderness where Israel begins rightful worship, as a nation, for the first time. And there's more than that: it's in the wilderness that God begins to teach the people about grace.

Remember, in Egypt, the Israelites weren't being punished for their sin. The Israelites slipped into slavery, not because they had strayed from God—they simply fell under the oppression of the Egyptian regime. The Egyptians were punished, and the Israelites were saved. But now we have a new situation. The Israelites have chosen the path of amnesia, whininess, distrust, unfaith. Whereas Abraham, Isaac, and Jacob were faithful with a few doubts along the way, Israel here believes that God is all-out against them. They're ready to go back to Egypt.

It's going to get pretty annoying to see the people that God delivered dissing and dismissing God as we walk through the Old Testament. It makes Moses mad, for one. Moses is like an older sibling here. He is the intermediary between the Israelites in the back seat and God in the front. He asks them, why do you quarrel with me? Moses cries out to the Lord, what shall I do with this people? What do you think Moses wants God to let him do?

When the people are dissing and dismissing God, and threatening to stone Moses, what do you think Moses thinks would be fair? Do you think Moses is thinking maybe it's time for another plague of frogs—this time, against the Israelites?

But you see, the wilderness is a teaching place, and it's here that Moses, and Israel, must learn that with God, it's not about what's fair. The Scriptures often describe God as hard, inflexible, solid, unmoving, firm: Our Rock. Our Rock of justice, fairness, righteousness; there are certain rules, laws which can never be broken. The laws that are about to be inscribed on tablets of rock just three chapters from now.

But God chooses to teach us grace before he teaches us the law, and not after. Because grace is at the center of it all. The law is a gift; grace is the greater gift, the greatest gift, and it's grace that God keeps teaching us over, and over, and over. The unemployment insurance kicks in. The whiny children are taken to McDonalds. Water comes from the inflexible rock. Over and over, when we diss and dismiss God, God delivers us again.

We keep dissing and dismissing the God who delivered us, and God keeps delivering. There are no lengths to which God will not go to deliver us, no way in which we can offend God too much.

When Jesus hung on the cross all day, teased, tormented and tortured, he cried out from the cross "I thirst." They gave him vinegar. We did not show Jesus the kind of grace God showed us. But when the soldiers stuck their spears in Jesus's side, what gushed out? Blood…and water. The Rock of our salvation allow himself to be struck; and everyone who knew Jesus heard his words in echo in their hearts: "I am the resurrection and the life. Whoever drinks of the water that I give him will never thirst. The water that I shall give him will become in him a spring of water, welling up to eternal life."

Moses, who God delivered from death in a basket on the waters of the river; Moses, who stuck his staff in the waters of the Nile; Moses, who watched God part the waters of the Red Sea, has forgotten that water is God's sign and seal of grace.

Grace is a difficult and a weird concept for those of us who have taken first grade math. The author Philip Yancey wrote that grace is atrocious math. Grace is one plus one equaling three. Grace is illogical; grace is unfair. Grace is scandalous; McDonald's for the whiny kids; the father running to his lazy, ungrateful son; water coming from a rock. Grace is, Annie Dillard wrote, like a man holding his teacup under a waterfall. Grace is the truth that we can forget God all we want but God forgives all our forgets. Grace is the reality that the people can diss and dismiss God, but God keeps delivering. Thank God that God is so unfair.

Thank God that forgives our whininess, our amnesia, our lack of faith, our sin, our failure. Thank God that grace comes before law. Thank God that God is holding the teacup of your failures under the waterfall of his love.

In the name of the Father, and the Son, and the Holy Spirit, Amen.

Week Six: God's Backside
Exodus 33

The readings we had for this week may have seemed technical, repetitive, boring, and weird, full of strange commands like how to cut apart a goat and burn it on the fire. But all these chapters focus around a central theme: how do we encounter God? It's an important question: maybe it's *the* important question. If our lives are in the hands of Almighty God, wouldn't you want to get to know Him, to communicate with Him, perhaps even to influence Him in some way?

Here's an analogy: there probably isn't a person in this room who wouldn't want to spend an hour alone with the President. Whatever you would want to do with that hour, I could only speculate. But I doubt anyone here would turn down the opportunity. If an hour with a person of such smallness as the President is such an exciting idea, what a gift it would be to have an encounter with Almighty God!

Without any disrespect to the office of the presidency, God is far, far more powerful than any one man could ever be. President Teddy Roosevelt knew this. Before going to bed, he would see if he could find a certain spot of light in the sky. Then he would recite, "That is the Spiral Galaxy in Andromeda. It is as large as our Milky Way. It is one of a hundred million galaxies. It consists of one hundred billion suns, each larger than our sun." Once he was reassured of his smallness, he would go to bed.

At this point in Exodus, the nation of Israel was just beginning to comprehend the significance of their opportunity to encounter God. They were starting to get an idea of the awesomeness and majesty of who God was, the God who has all the suns of all the galaxies of all the universe in his hand. They had been used to the gods of other nations, who could be made of stone or metal, with human hands; carried around conveniently, worshiped, and disposed of for another god when they no longer served their purpose.

By contrast, God's people begin to understand that this is a God who cannot be encountered according to our convenience, but according to His command, and that furthermore, this God wants nothing less than to be first in their lives, and that moreover, they must order their entire lifestyle to His commandments: their response is one of outright terror. Terror, and the knee-jerk desire to go back to an easier god, a god of their own making, a god they can encounter on their own terms. And this is how we get golden calves.

The golden calf signifies yet another break between the relationship between God and humankind, and it has terrible consequences. Not only the slaughter of three thousand of God's own people (by the way, Moses says this bloodshed is the will of God, but it is never confirmed that God ordered this bloodshed) but also God's decree, in Exodus 33:3, that he will no longer go with them. God will, instead, send an angel to guide them, but their unholiness cannot live with God's holiness (by the way, the incompatibility of God's holiness and human sinfulness is the core theme of Leviticus).

Moses is pretty upset with God's decision. So, Moses has it out with God. The chapter we heard today is a wonderful glimpse of the intimacy between God and Moses. Moses, who has seen God face to face, is pretty upfront with the Lord; one commentator noted that he's got some *chutzpah*. The Message translation captures Moses's attitude: "If I am so special to you, let me in on your plans. That way, I will continue being special to you. Don't forget, this is *your* people, your responsibility."

Moses basically tells God, you can't take your presence from us, because without you, we've got nothing. So God assures Moses that his presence will remain with them, albeit in a different way. But Moses still isn't satisfied. He desires an encounter with God, a reassurance that all is still well between him, personally, and between the nation, communally, and God. He demands, "show me your glory."

Commentator Fred Hozee makes an important point: that in Hebrew, "glory" and "heavy" come from the same root. God is glorious means, God is heavy, God is weighty. God is not to be taken lightly. God's glory is such that it could overwhelm us; it could crush us like a bug. So therefore, encountering God is not something to be taken lightly. We shouldn't be surprised when God seeks to control the terms of His encounter with us!

God grants Moses's request, but on God's terms, not on Moses's. Even though Moses has seen God face to face before, this time Moses will only see God's back. I must confess to you that the first time I encountered this passage was in Sunday school when a bunch of giggling kids told me there was a whole chapter in Scripture about God's backside. Moses will only catch God's backside, a glimpse of God's glory, of the weight of his majesty and holiness. Why can't Moses see God face to face now, when he could before? The rabbinical commentators noted that here, Moses is trying to control the encounter. God shows Moses mercy, just as he has shown the people mercy;

but God also sends a message: I am God, and you, my son, are not. I will show my glory to you in my time, and in my way.

We no longer have to carry around a tabernacle with bronze pole holders and lots and lots and lots of acacia wood; and, thank the Lord, setting fire to goat parts is not part of my job description. But God still dictates how, and when, we will encounter him. We can make ourselves open to God; we can be good listeners. But ultimately, we can go on a retreat; we can pray; we can have a perfect worship service with pitch-perfect music and amazing preaching, but it's totally up to God when to communicate with us, when we can catch a glimpse of his glory. That's what makes the life of faith challenging and that's what makes it beautiful.

At Bible Study at the homeless shelter on Friday, a man named Tony asked me if I'd ever heard the voice of God. And I had to admit that I have not experienced God's voice as an audible sound. I know people who have, but I have not had that experience. And I've never seen an angel. My encounters with God have not been concrete, physical experiences. For me, there have been times in my life when a thought simply popped into my head, when I was thinking of something totally different, and I knew somehow that it was God. That's actually how I knew I was expecting a child this time around; the thought was just there, sure and certain, days before science confirmed it. But I haven't heard an audible voice. I haven't seen a physical presence. I guess I've mostly encountered God's back side.

Last week, for example. I saw a name, printed out on our annual report, that I hadn't seen in a while. We baptized Robert a year ago Valentine's Day. And I hadn't seen Robert at all since he left the homeless shelter last March. I have to admit, it saddened me to see Robert's name under the baptisms, thinking, there's someone I'll never see again.

After the congregational meeting, members of our church gathered for a movie showing, but I was interrupted partway though. And, of course, my husband Dan informed me that Robert was here, and he had brought ten bags of clothes for people in need. It turns out Robert has a job working in a group home; one day, he would like to start a group home of his own. He has a godly girlfriend; and he was well-dressed because he was going home from worship at his new church.

Robert has had some help in getting his life together, but ultimately, he gives the credit to God. He says he encountered God in our little Bible studies at the shelter, and that he considers our font the birthplace of his new life. That

God engineered all of the difficulties he went through to change him fully and forever.

God might not part our Red Seas; God might not raise the dead in our lifetime. You and I might catch only glimpses of God's presence, hear only snatches of God's voice. God encounters us on His terms, not ours; we may see only, well, God's backside.

But you know what? It's enough.

It's enough to have faith for today.

"For now we see in a mirror dimly, but then, we shall see face to face."

In the name of the Father, and the Son, and the Holy Spirit, Amen.

Week Seven: The Best Way to Live
Leviticus 23

I want to speak to those of you who have fallen away or fallen behind in your Bible reading: We believe in a God of grace! Go ahead and join us on today's readings and don't lose sleep over the days you have missed. Falling behind is an opportunity to turn back to God. For those of you who are still on track, congratulations! You have made it through some of the most challenging passages of the Bible. These passages are challenging because they are so dense with meaning that they require a lot of interpretation. So, I want to encourage you to take the time to think about and interpret what you're reading. If you have the Daily Walk commentary, or if you have a Study Bible, you'll be able to gain a lot more from what you are reading. Because these chapters are packed with good news for us today! And I hope to show you that by studying Leviticus 23.

First of all, let's take a minute to appreciate that God commands us to celebrate! God commands the people of Israel to observe certain holidays, and most of these holidays are festivals. They're parties! They involve a break from work to rest and rejoice in the goodness of God, and to be together as a community. I like the Charles Swindoll quote: Americans tend to "worship our work, work at our play, and play at our worship." We are called to reclaim the practice of Sabbath, to actually make rest part of the rhythm of our lives.

We as a church and as individuals need to be people who know how to relax and enjoy life. Our culture teaches that fun comes from spending money, gambling, alcohol and drugs, sex. But the message of Leviticus is holiness. And being holy means being set apart, being different.

We are called, as ducks with sunglasses, to show people holy ways to have fun. This is why we as a church need to celebrate together, to spend time together, to have fun. This is why coffee hour is important; baseball games are important; movie nights are important. We need to find holy ways to enjoy life as a community and be people of joy.

So, let us take a closer look at the festivals God outlined for His people. Each one of them had a historical meaning, a prophetic meaning, and a personal meaning. Each one of them pointed to God's work in the past, God's work in the future, and God's work for us today.

Begin with the Passover and the Festival of Unleavened Bread. These festivals were to remind the people of Israel of their deliverance from Egypt. It must have been difficult to remember that they were once enslaved; but we know that one of the best ways to trust God today is to remember what God did yesterday. There's a saying in the Black church: "He never failed me yet." That's what Israel is called to remember in the feast of Passover. Christians also believe that God was pointing His people to the future: reminding them of the sacrifice of the lamb to teach them about the sacrifice of the Lamb, Christ. We believe that when the blood of Christ covers our doorposts, covers our lives, the angel of death will pass over us, and we can share in His resurrection. So, when John the Baptist says, "Look! The Lamb of God who takes away the sin of the world!" anyone who had grown up celebrating the Passover would see that God's prophecy was being fulfilled.

Finally, the seven days of unleavened bread had a personal meaning. The New Testament says: "false teaching is like a little yeast that spreads through the whole batch of dough!" Galatians 5:9. Yeast, or leaven, was a symbol of sinfulness in the Old Testament. Why? Because yeast causes bread to rise and get all puffed up. What does sin do but makes us all puffed up? Sin happens when we put ourselves before God and others. We think of ourselves as the center of the universe. We rise up in our own estimation. And this can happen in a positive or negative way. Do you know someone who is always saying, "woe is me, my life's a disaster, I'm a wreck"? We can become down on ourselves such that we see ourselves negatively as the center of the universe. And we all do it. So this festival calls us to put God first and remind ourselves to be humble. Humility isn't thinking less of yourself, it's thinking of yourself less. And that's what the festival of unleavened bread calls us to do.

The next festivals are the feasts of harvest. The first is the feast of first harvest, in which God called the people to give Him the first fruits of what they grew. It was a reminder that without God, we have nothing at all; that the blessings we enjoy aren't because of our labor, but because of God's love.

This goes directly against what our culture preaches, that God helps those who help themselves. The Scriptures tell us that God helps those who can't help themselves. Today, we are still called to give to God first. I remember recently we had a party at our house, and before we had the cake and ice cream, my one-year-old son said, "say grace?" I mean, the dessert really deserves its own grace.

We should think of God before we enjoy our paycheck, our dinner, even before we enjoy a party with family and friends, we should first recognize God's blessings with an offering, of time, of money, of prayer. Because after all, he gave us His best: "Christ has been raised from the dead. He is the first of a great harvest of all who have died." 1 Corinthians 15:20. This festival teaches us that Christ is the firstfruits of those who died; that God is coming back to gather us up in the final day of harvest, when we will share in the joy of His kingdom.

The next festival of harvest comes fifty days later; it's called Pentecost, which means fifty. Fifty days after the first harvest, the people of Israel celebrated the harvest again with more offerings to the Lord. Because we aren't called to give God 10%, or 30% like we give the government; we are called to give God 100%, to place all we have at God's disposal, to look at our lives and ask: what does God want me to do with this? That's why Israel was called, when they harvested, to leave the corners of their fields for foreigners, for strangers, for the poor. You will notice that throughout these chapters, God explicitly calls the people to treat the foreigners, people who worshiped idols, with grace and love. In the same way, God calls us not to use all we have on ourselves, but to give to others, whether they share our faith and culture or do not.

And giving to others refers not just to physical gifts, but to spiritual gifts as well. How many of us hoard our salvation? We know we're saved; we think of Christ as the center of our lives; but tell others about Him? No, too risky. Too scary.

From time to time I get obsessed with stories of the Titanic. It's just such a fascinating event, on so many levels. But the one part that disturbs me the most is that almost none of the lifeboats were filled to capacity. People were sitting in half-full lifeboats as human beings called to them, screamed for them; the people in the lifeboats even beat others down with their oars, and not a single lifeboat went back. They were scared of being pulled under, of being drowned themselves. They were scared that the lifeboats would get too full. So, they sat, and listened to the screams.

How many of us are sitting on lifeboats, just watching others drown? We know the way to safety and salvation; but we don't want to share. So, we just let them drown in their sin and pain and brokenness.

The message of Pentecost was that we are called to share with others, physically and spiritually, even others very different from ourselves. That's why it was on Pentecost that the church broke out of its little locked-up room and went out into the streets, preaching to people from all over the world. They were sharing not physical bread, but Jesus, who is the spiritual Bread of Life.

The next festival is the Feast of Trumpets. This is how we know we serve a joyful God: He wants us to blow noisemakers on the New Year! God put a New Year celebration right in the Bible! God wanted the people to celebrate new life, to celebrate a fresh start. He wants us to see how he is making all things new, and he is pointing us to that great day: "when the last trumpet is blown. For when the trumpet sounds, those who have died will be raised to live forever. And we who are living will also be transformed." 1 Corinthians 15:52.

Next, we come to the Day of Atonement. And this is the only one of the holidays God institutes that is more a fast than a feast. This is the time for God's people to come before God, and deny themselves, and to be purified from their sins. They did this by coming before God.

When the Temple was built, it was built in a series of concentric rings, and you could only enter in so far as your status allowed. Gentiles, non-Jewish people, could not come in whatsoever. Jewish women could come into the women's court; Jewish men could come into the Israelite's court; Priests could come into the inner court; and specially designated priests could come into the holy place, when they were performing rituals or prayers. But the Holy of Holies was where God lived, and it was separated from the holy place from a beautiful curtain, which, as you read, was beautifully embroidered in blue, red, and violet. That curtain could only be entered into by the high priest, and only on one day a year: The Day of Atonement. So, think of the significance of Matthew 27:51: "At that moment the curtain in the sanctuary of the Temple was torn in two, from top to bottom."

Since this place was so sacred to the Day of Atonement, all those who heard what had happened knew that God had fully and finally atoned for their sins: and that God had allowed all people, Jewish and Gentile, male and female, to enter into life with Him.

As Christians, we recognize God's atoning death on Good Friday. Many Christians like to go from Palm Sunday to Easter, without stopping at the difficult places in between. But we are called to recognize how our sin separates us from God, to thank God for His atoning sacrifice in Christ.

Finally, we have the festival of booths, or some translations call it the festival of shelters or tents; it was a festival where the people of Israel had to make tents and live in them, to remember their days of wandering in the wilderness, and give thanks for God's deliverance. I kind of think it's God's way of making people go camping. Now, a lot of us hate camping. At my house, we like a comedian named Jim Gaffigan who says, "why would you want to burn a couple of vacation days sleeping on the ground outside? You'll wake up freezing and covered in a rash. If it's so great outside, why are the bugs all trying to get into my tent?" But whether you like camping or hate it, God calls us sometimes to sacrifice our creature comforts for the sake of His kingdom. Reinhold Niebuhr is accredited with saying that "The Gospel was meant to comfort the afflicted and afflict the comfortable."

I've been on a lot of short-term mission trips; I made it a point to go to not only several third-world countries, but to some of the poorest places in America: the Appalachian communities, the Native American reservations, and communities of migrant farm workers. I can tell you that we in the United States are very financially blessed. The trip that was most important in my sense of call to ministry was in the Philippines. I'm a person who's enjoyed a lot of comforts; I'm white, my family is upper middle class, I'm straight, I've had a lot of privileges and access to education. So, I guess I've tried to keep my comfort in check by serving wherever I can. One opportunity I had in college was to go to the Philippines. On the other side of the world, far from my home, I was in a corrugated tin shack, where the family served us a plate of chicken and a can of Coke, because everyone knows Americans like chicken and Coke. I was partway through the plate of food and the can when I realized that plate and that can were intended for ten people to share. That night, my friend Rachel and I shared a sleeping mat. There was one mosquito net, and the family, a mother, father, and little boy, gave it to us, leaving themselves exposed to the possibility of malaria. We lay under that mosquito net and listened to the rats scurry overhead. In the morning, the mother kindly gave us tissues to clean our nostrils from the black dust that we had collected overnight, in this place where companies, many of them American companies, don't have to follow environmental regulations. The mother whom my now-husband, Dan, stayed with had lost two of her children to respiratory disease.

That trip afflicted this comfortable girl, albeit in such a small way and for such a short time and led me to reprioritize my life. It eventually led me into ministry.

God calls us to step out of our comfort zone sometimes; to leave our nice warm houses; to live in tents; to be reminded that this Earth is not our home. That this life is just a journey; that our bodies are but a shell, and to place our trust, not in the things of the world, but in the things of God.

So make time for God. Make space for God. Step out of your comfort zone. Reach out of your lifeboat. Be holy. It's not just a good thing to be. It's what God has been commanding us to be, in hundreds of ways, for thousands of years, here, in the middle of Leviticus, and in so, so many places. It's also the best possible way to live.

In the name of the Father, and the Son, and the Holy Spirit, Amen.

Week Eight: Fight Snakes with...Snakes?
Numbers 21

If you think about it, it actually comes as no surprise that the Bible can be challenging to read. After all, it is God's Word. Who says it will be easy to understand, and to apply to our lives? God's thoughts are far from our thoughts, and God's ways are far from our ways. In order to understand the Bible, we have to look at the passages in the context of the cultures in which they were written.

Take the laws that seem fairly arbitrary and strange, like the law against mixed fibers found in Leviticus 19:19, "You shall keep my statutes. You shall not let your animals breed with a different kind; you shall not sow your field with two kinds of seed; nor shall you put on a garment made of two different materials." God's Law doesn't forbid all mixed fibers, just the combination of linen and wool. It's laws like these that lead people to argue that the Bible has no relevance, no significance for today, and we should just throw out the whole thing. But that would be kind of like saying we should ignore the Constitution and the Bill of Rights because, according to dumblaws.com, in Detroit, Michigan it's illegal to scowl at your wife on Sunday. (Ladies, you're welcome.) We have to look deeper at the reasoning for the law.

The medieval Jewish scholar Maimonides explained that in Canaanite, idol-worshiping cultures, it was common practice to plant different types of seed together, or weave different kinds of fibers together, as a fertility rite; you were "marrying" different things together, and that would lead to greater fertility. It was, we might say, a way of doing magic. God wanted his people to stand out from others; to be set apart, to be holy; and to trust God rather than relying on magical rites. That message is still helpful for us today; so many of us try to control our own lives, through magical thinking; if I wear these socks, my team will win. If I eat right and exercise, I'll never get cancer. The truth is, we aren't in control, and we aren't meant to be. God invites us, rather than magical thinking, to trust in his power and love, that he will provide for us in every circumstance.

Apart from the seemingly strange laws, a lot of people, myself included, are highly disturbed by the violence in the first five books of Moses. Particularly, it's disturbing when God himself sponsors violence, or actually just comes out and kills people. Like the followers of Korah, the Levite who wanted his tribe to have more of a role in the Tabernacle than just hauling it around; they get swallowed up by the earth. Or the ten spies—remember, of the twelve who peeked into Canaan, only Caleb and Joshua were optimistic—in response to the ten spies' lack of faith, they get killed by a plague. To our eyes, it looks disproportionate. But this kind of thing seems to be happening all the time in the book of Numbers. In the passage we read today, the people get bitten by snakes, apparently for being too whiny. Don't we believe in a loving, merciful God? How can we reconcile the God Jesus described with the God who kills thousands of people in a moment?

But God is not safe. A recent study of young Americans described the typical young person as a moral therapeutic deist. What in the world does that mean? Most young Americans believe there is a God, who created them, teaches them right from wrong, and helps them when they need it. This kind of god can be called upon in our hour of need but doesn't necessarily need to be part of our everyday lives; doesn't need to be worshiped or feared. This is a domesticated god, a tamed god, who shows up conveniently to help us and then quietly lets us be. This is not the God of Scripture. Put simply, He is not a *safe* God.

In the Chronicles of Narnia, C.S. Lewis uses the biblical image of the Lion to describe God. In a passage from *The Silver Chair*, a little girl named Jill first meets this Lion as He is sitting next to a stream. And it just so happens that what she most desperately wants and needs is a drink of water.

"Are you not thirsty?" said the Lion.

"I am dying of thirst," said Jill.

"Then drink," said the Lion.

"May I — could I — would you mind going away while I do?" said Jill.

The Lion answered this only by a look and a very low growl. And as Jill gazed at its motionless bulk, she realized that she might as well have asked the whole mountain to move aside for her convenience.

The delicious rippling noise of the stream was driving her nearly frantic.

"Will you promise not to — do anything to me, if I do come?" said Jill.

"I make no promise," said the Lion.

Jill was so thirsty now that, without noticing it, she had come a step nearer.

"Do you eat girls?" she said.

"I have swallowed up girls and boys, women and men, kings and emperors, cities and realms," said the Lion. It didn't say this as if it were boasting, nor as if it were sorry, nor as if it were angry. It just said it.

"I daren't come and drink," said Jill.

"Then you will die of thirst," said the Lion.

"Oh dear!" said Jill, coming another step nearer. "I suppose I must go and look for another stream then."

"There is no other stream," said the Lion.

Our God is not safe. He is not tame. He cannot be made to do what we want, when we want, and then disposed of until we need Him again. He made all that is and holds all things in His hands. Life, death, and eternal life are His to determine, not ours; there is no other God, no other Source of life and of love, no "other stream." And in Scripture, at certain times, He chooses to teach us eternal truths through eternal means.

As here, in the story of the snakes. The Israelites, yet again, are complaining about the wilderness conditions. The wilderness is an intentionally boring place. Manna every day. Tents every night. And why? Because it's a teaching place. It's a blank slate. Because when your chalkboard's all filled up, there's no room to learn.

But the people don't like being in this teaching place; they're sick of manna and tents, and they've come up with their own solution: let's go back to Egypt! Bricks without straw? No big deal. The slaughter of the firstborn? Meh. The food was to die for! By now, the Israelites' complaints are familiar. They're even funny: verse 5 says, "There's no bread to eat!" And, "We hate this bread!" Well, which is it, Israel? But this time, God sends a different answer: Snakes.

Like Indiana Jones's lament: why did it have to be snakes? Well there's a very good reason. Where have we seen snakes before? Remember all the way back in Genesis 3? When the snake tells the woman, here, eat this fruit, and be like God? When humankind substitutes its own judgment for God's? That's what the Israelites are doing here. They have substituted their own judgment for God's. So God's punishment has a message: you've tried this before. I want to give you milk and honey, the Garden of Eden, the Promised Land. This is the path lined with vipers, and it ends in death!

As people begin dying, they cry out to God for help. They ask God to take away the snakes. But God doesn't take away the snakes. He also doesn't send over poison control with some anti-venom. What does He do? More snakes! God's answer is to command Moses to make a snake and put it on a pole, and hold it above the people. Whoever looks at the snake will live. Now, this makes no sense at all from a logical standpoint. Fight snakes with…snakes? Isn't that like fighting fire with fire? (Actually, firefighters *do* fight fire with fire.)

God's command makes all the sense in the world from a spiritual standpoint. The bronze snake would only work when people looked at it! God wants the people of Israel to recognize what they have done; to see that this is the old pattern, the old enemy; to recognize that this way of life, trying to substitute our morality, our plans, our judgment, for God's does not work. God won't take away the snakes, because it's the snakes we need to see. We need to recognize the consequences of our sin. We need to see what it is that we've done. We need to see the snake lifted high.

If you've never seen it, *The Bridge on the River Kwai* is about some British prisoners working at a Japanese POW camp. Their job is to build a bridge. And the British officer in charge of this detail, Nicholson, gets obsessed with this bridge. It will be the greatest bridge ever built. It will symbolize the strength and might of the British people. It will be his life's work. And then, as the bridge is finally completed, Nicholson finds dynamite, and wire; he learns that this bridge is central to Japan winning the war; that this bridge was never meant to be built. He cries out, "my God, what have I done?" He is shot, but in his dying act, he stumbles towards the detonator and collapses on the plunger just in time to blow up this bridge, his life's work, sending the enemy train plunging into the river.

Sometimes we get so caught up in our own plans, and thoughts, and judgments that we lose sight of what's important. We get so caught up in our whininess that we want to go back to Egypt and miss the Promised Land. God has to show us the consequences of our sin; sometimes those consequences are very hard to face.

When we look up, and realize, "My God, what have I done?"—where our own wisdom, our own judgment, our own decisions as to justice and righteousness lead; they lead to the snake lifted up; they lead to Christ, hanging from the cross. It is only then, when we look up, and recognize the great price of our sin, that we can be healed.

So if you are in a wilderness place, if you are tempted to turn back, if you are tempted to substitute your own judgment for God's—look up. Look up and remember. Remember that God is much, much bigger, much, much wiser, than we are. He is not safe; but He is Good. Remember, and be healed.

In the name of the Father, and the Son, and the Holy Spirit, Amen.

Week Nine: Because I Said So
Deuteronomy 11

Raising kids gives me a lot of respect for God's position vis-à-vis the Israelites. We keep trying to teach them; they keep resisting. Do you remember when you resisted your parents' rules—"why do I have to?" and they said, "Because I said so!"? And if you're a parent, do you remember the day your whiny kid drove you nuts asking "Why do I have to?" and you found yourself saying, "Because I said so!"?

The other day, our son (JP) was banging his toys on the piano. My husband (Dan) said, "Stop banging your toys on the piano, or you're going in timeout." JP started playing with the toys on the piano bench, and asked, "Me play toys on piano bench?" Dan slowly nodded his head. Then JP climbs onto the bench and asked, "Me sit on piano bench?" Dan said, "Okay, but remember, you can't bang your toys on the piano." Then JP begins banging his toys on the piano. Dan took away the toys and said, "You broke the rules, now go sit in timeout." JP scrunches up his face, punches his fist in the air, and says one word: "Never!"

There's a part of all of us that hears rules and says, "Never!" We all have these little corners of our soul that get a kick out of jaywalking or sneaking through a red light. Especially as Americans. We've all got that wild West streak, that desire for independence from rules.

This lawless streak, this rebellion against set rules, has become even more characteristic of our culture in recent years. Who reads etiquette books anymore? Rules are unpopular. Yet this passage in Deuteronomy tells us, in no unclear terms, that we need not only to follow these rules, but to uphold them as the centerpiece of our lives. Deuteronomy contains the sermons that Moses gave to the people before they entered the Promised Land. By this time, many of the Israelites had been born in the wilderness. The old generation was passing away. So, Moses found it necessary to restate the law and explain it. There are two key passages in which Moses stresses the importance of the Law: Deuteronomy 6, which is called the Shema in the Jewish tradition and is repeated daily, is the command to learn the law addressed to individuals; Deuteronomy 11 is the command to learn the law addressed to the community, and says "commit yourselves to this word."

Notice that God calls us not to follow the law, but to commit to the law. Our commitment is not just a matter of what we do, but what we believe; the law is not just for our head to understand or our hands to perform, but for our hearts to believe in; more about this later. This command to commit ourselves wholeheartedly to the law brings up three basic questions for me: What is the law of God? How do we commit to the law of God? And, why do we commit to the law of God?

First: what is the law of God? A very good question came in through email: It seems that God is calling and directing the new community of the Jewish nation of Israel, but how many of these laws or directives from this drama apply to our lives today? I am not sure exactly how we discern what does and does not apply to us especially after receiving Christ and the New Testament teaching? As I was thinking about this question, I believe we as Christians have clear direction from Jesus as to how to interpret and apply the law to our own lives.

Jesus taught us that the greatest commandments are these: Love God with all your heart, and all your soul, and all your strength, and all your might, and love your neighbor as yourself. It all comes down to love. When we consider our actions, how do we love God, and love others, in the best possible way? Here in Deuteronomy 11:22, Moses summarizes the Law: "Show love to the Lord your God by holding fast to him and walking in his ways." There is a heart piece here: hold fast to God. We must actually commit our hearts to God, not just our heads; we have to trust him. But there's also a practical piece: *actually* walk in his ways. How do we show our love? By our actions. We demonstrate our love of God by holding His will above our own, by obeying His commands, by walking in His ways.

Jesus said that all the law boils down to loving God and loving our neighbor. Just as God sent the law to Moses on Mount Sinai, Jesus delivered the law to the people in the Sermon on the Mount, by teaching them how to observe the law. The law was not about the letter but about the spirit. For example, if you became very angry with someone, you were breaking the sixth commandment; thou shalt not murder, because your thoughts were murderous. Sometimes, therefore, the law means doing more than the letter. At other times, the law means disregarding the letter in order to keep the spirit of the law. Jesus healed on the Sabbath; he interrupted his worship to lovingly serve others. But to withhold healing from people who desperately needed it would violate the greater commandment to love your neighbor just as you love yourself. Therefore, as Christians, we are called to look at all our thoughts, words, and actions and ask, does this show love and respect to God and my neighbor?

Jesus's summary of the law did not mean that Christians follow no rules. To the contrary, when we look at Jesus's teaching, we see a clear focus on the Ten Commandments. And the Jewish tradition is to hold these commandments above others; Moses repeated the Ten Commandments in Deuteronomy, as he helped a new generation to learn God's central law. The

Ten Commandments are so important that we see them even across cultures. When you study other religions, you will find that nearly all religions prescribe something like these ten basic rules.

Beyond these basic laws, we have so many more. So, the question is this: how many of the 613 laws of Moses are we supposed to follow? In the Sermon on the Mount, Matthew 5:18, Jesus said that not a jot, not a tittle of the law would pass away; all of the 613 laws are relevant for us today. We might not be called to follow the letter of a particular law anymore, but the spirit of the law still informs and teaches us. For example, the ceremonial laws about animal sacrifice are no longer required, because Christ is the great sacrifice, for once and all, for all our sin. The curtain of the Temple was torn in two at the moment of Christ's death, as humanity was no longer separated from God. However, the spirit of sacrificing our best to God is important today, as we are called to give our time, talent, and treasure to furthering God's work in the church. We have to take each law and consider it in light of the Ten Commandments and in light of the Greatest Commandment and apply it to the situations in which we find ourselves. I know that's not an entirely satisfying answer; I know you want me to tell you which of the 613 go in Column A and which go in Column B. But what Jesus saw is that when we blindly follow the Law without paying attention to the spirit of the law, we end up becoming people of judgment and hypocrisy rather than people of love and grace. All of the law is God's Word. All of it is relevant for us today. As we interpret and apply the law, we have to read carefully and listen to the direction of the Holy Spirit, and above all, be people of love and people of grace, rather than people of pride. We remember that the church is not a hotel for saints, but a hospital for sinners.

The second question: how do we commit to the Law of God? Deuteronomy 11:18-19 gives us direction: Tie, teach, and talk. First, tie them to your hands and to your heads. In the Jewish tradition, men wear phylacteries, little boxes inscribed with verses from Deuteronomy, strapped to their hands and foreheads. God gives us a symbol that the Word of God should be in our head, in our thinking, and in our hands, and in our doing. Even if we do not literally wear Scripture on our person, sometimes we need visual reminders of what we are called to do and to be. Rev. Terence Fretheim, interpreting this passage, remembered how in his home growing up, verses of Scripture were embroidered and hung on the walls. Perhaps we are called to go back to that; but however we do it, God knows we need to be reminded, daily, of His law for our lives.

Second, teach them to your children. It was very important to God that the next generation not forget the wisdom of the past. You and I are called to reach out to the children of our community, many of whom are in great emotional and spiritual need and share the Word of God. This is what we have done at Starr Presbyterian Church through our Parents' Relief Week, and we are called to find new ways to reach out to the children and families around us, who need to know about God's love and God's law.

Third, talk about them, in your home and out of your home. How can you share the Word of God outside your home? How about putting a Bible verse on your email signature? Sharing Scripture on Facebook? Or what about in the checks you write? You can buy personal checks that have Bible verses on them; so whoever is cashing your check can read, "Trust in the Lord with all your heart and lean not on your own understanding." Is Scripture a part of your everyday vocabulary? There's a fine line here between sharing our faith and being too preachy; but the more that Scripture enters your heart, the more that Scripture becomes part of your conversation. Some people simply exude Scripture, simply and gracefully; that's how I want to be.

And the third question: why do we commit to the Law of God? In Deuteronomy 11:26-28, God is pretty upfront with His people: you have a choice. You have a choice between blessings and curses. For the people of Israel, as we will see, following or breaking the law had historic consequences. But Christians believe that the curse of sin was washed away by Christ's blood at Calvary; that we are no longer under a curse because of our failures. So why follow the law? Because, as I keep saying up here, God gives us the best possible way to live. The law is there to keep us safe, and healthy, and whole. Loving God and loving our neighbors, keeping the letter and the spirit of the Ten Commandments, studying the Law of God, will give us better lives, better families, stronger communities.

Rules are there to help us! Just two examples: one from society first, remember the days of Emily Post and etiquette books, when there was a proper way to eat a lemon? Such a rule seems silly and unnecessary today. Etiquette has become something of a forgotten art. And do you know what that leads to?

Lemon juice in the eye of your dining companion. The proper way to eat a lemon is to hold one hand over the other when squeezing it. That rule is based on the best way not to get lemon juice all over the place. So there's actually a reason for the rule related to loving your neighbor as yourself. The second example: thou shalt not covet, that is, want something that's not yours. It's the Tenth Commandment, but it's one that people don't talk about much anymore in the days of advertising. Actually, the Old Testament has a lot to say about not borrowing and not lending—including laws against charging interest (which Wall Street long ago set aside.) I submit to you that today, we have a society based on coveting, based on wanting what's not yours, and that leads people to buy things they don't need with money they don't have. We buy clothes because we think they'll make us look attractive, instead of being content with what we look like and accepting ourselves as beautiful in God's sight. Or we buy big houses and fancy cars, so we feel successful, instead of feeling good about our work no matter what we earn. What does this cycle of coveting lead to? The average American has over $16,000 in credit debt, $28,000 in auto loan debt, and $172,000 in house debt. This debt creates stress in personal life, strain on marriages, and strain on communities. Maybe it's time to go back to "Thou shalt not covet!"

Rules help us remember what's right; rules give us boundaries to keep us in check. The law is a gift; when we keep the letter and spirit of the law, we have fuller lives, better families, stronger communities. We have a choice between life and death, blessings and curses. We have a choice whether to say "Never!" or just quit banging our pianos. We have a choice whether to squirt lemon juice in our neighbor's eye. And, at the end of the day, why do we follow the law? Not because I said so, but because God said so. And He probably knows better than we do.

In the name of the Father, and the Son, and the Holy Spirit, Amen.

Week Ten: God Wins
Joshua 6

How can we consider the book of Joshua the Word of God? In Joshua, the people of Israel carry out total destruction, or *herem*, in Canaan. God explicitly commands them to "show no mercy." After the destruction of these cities, we hear, over and over, the refrain: "They completely destroyed everything in it with their swords—men and women, young and old, cattle, sheep, goats, and donkeys."

I think it's important to recognize that the idea of genocide is appalling to us because it's against our deepest beliefs about what is good. And I believe that our deepest beliefs about what is good come from God himself. By our own nature, there is nothing appalling to us about violence. Recently my family was watching *Planet Earth*, and I learned again the scary truth that when a male bobcat or lion or tiger mates with a female, he also goes ahead and kills her children by another mate, so his own offspring will have a better chance. I think human nature is not necessarily less violent than this. It's only because of God's work in our lives that we believe in loving our enemies. It's only because of God's work on our hearts that these texts are even disturbing in the first place.

And this brings me to my first point: God works with what He has. We have to look at the context of these texts. We have seen how far humanity has fallen, and how violent and cruel, idolatrous and immoral humans have become. When these texts were initially written, the language of total destruction of the enemy was standard in any national military conquest account, and it was almost always hyperbole. In Joshua, God is working for the survival not of a race of people, but of a better way of thinking and living. Remember, God chose Abraham and Sarah so that *all nations of the earth* could be blessed through them. God is calling for the Israelites to destroy these cities in order for the practices of idol-worship and lawlessness to end. As we read the rest of the Old Testament, it will become clear that the God-fearing nation-state is not the best model. Israel does not hold fast to God's laws. In the fullness of time, God will send salvation to all people, not just one nation. As travel becomes easier, and literacy increases, the sharing of God's message beyond one nation becomes possible.

We also have to know an important detail that Joshua leaves out, but that modern archaeological study has shown us: at the time of the Conquest, these Canaanite cities were ruled by Egyptian overlords, who continued their forced-slavery ways among the Canaanites. The Israelites don't go in and attack little villages and family farms. They attack big cities and they take down the kings. Remember the catalogue listing all the kings Joshua took out in Chapter 12? Scholars tell us, these kings were probably Egyptians, and not good guys at all.

Furthermore, when people ask for mercy, when people desire to make peace, the Israelites grant their request. We see this in the story of Rahab and her family, and also in the story of the Gibeonites. In Chapter 8, we hear that all of Israel, both the Hebrew people and the foreigners, heard the law. Who were these foreigners? I think there were more than just Rahab and her family who became part of the emerging nation.

Finally, we have to look at the context, not only in terms of the time in which it happened, but the time in which it was written down. Most scholars believe that these stories were transmitted orally and were written in their final form at the time when Israel was in exile in Babylon. Knowing this, how do we approach the Book of Joshua? Does anyone here think that the message of Joshua is that we, today, should conquer our unbelieving neighbors? Obviously, the answer is no. First, the events described are miraculous. We aren't dealing with human beings deciding to wage war, like the Crusades. This is God's action. Second, when we read this book alongside the message of Jesus to "love your enemies," violence of this type cannot be condoned.

Scholar Matt Lynch of the Western Theological Centre suggests that, knowing this context, we shouldn't so much ask why God authorized violence, but instead, 'What might the book of Joshua be doing?' And when we look closer, we see that there are two important messages.

The first message is: totally destroy your idols. Reading the Book of Joshua in the context of the Old Testament, the concept of total destruction, or *herem*, which Joshua undertakes is not the total destruction of people. Throughout the Old Testament, God calls for a *herem* against idols. When the Book of Joshua was written, its message to the people was to totally destroy their *practices* of idol worship, sin, and lawlessness, so that they could once again enter into their land and live in peace. Therefore, we should read it today as a commandment to totally destroy everything that separates us from God. As Jesus said, "If your hand causes you to sin, cut it off." (Matthew 5)

The season of Lent is an opportunity to rid ourselves of idols. Why do we give things up in Lent? Not out of some magical thinking that we'll be blessed because we do, or out of a sense of obligation that we have to, but because sometimes it helps us to get rid of distractions that have the potential to become idols. For that reason, maybe total destruction of the television or Facebook would be a good practice for us this Lent.

The second message of *herem* is: God wins. Get on His side. If we read Joshua in its context, we see it is a message to the Israelites, living in exile, who could have given up at any time: God will prevail, and so will we. This is not really a military story: it's way too one-sided! As any Civil War or World War II buff will tell you, you've got to have two great powers stacked up against each other. Here, there's no real battle: against God, no one will prevail. When your Commander in Chief has the power to make the sun stand still, it doesn't even matter what kind of earthly weapons you have.

Jericho was the greatest stronghold of the Canaanite kings, and it stood right in Israel's way. They were confronted with their greatest challenge as their first challenge. They were few in number, without great weapons, and the walls of Jericho, scholars tell us, were six feet thick and about twenty-six feet high. The devotions many of us read asked us, what is your personal Canaan? What is your personal Jericho? What is that seemingly impenetrable wall you are facing today?

You can't climb over it. You don't have the weapons to knock it down. And nobody's about to open the door for you. So, what do you do? You walk, and you wait. The battle of Jericho isn't a battle at all: it's worship. It's a seven-day march, reminding the people of the seven days of Unleavened Bread, and ultimately, the seven days of creation. The battle starts and ends at the Altar of Gilgal, an important place of worship. There's music, like in every worship service; the priests lead the people. They carry the Word of God with them: that's what's in the Ark of the Covenant. And at the end, people are called to be silent, and to listen for God. This is our model for how to face the six-foot-thick walls in our own life: walk, and wait; be silent, and carry the Word of God with you.

There are several people in my life who annoy me, because when I come to them with a problem, their question is always the same: "Did you pray about it?" But the book of Joshua teaches us that we are to encounter the Jericho's of our lives first and foremost, by prayer. I remember a couple of years ago when we were looking for five hundred dollars to send our young people to a Christian conference. Where would we get the money? Just as I began to get concerned, we got a call from a mission group that wanted to stay at the church. They didn't have much, but they could give us a little; say, five hundred dollars. This was not surprising to me. In my years at the church, I've asked several times if people might come forward to give scholarships for kids to go on mission trips. Whether it's a thousand dollars or three hundred, the money that comes in is exactly what we need for the trip. Sometimes I wish God would throw in a few extra dollars!

Joshua is not a story about the Israelites' fighting strength but about their faith strength. I think the clearest evidence of this is the stories of Canaanites who were won over by the power of God. Rahab, a Canaanite prostitute, is the last person you'd expect to be an example of faith; but it's her faith that's lifted up in the book of Joshua. She displays hospitality to others; she trusts in God; she places her household in God's hands, and she is saved. By contrast, Achan is an Israelite by blood, but he sees the battle of Jericho not as an exercise of faith, but as an opportunity for financial gain, and all of Israel feels the consequences of his lack of faith. The story of Rahab, like the story of the Gibeonites, demonstrates that it's not the Israelites' race that is important; it's the faith that God is teaching them in order to save all of the world. God's plan, all along, was to offer salvation to all people, to break down the boundaries between nations, to break down the walls that divide Jericho from Israel, and to offer salvation to all people. We see this in the most unlikely of people—Rahab, the Canaanite prostitute, who becomes an ancestor of Jesus.

The message is this: God wins. Get on His side. This salvation work, begun in Joshua, is completed by the one who shares his name—Jesus, or in Hebrew, Yeshua, Joshua. A Canaanite person comes up only once in the New Testament. Do you remember where? It's when Jesus heals a Canaanite woman in Matthew 15:22-28. He engages in this dialogue with her, whereby she convinces him that people outside the nation of Israel are worthy of God's healing love. But I believe Jesus engaged in that dialogue, not because he really believed she was a "dog under the table, entitled to crumbs left behind," but because even when you read the Old Testament, you see that God truly wanted to bless all families of the earth.

God wins. When we try to fight our own battles, we will lose, every time. But when we give the battle to the Lord, He casts out the demons, he destroys the idols, he breaks down the walls. So keep walking. Keep waiting. Keep praying. Keep silent. Carry the Scriptures with you. And watch the walls come tumbling down.

In the name of the Father, and of the Son, and of the Holy Spirit, Amen.

Week Eleven: Mighty Warrior
Judges 6

When Rick Warren founded Saddleback Church in 1980, someone asked him, "how big do you think this church will get?" Rick replied, "we'll have 20,000 members." The questioner joked, "Who do you think you are?" Rick answered, "it's not about who I am. It's about who God is." Today, Saddleback has about 29,000 in worship on an average Sunday. The story of Gideon tells the same story: It's not about who you are. It's about Whose you are.

Gideon is one of the greatest warriors in the history of Israel, but he's also a very human person. He's a man tempted by idols. He struggles with self-worth. He's a man riddled by doubt. He's kind of a high-maintenance believer. And that's me; I question God; I question myself. Maybe there's some Gideon in most of us.

God encounters Gideon at a time of great suffering for the people of Israel. As we learned, the Israelites, first of all, are still struggling with the presence of the Canaanites, all these other people who are now living alongside the people of Israel in the Promised Land. And this is a struggle for God's people because it is difficult for them to maintain their faith, to keep God's commandments, to maintain worship, and to teach their children the faith among all these people who worship other gods. In fact, when God encounters Gideon, he, like most people of his time, had a Baal altar and an Asherah pole right next to his place of worship for Yahweh. Not only was Israel dealing with this struggle from the interior, but also with the constant pressure of the Philistines on the west, and on the East, you've got the Edomites, the Moabites, and the Ammonites. So, the only thing Israel doesn't need is something more to deal with.

Do you ever feel like you're surrounded on every side already, and then you get clocked with one more thing? The one more thing is the Midianites, who aren't even on my map, who come from all the way in the southeast and begin attacking Manasseh, which is Gideon's tribe. Gideon is so afraid of these Midianites that when we find him, what is he doing? He's having to hide in his wine press in order to harvest his grain. He's living in fear.

This reminds me of when I was in Costa Rica on a mission trip, and we needed a piece of construction equipment to finish our project. I figured if we needed the equipment to finish our project, we might as well just buy it there, spend a hundred dollars or so, and we could beg forgiveness when we got back. So, we went to the store and bought this piece of welding equipment and brought it back to the church we were working on. But the pastor of the church, Gustavo, who also did the welding, because that's what you do there, everyone knows how to do construction, he made us use the equipment inside. Because, he explained, if anyone knew he had this $100 piece of equipment, they'd kill him and steal it. That is how Gideon is living; he is living in fear.

Now God comes to this scared idol-worshiper who is doing chores in his basement, and this is what he says: Mighty Warrior, the Lord is with you! Gideon is anything but a mighty warrior at this moment. But God doesn't look with human eyes. So, my question for you is this: Who does God say you are?

You might see yourself as weak, ugly, broke; you might say, I can't do that, I'm divorced, I'm gay, I'm disabled—but that's not what God sees. You might be hiding your faith in the basement, doing your Bible reading in the dark, because you don't have the courage to proclaim your faith to others; but God has called you to do just that. Gideon calls himself the least in his family, and his family is the weakest in their clan. God calls him Mighty Warrior. Who does God say you are?

- God says you are his child: John 1:12, "But to all who received him, who believed in his name, he gave power to become children of God."
- God says you are his chosen one: Ephesians 1:4, "Just as he chose us in Christ before the foundation of the world to be holy and blameless before him in love."
- God says you are the salt of the earth: Matthew 5:13, "You are the salt of the earth; but if salt has lost its taste, how can its saltiness be restored? It is no longer good for anything but is thrown out and trampled underfoot."
- God says you are light of the world Matthew: 5:14, "You are the light of the world; A city built on a hill cannot be hid."
- God says you are a temple for his Holy Spirit: 1 Corinthians 6:19, "Or do you not know that your body is a temple[a] of the Holy Spirit within you, which you have from God, and that you are not your own?"
- And that God lives in you: 1 John 4:4, "Little children, you are from God, and have conquered them; for the one who is in you is greater than the one who is in the world."

- God says you are more than a conqueror through him who loves you! Romans 8:37, "No, in all these things we are more than conquerors through him who loved us."

We might look at our church and ask, how can we possibly take care of our own members, much less reach out into the world to help people in need, and share the love of Jesus Christ? But God says: Upon this rock I will build my church, and the gates of hell will not prevail against it! Matthew 16:18 This is what God says about us! Will we spend our lives trying to prove God wrong, or will we prove God right?

Now Gideon is one who asks difficult questions. When God calls out to Gideon, "mighty warrior! The Lord is with you," Gideon doesn't say, "awesome! Let's go get some Midianites." Instead, he says, If the Lord is with us, why then has all this happened to us? Where are all his wonderful deeds? Judges 6:13. The answer to Gideon's question comes a bit earlier in the chapter. In Judges 6:6, we learn that it's only when the Israelites cry out to the Lord that God responds by seeking out Gideon.

We've seen this before; sometimes you have to admit that you can't handle this on your own, that you need God's help, before God comes to your aid. But God doesn't chastise Gideon and say, hey, you idiot, maybe I've held off helping you because, I don't know--you've got idols in your living room! Instead, God answers Gideon's questions with his presence. God says, "I will be with you." And Gideon tests God! Over and over again, like a child, Gideon checks to see—are you still there, God? What if I go away for a little while, will you still be there? Yes, Gideon. Of course, Gideon. And then God shows his presence to Gideon; he sees the angel of the Lord; his offering burns up before his eyes. He's seen God! And yet. Gideon keeps questioning and testing God, and God keeps responding. Later in the chapter, Gideon has assembled the army, and is ready to fight the Midianites. But he needs another sign. So he lays out a wool fleece, and if the wool is wet, and the ground is dry, he will know that he should fight. So he lays out the wool, and a whole bowlful of water is in the fleece; but the ground is dry. But Gideon still needs more evidence. Gideon goes back to God, and says, God, I'm still not sure. This time, could you make the ground wet, and the fleece dry? Yes, Gideon. Of course, Gideon.

Gideon has trouble trusting; he wrestles with doubts and fears. Why does God jump through Gideon's hoops? Why does God give Gideon the signs he needs? Why doesn't God give up on Gideon? After all, we see in other places that God doesn't always answer our calls for signs and wonders. Lent is a good time for remembering Jesus's walk through the wilderness, the forty day fast that inspires us. Remember that, on the mountain, in the wilderness, Satan tempts Jesus to do all kinds of miracles and wonders, and Jesus refuses. Matthew 4:7, Jesus says, "you shall not put God to the test." So why doesn't God give up on Gideon?

I think there's a difference between seeking to prove God wrong and asking for help along the way. Satan sought to prove God wrong, by tricking Jesus into doing something He was not meant to do. Gideon sought encouragement and guidance from God, but I believe that he would have followed God's calling whether or not God gave him the specific signs he asked for. The truth is, if you and I are honest, we will see that God hasn't given up on us. Look back on your life. God has shown you, over and over and over, He is with you. God has shown us, as a church, over and over and over, he is with us. Yes, Gideon. Of course, Gideon. No, I won't give up on you.

We have to be looking for the burning bushes; we have to have our eyes out for the wet fleece. If we keep our eyes open, there are God sightings everywhere around us. So, what will it be: faith, or just more fleece?

God has given us every sign we need. God is calling: Mighty Warrior! Chosen One! Child of My Heart! I am with you! And I want you to be a light unto the world! Which will it be? Faith or fleece? Test or trust? Will you test God, try to prove God wrong about yourself, about us? Or will you trust God means what He says? Will you be the light of the world? Will you step forward, in new and creative ways, to reach out into the community, to reach out to family and friends, with the love of Christ? Or will you hide yourself away, try to prove God wrong, we're not a city on a hill, we're not the hands and feet of Jesus, we're not anything at all—or will you prove God right, by being the mighty warriors we were meant to be?

In the name of the Father, and of the Son, and of the Holy Spirit, Amen.

Week Twelve: Seeds in Winter
Ruth 4

If you ever become convinced that the world's gotten as cruel and violent and chaotic as it could possibly get, read the book of Judges in the Old Testament. It's like the Wild, Wild West times a thousand. The book is absolutely spilling with blood…a king gets stabbed by an assassin while he's supposed to be relieving himself, a woman stabs a leader through the head with a tent peg, a group of men rapes a concubine, then her lover sends her dismembered body to unite his allies against the wrongdoers. These do not make for easy Sunday school lessons or good bedtime reading. Amidst this backdrop, the story of Ruth comes as a breath of fresh air; a sweet romance, a new baby, and grandma who finally gets to retire.

Maybe the book of Ruth gets overlooked because we tend to think that's all it is—a nice story, a biblical date movie. But that's not all that's going on here, not by far. The book of Ruth contains some of the most important messages of the Bible; it shows us the character of God and what it means to live as a follower of Christ.

The story begins with a great tragedy; a man leaves his ancestral home of Bethlehem due to a famine; he then dies, leaving two sons; both of the sons marry foreign women, then both of the sons die childless, so there are three widows left behind. Two of these widows are still of childbearing age, and thus have good marriage prospects; but their mother-in-law, Naomi, is left essentially destitute. Some commentators note that Naomi is like the female Job; everything she had has been stripped away.

There's another layer to this that we don't understand because it's out of our cultural context. When Elimelech, Naomi's husband, left Bethlehem, he left his land behind; he probably rented it to a caretaker. But that land was not his to give. You see, the land of Israel was given to the Jewish people by God. Each tribe was given a certain piece of land, and within each tribe, different clans held each piece of territory, with the understanding that they did not really own the land—it was God's property, given to the Jewish people as caretakers. Therefore, if a man died childless, leaving no sons to take care of the land, it was not only a legal problem but a theological problem—the family is not fulfilling its covenant with God to care for the land God has provided.

Naomi gives her daughters-in-law permission to go, find husbands, and try to survive. Orpah follows this directive; but Ruth clings to her mother-in-law.

It probably will come as no surprise to you that this is not a natural relationship between a daughter-in-law and a mother-in-law. When we look at the book of Genesis, when a man marries, he must leave his father and mother and cleave to his wife; some translations say he clings to his wife. In premarital counseling, this is one of the first things I cover; when you marry, your spouse becomes your first priority, and you must leave your family of origin behind. We call it leaving and cleaving. Many of the problems a couple experiences in marriage come about because one or the other spouse hasn't really left their parents behind. It's natural, therefore, that there is some stress in this process, especially for the parents. I mean, my husband Dan has already told the kids to write off everything I say and do for a year when the boys get married.

So what Ruth does is the opposite of human nature. We see in verse 1:14:

Then they wept aloud again. Orpah kissed her mother-in-law, but Ruth clung to her. (Rut 1:14 NRS)

The word for "cling" in this verse is the exact word for "cling" in Genesis 2:24: *dabaq*. Ruth has clung to her former mother-in-law instead of to a husband; it is the opposite of her natural inclinations; it is not in her financial or social best interest. But this is what love does. Ruth, who has come to know something of the God of Israel and his covenant love, will not forsake this woman in her time of need. She will not allow the family land, its covenant promise of God, go forsaken. Rather, she gives up her own power and prospects to hitch her wagon to this old woman.

JK Rowling once wrote, "If you want to know what a man's like, take a good look at how he treats his inferiors, not his equals." Ruth's heart is shown in this moment, as she willingly empties herself to cling to this woman, against her nature and probably her better judgment. This is, to me, a prefiguring of what Christ did for us. Why would he willingly forsake heaven itself, to lead the life of a worker, an itinerant carpenter, with no family, no home, no wealth—to be betrayed and cast away by his people, and to die the ignominious death of a slave? Love. The covenant love of God, which willingly gives up worldly power for the sake of the beloved.

We learn something else from Ruth's selfless act: taking care of your family. In-law strife hits close to home for many of us; I hear about it all the time as a pastor, the difficulties within families. Yet Scripture directs us to, for lack of a better phrase, love the ones we're with. "What can you do to promote world peace?" Asked Mother Theresa. "Go home and love your family." When you and I meet God, He will ask how we loved our neighbors, which basically means those closest to us. This means all the peoples and cultures of metro Detroit, it means my homeless neighbors, my African-American neighbors, my Jewish neighbors, and my gay neighbors. But, perhaps hardest of all, it means my family. How did you treat them? Did you forgive them when they were difficult? Care for them when they were sick? Did you give up some measure of your own position, your own power, to love someone who needed love?

Ruth clings to Naomi; and the two set out for Judah. Once there, it's clear Naomi is in charge, and she has a plan; Boaz can serve as the kinsman-redeemer. This means that he will take over the land, marry Ruth, and have children who will, under Jewish law, technically be the sons of Naomi and Elimelech. The land covenant will be fulfilled; Naomi and Ruth will be cared for; and there will be new children of the covenant. All that remains to be done is, well, some old-fashioned matchmaking.

Naomi sends Ruth out to whet Boaz's appetite; it's clear her plan is working, since Boaz makes sure there's some extra wheat for Ruth to glean. This, apparently, is the biblical equivalent of swiping right.

So the ladies take it to the next level. Naomi sends Ruth in to the threshing floor for a not-so-blind date. But she doesn't go in without her war paint. Naomi says, "wash yourself and put on your best clothes."

Then Ruth comes in, lays down next to Boaz, and uncovers his legs. Now, I know your translation says feet, but I've done some more exegesis on this than may be strictly necessary, and the scholars are pretty sure the Hebrew actually means legs. What Ruth is doing isn't sinful, but it's most definitely suggestive.

This is not some delicate flower hanging back and waiting for a gentleman to make the first move. Ruth is using everything she's got here. Here's my question to you—do we use everything we've got? In the church, we're apt to think that people will be drawn into our doors by, I don't know, the strength of our worship, the work we're doing in the community, the Scriptural command to remember the Sabbath and keep it holy. Especially as Protestants, we tend to engage the mind in worship more than the body. But we need to remember human nature once in a while. People need to worship with their eyes, noses, mouths and hands as well as with their ears and brains. Our worship engages the senses much less than the worship described in the Old Testament, which was a sensual feast. From the opening praise to the coffee hour, we need to redirect human passions to a holy purpose, just like Ruth did.

So Ruth and Naomi's plan works. Skipping ahead—and I'm not nearly plumbing the depths of this amazing story—Boaz acts as the kinsman-redeemer, secures the land, marries Ruth, and together they produce a son for Naomi.

But the story does not end here. This child, Obed, is the grandfather of David, Israel's greatest king, and what's more, he is the 27th great-grandfather of Jesus Christ, the great kinsman-redeemer who saved us all.

This is a joyful story with a happy ending; but I want you all to remember something. While this is going on, this woman's act of self-emptying love, this man's act of both passion and commitment, while this is all happening in this little corner of Judah, the children of Israel are still running around bashing people's heads in with tent pegs and cutting up each other's concubines. Good things are happening; but the story of Ruth and Boaz does not make the headlines of eleventh-century Jewish newspapers.

Could it be that the things God is doing today, aren't making the headlines? Could it be that, even though sometimes our world looks like it's going to hell in a handbasket, even though our churches are struggling, our nation is more divided than ever in history, and the values which used to govern our society are all but lost—God is planting the seeds of a bright future?

When my husband Dan and I first walked through our house, the real estate agent must have thought we were crazy. The house had been vacant for many months and was in foreclosure. In 2008, there was a lot of that going around. The paint was peeling; the kitchen cabinets were falling apart. The ceiling had actually caved in in more than one location. There was black mold throughout the bathrooms. And yet we walked through that place as though it were the Taj Mahal. We were thrilled to have found it, it was exactly what we wanted, we told the guy; a couple of hours later, we were homeowners.

Why? Because we weren't looking at the house as it was; we saw the potential. The bones, the layout, the limestone details, the solid plaster walls, the cute 1940s details like a doorbell inset and a telephone shelf that gave the place a special character. It was an investment—we were buying when everyone else was selling, and we'd never be able to buy into our neighborhood if we were looking today. Warren Buffett once said, "Whether we're talking about socks or stocks, I like buying quality merchandise when it's marked down. In the winter, when everything looks cold and dead—under the frozen ground, the seeds are just beginning to wake up.

This is why we need to have a God's eye view of our situation. When we look at the headlines, it's easy to get discouraged—but our God works behind the scenes. The work you and I are doing for God now, it is more important than ever. Don't get distracted by the headlines; don't try to fix the present. Focus on the future God is working, even now—through ordinary people, choosing the right, choosing to love, choosing to commit, God is redeeming the world.

Week Thirteen: Leadership
1 Samuel 16

We've been reading 1 Samuel this week, and 1 Samuel is an account of what leadership looks like. Sadly, the failings of leaders in government, in the church, and in business are so well known that we no longer have any real level of confidence and very little respect for our leaders. The other day on the plane, my husband Dan was wearing a fleece jacket with the badge of the office of Michigan Attorney General on it, because his job is with the Attorney General's office. The ladies sitting next to him on the plane said, "wow, you're really brave to wear that in public." Now, the badge on his fleece didn't refer to the person who holds the office, but to the office itself, which is much larger than one person and encompasses people of every political persuasion working for the good of the state.

We've lost our respect for the office of leadership. And that's a bad thing, because without leaders, you can't really get anywhere. We saw this in the book of Judges: there was no king in Israel, everyone did what was right in his own eyes. We need leaders, and we as Christians are called to become better leaders ourselves.

Perhaps you are saying to yourself, but I'm not a leader. First of all, if you are an elder, or a trustee, or if you are a liturgist, or if you are a worship leader, or if you lead a group within the church, you are a church leader. But more than that, we are all called to be leaders in some area leadership and guidance to your whole family. There's a lady I visit who's living in a nursing home today, but her family is still looking to her for guidance and assistance as a leader of the family. Your family needs you to teach and guide them with what you have learned. Many of us are also professional leaders. We have teachers here, we have small business owners, and people in positions of authority within a larger organization. So how can you and I be better leaders?

1 Samuel tells the stories of three major leaders; Samuel, Saul, and David. First, we have the story of Samuel, the priest and judge of Israel. The people begin to call for a king rather than a judge, and Samuel sees that his own children are not up to that task, so he spends the final years of his life seeking a king. First God calls Samuel to anoint Saul. And Saul is a great choice; he's tall, he's good looking, he's a great warrior, he seems to be very religious; great candidate for king. 1 Samuel 9:2, "He had a son whose name was Saul, a handsome young man. There was not a man among the people of Israel more handsome than he; he stood head and shoulders above everyone else."

But after a while, Saul starts to make some missteps, and God does something really unexpected; he tells Samuel to anoint a better king. Now this is a strange and a difficult thing. Some of you have commented that the rejection of Saul seems to come really fast, without a lot of provocation, and it's difficult to read about. And you're not alone; this is really difficult for Samuel. Actually, it's even difficult for God. 1 Samuel 15:34, "Then Samuel went to Ramah; and Saul went up to his house in Gibeah of Saul."

Samuel and God both grieve for Saul. We don't know how long they grieved, or how they grieved. But they grieved. Now Saul made some mistakes; he made a vow that he would kill anyone who had something to eat before a battle, which is probably poor battle strategy; he took plunder for himself from a city that God wanted totally destroyed, which never really works, and he offered a sacrifice when he wasn't supposed to. But most importantly, it's God's way to choose leaders based not on the outward characteristics, not on their credentials, how many degrees they have or how good-looking they are or how much money they've made. If those things made a good leader, we'd look at the life of Jesus, for instance, who died a slave's death without enacting major social change or making a lot of money, and we would say, that's not a good leader. But what really makes a good leader is not the outward characteristics that the world values, but the inward character of the heart. And ultimately, if you focus on your inward heart, you will do a lot more good for people than if you focus on outward success.

So the first lesson of leadership is this: Good leaders are honest and humble. Honesty is so important in our leaders. When you're honest with people, you gain their trust. You can't lead people if they won't follow you, and they won't follow you if they don't trust you. So good leaders need to be honest. We see this in Samuel. First, Samuel is honest in with himself and with others. When God calls Samuel to anoint a king, what would be the easiest thing for Samuel to do? Anoint himself. Or anoint one of his sons. But Samuel is an honest person, and he accepts the fact that he himself and his sons have been rejected. Then God rejects the person that God has earlier called to be anointed; God rejects Saul. But Samuel doesn't pretend like he's a superhuman; he's upset when someone who he has trusted and gotten behind turns out not to be the right man for the job. Samuel grieves. Samuel is honest, which makes him a good leader.

And as we see later in the story, David is honest too. We all like David and Goliath, David the shepherd boy, David who plays the harp. When I was a kid, we got a Nintendo. This was a huge deal for my family. My mom got us this game called Bible Adventures to kind of counteract the evil force of video games coming into the house. And in Bible Adventures, you got to be David. There were two levels; first you got to save the sheep, then you got to fight Goliath. There was no Bathsheba level in Bible Adventures. There was no level where you slept with another man's wife and had her husband killed to cover it up. There was no game in which you pretend to be loyal to the Philistines while raiding and killing entire villages. There was no level in which you quash a rebellion by his own son. These are the stories of David no one likes to remember. But in some ways, they are the most important stories. Because David is very human. But David is also very honest. He doesn't do the typical politician non-apology apology: "mistakes were made." He doesn't minimize his actions and the harm he has caused. Rather, he is honest, he seeks forgiveness, and he tries to make amends. We see this in the Bathsheba story:

2 Samuel 12:13, "David said to Nathan, "I have sinned against the Lord." Nathan said to David, "Now the Lord has put away your sin; you shall not die.""

Psalm 51 is our model for repentance in the Bible. It's the text we read every Ash Wednesday, and it's held up as a prayer David prayed after he went in to Bathsheba.

"Have mercy on me, O God,
   according to your steadfast love;
according to your abundant mercy
   blot out my transgressions.
Wash me thoroughly from my iniquity,
   and cleanse me from my sin.
For I know my transgressions,
   and my sin is ever before me.
Against you, you alone, have I sinned,
   and done what is evil in your sight,
so that you are justified in your sentence
   and blameless when you pass judgment.
Indeed, I was born guilty,
   a sinner when my mother conceived me.
You desire truth in the inward being;
   therefore, teach me wisdom in my secret heart.
Purge me with hyssop, and I shall be clean;
   wash me, and I shall be whiter than snow.
Let me hear joy and gladness;
   let the bones that you have crushed rejoice.
Hide your face from my sins,
   and blot out all my iniquities.
Create in me a clean heart, O God,
   and put a new and right[b] spirit within me.

> Do not cast me away from your presence,
>   and do not take your holy spirit from me.
>
> Restore to me the joy of your salvation,
>   and sustain in me a willing spirit.
> Then I will teach transgressors your ways,
>   and sinners will return to you.
> Deliver me from bloodshed, O God,
>   O God of my salvation,
>   and my tongue will sing aloud of your deliverance.
> O Lord, open my lips,
>   and my mouth will declare your praise.
> For you have no delight in sacrifice;
>   if I were to give a burnt offering, you would not be pleased.
> The sacrifice acceptable to God is a broken spirit;
>   a broken and contrite heart, O God, you will not despise.
> Do good to Zion in your good pleasure;
>   rebuild the walls of Jerusalem,
> then you will delight in right sacrifices,
>   in burnt offerings and whole burnt offerings;
>   then bulls will be offered on your altar."

David was a good leader because he was honest with himself, with his people, and with God. He was also a humble leader. Humility is not thinking less of yourself, it's thinking of yourself less, and David puts the needs of others and the desires of God before himself. Consider what happens after David is anointed. Does he swoop in and take over the palace? No. He goes to be a servant of the current king, to play the harp for him. And then he spends the prime years of his life on the run from that same king. Who shows the greatest respect for Saul's anointing? David. David will not kill Saul and does not want others to do so. Because Saul was anointed by God and David respects that. David rejects Saul's armor when he goes in to fight Goliath. It's too big for him, too heavy for him. He is honest enough with himself, with others, and his God to think no more of himself than he ought. This is in contrast to Saul. God turned away from Saul because Saul offered a sacrifice. This seems really unfair to us; I mean, isn't Saul worshiping God? Isn't that a good thing? It feels like when God rejected Cain's sacrifice but accepted Abel's.

But this is the key: Saul wasn't humble. You see, in ancient Israel there was a system of three leaders: prophet, priest, and king. There was a kind of separation of powers. The king provided protection and prosperity, the priest provided worship and care, and the prophet's job—well, the prophet's job was to criticize the priest and king, to make sure they are following God's will. So when Saul offers up a sacrifice to God, he is taking on not just the role of king but also of priest. He's violating that separation of powers and making himself more powerful than he ought to be. As we will see, there's only one person who can fulfill the roles of prophet, priest, and king, and that is the messiah. I often think that I need a sign on my office door: Two things I know: The messiah has come, and I am not him. As leaders, we are called not to think more of ourselves when we become leaders, but to think first of others and of God's vision. So: good leaders are honest and humble. And, good leaders are courageous and called.

We look at all the reasons why God may have called for David's anointing, but maybe the most important one was the public tagline about David: 1 Samuel 29:5, "Is this not David, of whom they sing to one another in dances, 'Saul has killed his thousands, and David his ten thousand?'" Even though it seems pretty violent to us, this was a time when the people needed protection. God was building a nation, and he needed a great warrior. David's courage was evident from his days as a shepherd, when he protected the sheep; now he is called to be a protector of a greater flock. As leaders, we need to be courageous, and call the people to be warriors for what we know is right. We also need to have to courage to protect others and look out for the best interests of our people.

Finally, all the rest of the examples of leadership come down to this: it's about calling. Good leaders are obedient to God's voice and God's calling. Why isn't this book of the Bible called 1 David? Why is it called 1 Samuel? I believe it's because Samuel's entire life is about calling, and leadership means listening to God's call. As a young boy, in the middle of the night, Samuel hears a voice calling, "Samuel." And he says, "Here I am, Lord." And what is leadership but saying: here I am, Lord. Samuel was excited to anoint Saul because he looked like a great candidate. Then Samuel wanted to anoint one of Jesse's older sons because they were so tall and good looking. And this is very human; for the past half century, Americans have always elected the taller of two presidential candidates. But Samuel is one who listens for God, and God isn't interested in looks or degrees or money or credentials. God looks at the heart. His heart beat with the beat of God's heart. In the end, like all callings, David's calling is a mystery; it has to do with something only God can see or understand.

I don't understand why God calls who He does. Do you know how many times I wish God had called someone else to ministry? Only every day. But we don't do this because it's easy. We do this because when he says, come, follow me, and I will make you fishers of men, we lay down our nets. We do this because when we heard him calling in the night, we didn't roll over and go back to sleep. We said: here I am. Send me. We don't do this for the world's accolades; we do this because we know that it's through the cross that we find our salvation. So we pick up our crosses, and we go. We lead.

Where are you called to lead? What is the task for which God has anointed you, unlikely you? Whatever your calling, I suggest to you this: listen for Him calling in the night. Be faithful to what God has called you to do. Become a man, a woman, after God's own heart. If we had more people doing that, men and women in leadership, who were humble, who were honest, who were courageous, and who were faithful to the call you imagine what we could do. We could inspire greater trust and greater hope for a greater future for the world.

In the name of the Father, and the Son, and the Holy Spirit, Amen.

Week Fourteen: Courage
2 Samuel 12

David didn't wake up and say, "Today I will commit adultery and tomorrow, murder." After all, Satan doesn't wear a name badge, he just shows us the cheese on the mousetrap. In this case, the cheese was Bathsheba, bathing in the afternoon window, the water catching the sunlight on her hair. Like how quicksand appears to be solid, leaves and twigs resting on its sandy surface, so you never know until it's too late.

We don't know if this is the first time that David seduced, or raped, another man's wife. Indeed, his power was such that Bathsheba truly had no choice in the matter. There has been a lot of preaching wondering why Bathsheba was bathing on the roof. But the text doesn't say she was on the roof, it says David saw her from the roof. Notice that in Nathan's lamb story, did the lamb present herself to the rich man, saying, "Hi, I'd like to be your supper."? No, the lamb is slaughtered. In my reading of the Bible, David stands squarely to blame.

This could have just been a one-night stand, but David gets Bathsheba's text message, "I'm pregnant." And David knows he's stuck. The quicksand is reaching his ankles, and like anyone would do, he tries to pull himself out. We watch David's painful struggle, the cover-up attempt. David comes up with a plan. Call Uriah home and get him to sleep with Bathsheba. Sure, it wouldn't hold up to a paternity test, the math might be a little off, but really, where's the harm? So, he calls Uriah home, and he orders him, go home and wash your feet. Which is a Hebrew euphemism for, have sex with your wife. But Uriah, the Hittite, not even a true Israelite, cares more for the troops on the field than does David, Israel's king. Uriah the Hittite won't go home while the troops are in the fields. And David feels the quicksand moving up his calves. So David moves on to plan B. Get Uriah drunk. But as one commentator remarked, Uriah drunk is more pious than David sober. There is no easy way out of this. David feels the quicksand reach around his waist. And maybe he even justified it to himself, for the good of the nation, for all who believe David is this God-fearing king, he has to preserve that trust. Plan C. David pens a letter. And, stopping at nothing in his own desire to see this thing buried, he gives it to Uriah himself. The letter is Uriah's death sentence. Joab the loyal commander does as his king asks. And he sends back word: Uriah is dead. David is now a murderer.

The thing about quicksand is, all your agitated movements, all your pulling and struggling to get yourself out, only sinks you deeper in. Contrary to popular belief, quicksand cannot kill you. It just sticks you in away from water, away from food, away from life, at the mercy of the elements, at the mercy of the first snake that slithers your way, and there is nowhere to go but the dirty, sticky mess you have gotten yourself in. The force needed to pull one foot out of quicksand is equivalent to the force needed to lift a midsize car. You know how you get out of quicksand? Someone else has to get a rope and pull you out.

Because I didn't live through the events myself, I learned about Watergate when I got the chance to visit the Gerald Ford Presidential Museum. The exhibit is really wonderful and if you get a chance to visit it in Grand Rapids, Michigan, I highly recommend it. President Nixon did everything he could to pull himself out. He used all the resources at his disposal, including the CIA, to cover up what he had done, but with every lie he just pulled himself in deeper. Until finally he was forced to hand over the smoking gun tapes, and the jig was up.

The Scripture says that the thing David had done displeased the Lord. Understatement of the year. The jig is up. So, God turns to Nathan. What's developing in Israel is this three-part system of prophet, priest, and king. And in this system, Nathan is the first of Israel's prophets, the first in the long line of guys with bad news that will take us to Isaiah and Jeremiah and the rest. But Nathan doesn't have a big part in 2 Samuel. There is no call story for Nathan; we don't know how he came to be in David's court. We meet him first in 2 Samuel 7:2. David comes to him and asks what they should do with the ark; a "house" for the Lord. And Nathan says, "Go ahead and do whatever you have in mind." But God then speaks to Nathan and tells him that it's God who wants to build David a house—a house of kings! And that it will be up to David's son to build the temple. Nathan, so far, has been the bringer of good news. A great guy for David to keep on the payroll. But this time, Nathan has bad news to deliver.

And Nathan has a choice. He could be obedient to the Lord, and perhaps forfeit his life. After all, David's already killed once. Who's to say he won't do it again? Or at least hand Nathan a pink slip? At this point in Israel's history, the prophet's role is brand new. Do they really need a prophet? Or is a priest enough to keep God happy? Is the prophet supposed to be honest and obedient to God's Word, or is he simply supposed to be the king's spiritual mouthpiece? Nathan chooses to be honest, and thus to risk his livelihood and even his life. And this choice has great implications for the nation of Israel. Because, as we will see, the kings will disappoint; the priests, too, will become corrupt; and it's the prophets who will lead the people back to God.

Speaking up and speaking out about injustice and sin is difficult. It's rarely stress-free. So why do it? Why not keep our mouths shut? Well, look at the alternative. The alternative is lies, cover-up, more quicksand. Simply put, Nathan fears God more than he fears the king. One author put it this way: "Courage is not the absence of fear, but rather the judgement that something else is more important than fear." My question for you today is: what are you afraid of? Well, isn't God more important than that fear? Courage is a choice; the choice of faith over fear. Sometimes our courage isn't like that of Nathan. We don't have one big life-or-death moment. Instead it's the courage to keep hoping. To keep loving. To keep working toward God's vision of justice, and hope, and peace, and not take the easy way out.

Nathan chooses faith over fear. He has the courage to speak the truth. And in making this choice, Nathan's faith sets a precedent that will keep the nation faithful even beyond the age of kings. Nathan shows everyone what a prophet, what a preacher, should really be: one who speaks God's truth, even when it's hard. But beyond courage, Nathan has wisdom. He finds a way to lead David into understanding what he has done. Nathan comes to him and says, king, there's a problem in your kingdom.

A rich man had hundreds of sheep, thousands of sheep, and a poor man had only one, which he loved like his own daughter. The rich man needed a sheep, but rather than take any of his own, he stole the only sheep of this poor man, and violently destroyed it for his own pleasure. David, furious, jumps to his feet and declares that this rich man deserves to die. Pop quiz: do you remember someone else who uses this same method? It's the wise woman of Tekoa, who in 2 Samuel 14 tells David a story that convinces him to forgive his son Absalom. 2 Samuel 14:13. Nathan and the woman of Tekoa use this clever strategy to get David to recognize that if one of his subjects acted in such an unrighteous way, they would surely be punished. David must submit himself to the same judgment.

And this teaches us something important: we are called to be brave, but we aren't called to be dumb. Speak the truth but do it in such a way that others will listen and actually change. Do the right thing but do it also in the right way. Sometimes the quick, knee-jerk reaction isn't the best way to solve a problem and might be the best way to get yourself in trouble. Nathan realizes that outrightly condemning David won't work. He must make David see for himself the error of his ways. And this is a principle you learn in business, in law, in therapy—it's much more effective to convince someone than to confront someone. Like Nathan, we are called to be smart about our courage, not only to protect ourselves, but more importantly because we'll be most effective if we think before we act.

One more lesson from Nathan: after his long indictment, David is muted. The king simply says, "I have sinned against the Lord." And just that fast, in that very moment, without qualification, without question, hardly have the words passed from David's lips before Nathan replies, The Lord has put away your sin. You will not die. A lot of people feel like Nathan lets David off the hook. How can he be sure that David is really sorry? That he really repented?

In the same way, when Nixon finally resigned and Gerald Ford became President, Ford's most unpopular act as President was to pardon Nixon of any wrongdoing, even before an official charge was filed in court. The museum showed letters upon scathing letters from the American people furious over the injustice of what Ford had done. Even the White House Press Secretary, Ford's close advisor and friend, resigned in protest.

But from a biblical standpoint, Ford's act was entirely right. Because when we turn to God, when we admit that we have sinned against the Lord, that's the moment the rope comes down. That's what grace is. There are no limits around it. We don't have to prove ourselves worthy of that grace. We simply have to receive it. And out of the mess, God pulls something beautiful. Thieves become theologians. Prostitutes become prophetesses. Druggies become disciples. Worriers become worshipers. From this 2 Samuel 12 mess of sin, lies, abuse and violence, God pulls a great-great-great-great-great-great-great-great-great-great-great-great grandson, Jesus.

What can God pull out of your mess? When we look at our lives, sometimes the problems we face look like quicksand. But if we stop trying to fix it ourselves, and instead turn to God; if we, like Nathan, are obedient to His Word, and face our problems with courage, with wisdom, and with grace, we can grab the rope. So whatever situation you are facing, at work, at home, in the church, let your faith be bigger than your fear. Rather than react, think before you act. And find a way to put out a rope. Find a way to show grace. Let God pull a bless out of your mess.

In the name of the Father, and the Son, and the Holy Spirit, Amen.

Week Fifteen: Jerusalem
1 Kings 5:1-13

On this day, Christians around the world celebrate the event that got Jesus killed; his triumphal entry into Jerusalem, where the common people proclaimed him King. The Roman authorities saw a rebellion fermenting, and the religious leadership of the Sanhedrin didn't like Jesus's challenge to their authority—which he displayed, soon after entering the city, by ransacking the Temple. Jesus knew that by entering the capital and confronting the religious and political powers, he was writing his own death warrant. But he was determined to go there. The Scriptures say Jesus had set his face toward Jerusalem. Matthew 19:1. Why Jerusalem? Why did Jesus have to go there? After all, it would be more convenient, today, if the place where Jesus died and rose from the dead were somewhere other than the land that's also sacred to Muslims and Jews.

We read about Jerusalem in the books of Samuel and Kings as the city where David and his line consolidated their power. Prior to that time, the area around Jerusalem may have had some historical significance as the location where Abraham sacrificed Isaac, but as we have seen, worship traveled with the ark, judges ruled from wherever they happened to live, and there was no one place in the Holy Land set apart as the Holy City. It's with David, Solomon, and the Davidic line that Jerusalem becomes the center of the people's political and religious life.

And that is precisely why Jesus had to go to Jerusalem: because God had some problems with both the political and religious situation of the city, and indeed, of the world. Jerusalem means a number of things, but the most agreed-upon meaning of the name "Jerusalem" is the city of peace. And then, as now, there wasn't a lot of peace in the city. The Roman occupiers maintained order through violence. They violated the Temple and installed priests loyal to them, rather than to God or the people. So, the Jewish people were looking for someone to come in and fix it, a savior who would ride in on a big tank with guns blazing and set everything right.

A few years ago, a documentary came out about education in America, called *Waiting for Superman*. The people of Israel were waiting for Superman. They were waiting for the promised Messiah, a new king from the line of David, who would show the Romans who was boss. They wanted David back. They wanted Solomon. The great kings of old. That's why they rejoiced to see Jesus riding in on a donkey. The people remembered 1 Kings 1, and they remembered Zechariah's prophecy: from Zechariah 9:9-10, that the king would come humbly, riding on a donkey colt.

So that is why they waved their palm branches—a symbol of hailing a king, or perhaps a reminder of the branches they waved during the festival of booths, which was one of the festivals we studied back in Exodus. They're excited for David to come back, or one of his line, and kick some Roman you-know-what, and restore a godly king on the throne. And can we blame them? Don't we want solutions, now, to the real physical and political and economic problems we face? Aren't we waiting for Superman? Don't we want God to heal our bodies, our finances, our nation? The people of Israel wanted to make Israel great again. And no matter how you feel about our President or his slogan, we do, all of us, long for a greater America.

But a great nation wasn't good enough for God. As we have seen, the good old days weren't always so good in Israel (perhaps the same is true, if we are honest, about our own history as well). The line of David turned out to be a disappointment. Even David himself was far from a perfect ruler. Although Jesus is proclaimed king, when he enters the city, it's not Solomon or David he thinks of. Instead, just after he enters the city, Jesus remembers what happened to the prophets, who truly spoke for God: Matthew 23:37 says, "Jerusalem, Jerusalem, city that stones the prophets, how often have I wanted to cover you as a hen covers her chicks under her wings!"

Jesus knows that his role is not just to restore power, but to share truth, and historically, truth doesn't go over so well. You see, the people want a king, but God is not interested so much in what we want. You see, He's tried that. When the people wanted a king before, He gave them a king. And in so doing, he preserved the nation, he preserved the faith, he preserved the relationship between himself and humankind. But as we have seen, it was not an ideal system, nor was it God's design from the beginning. He wanted the people to turn to him, love him, and follow him. If we all turned toward God, we would have no need of a king, because we would live in justice and righteousness and peace.

God thinks bigger than the political problem that the Israelites see, and bigger than the short-term political solution they envision. And God sends us not a physical savior, not a political savior, but a Savior of our hearts and souls. Not the savior we want, but the Savior we need. A Savior who will not ride into the city on a chariot, like the Romans, but on a humble donkey—and not just a donkey, but a young donkey, a donkey cold. A Savior who will not wear a crown of gold, like David, but a crown of thorns. A Savior who will not speak on a throne, like Solomon, but from a cross. A Savior who rules not from power, but from love.

We try to accomplish things from our power, from our strength. We try to fight for what we believe in. And some things can be accomplished through political power and military might. But not the great things. The kingdom of Israel fell. So did the empire of Greece. The Romans, too. The British Empire, on which the sun never set—it's history now. Hitler declared that the German Reich would reign forever—a few years is all it took before his tyranny crumbled. Political power, military might—they will fall. Superman might save us, for now. But what created the universe, what created life, what created you and me—the power that breaks down barriers and changes people and nations forever—is the power of love. And that's the power that, deep down, the people saw in Jesus. That's why they wanted to crown him king. They were right to do so. They just didn't think big enough. They just didn't know just how much his love could do.

I read a true story about what love can do, by a man named Richard Paul Evans. He writes:

> For years my wife Keri and I struggled. Looking back, I'm not exactly sure what initially drew us together, but our personalities didn't quite match up…We were on the edge of divorce and more than once we discussed it…. I was alone and lonely, frustrated and angry. I had reached my limit. That's when I turned to God. Or turned *on* God. I don't know if you could call it prayer–maybe shouting at God isn't prayer, maybe it is–but whatever I was engaged in I'll never forget it. I was standing in the shower…yelling at God that marriage was wrong, and I couldn't do it anymore. As much as I hated the idea of divorce, the pain of being together was just too much…why couldn't we get along? Why had I married someone so different than me? Why wouldn't *she* change?
>
> Finally, hoarse and broken, I sat down in the shower and began to cry. In the depths of my despair powerful inspiration came to me. *You can't change her, Rick. You can only change yourself.* At that moment I began to pray. If I can't change *her*, God, then change *me*. I prayed late into the night. I prayed the next day on the flight home. I prayed as I walked in the door to a cold wife who barely even acknowledged me. That night, as we lay in our bed, inches from each other yet miles apart, the inspiration came. I knew what I had to do.
>
> The next morning I rolled over in bed next to Keri and asked, "How can I make your day better?"
>
> Keri looked at me angrily. "What?"

"How can I make your day better?"

"You can't," she said. "Why are you asking that?"

"Because I mean it," I said. "I just want to know what I can do to make your day better."

She looked at me cynically. "You want to do something? Go clean the kitchen."

She likely expected me to get mad. Instead I just nodded. "Okay." I got up and cleaned the kitchen.

The next day I asked the same thing. "What can I do to make your day better?"

Her eyes narrowed. "Clean the garage."

I took a deep breath. I already had a busy day and I knew she had made the request in spite. I was tempted to blow up at her. Instead I said, "Okay." I got up and for the next two hours cleaned the garage. Keri wasn't sure what to think.

The next morning came. "What can I do to make your day better?"

"Nothing!" she said. "You can't do anything. Please stop saying that."

"I'm sorry," I said. "But I can't. I made a commitment to myself. What can I do to make your day better?"

"Why are you doing this?"

"Because I care about you," I said. "And our marriage."

The next morning I asked again. And the next. And the next. Then, during the second week, a miracle occurred. As I asked the question Keri's eyes welled up with tears. Then she broke down crying. When she could speak, she said, "Please stop asking me that. You're not the problem. I am. I'm hard to live with. I don't know why you stay with me."

I gently lifted her chin until she was looking in my eyes. "It's because I love you," I said. "What can I do to make your day better?"

"I should be asking you that."

"You should," I said. "But not now. Right now, I need to be the change. You need to know how much you mean to me."

She put her head against my chest. "I'm sorry I've been so mean."

"I love you," I said.

"I love you," she replied.

"What can I do to make your day better?"

She looked at me sweetly. "Can we maybe just spend some time together?"

I smiled. "I'd like that."

I continued asking for more than a month. And things did change. The fighting stopped. Then Keri began asking, "What do you need from me? How can I be a better wife?"

The walls between us fell. We began having meaningful discussions on what we wanted from life and how we could make each other happier. No, we didn't solve all our problems. I can't even say that we never fought again. But the nature of our fights changed. Keri and I have now been married for more than thirty years. I not only love my wife, I like her. I like being with her. I crave her. I need her. Many of our differences have become strengths and the others don't really matter. We've learned how to take care of each other.

When we treated God with cruelty and hate, when we hurt God and one another in unforgiveable ways, God didn't come down to show us who was boss. He asked "How can I make your world better? What more, beloved people, can I possibly do for you?", and we answered, "die." So He did. And in doing so, He defeated the powers of darkness with the power of love. He was not the savior we wanted, but the Savior we needed.

What do you want from God? Are you praying for healing, praying for success, praying for someone to come and save you? Someone already did. We pray for what we want from God. But what if, instead, we prayed for what we really need? Maybe it's not healing from the disease. Maybe it's the strength to carry on. Maybe it's not greater success. Maybe it's redefining what success really means. Maybe it's not waiting for Superman to come and save us. Maybe it's placing our trust more and more in Jesus, who already did.

This Holy Week, the world is already celebrating Easter, new life, all things bright and shiny and new, the triumph of the King. The world wants bunnies and eggs and holiday ham. The world wants easy answers. But we walk through Jerusalem. We watch the city of peace turn into a city run by cruel governors, corrupt politicians, and an angry mob. We see the worst humanity has to offer. And we see our salvation. Not in a king on a throne, restoring peace to the city for a time, but in a Savior on the cross, restoring peace for all people and for all time, not with the power of armies, but with the power of love. Come. Let us walk into the city of peace.

In the name of the Father, and the Son, and the Holy Spirit, Amen.

Week Sixteen: Resurrection
2 Kings

Easter is the most important day of our year as Christians. What is the biggest Christian holiday the world celebrates? It's Christmas. The world goes nuts for Christmas. The world goes crackers for Christmas. The world goes nutcrackers for Christmas. But Easter slips by in our culture without much fanfare. It's a long weekend maybe, nothing more. Easter hasn't been associated with the wild commercialism of Christmas. Maybe that's partly because Easter is so clearly about faith that it can't be commercialized and secularized. The world may say it's about the bunny, but everybody knows it's about the Lamb.

Because Christian faith makes no sense at all unless Jesus rose from the dead. Born from a virgin? Cool trick. Feeding of the five thousand? That's nice, but McDonald's does it every day. Sermon on the Mount? Nice speech. Even Jesus's death on the cross would be just another martyrdom in the cause of truth and justice if it weren't for Easter.

Jesus rising from the dead is at the very center of our faith. Our job is to go out and tell the world about the truth of Easter. In Acts Jesus tells the disciples what they are supposed to do: "You will be my witnesses in Judea, and in Samaria, and to the ends of the earth." Acts 1:8. Our job is to repeat the words we shouted this morning, not just in the safe confines of the church, but in the whole world: He is risen indeed!

So my question to you is this: do you believe He is risen indeed? Is Jesus risen, in your mind? Is Jesus risen in your heart? Is Jesus risen in your life? And for each of these questions, you will have the opportunity today to say it one more time: He is risen indeed! And not just to say it, but to really believe it, so much so that, like the women who came to the tomb, you have no choice but to tell the whole world.

So first, Is Jesus risen, in your mind? There are lots of historical proofs of the resurrection: the heavy stone, the lack of a body, the sudden, inexplicable change in the disciples. But even if you don't buy these historical reasons, consider Science, Scripture, and nature.

First, scientific theory about the origins of the universe is telling us that the universe had a starting point: there was nothing, and then there was light. What did God use to create the universe? Did He do it from one star? Or even one molecule? No. He made everything that is out of nothing at all. And if He did it once, if you can believe that miracle, can't we believe that God brought life from nothingness that Sunday morning? That God is in the habit of making all things new?

God has been trying to make this point to us for a very long time: "I make all thing new." God's message of Easter is all over the Bible. Nine people are raised from the dead, including the unnamed son of the Shunammite woman we read about this morning. Back in 2 Kings, God gave the people two prophets, Elijah and Elisha, and we believe their purpose was to prepare people for Jesus, because so many of the miracles they performed—feeding the hungry, raising the dead, healing the sick—were the same kinds miracles Jesus performed.

But God didn't just tell us about resurrection through the miracle workers of the Bible. He also placed our little blue planet in such a way that we experience seasons, a message of resurrection every year. The great reformer Martin Luther said that God speaks "in every leaf in springtime." Each daffodil, each crocus, each lily is God's way of explaining to us: I like to make things new. Butterflies arise from their tomblike cocoons. A seed dies so that the seedling can emerge. We see all throughout nature the truth of resurrection.

We all have questions, we all have doubts. But ultimately, one side has to win. Is it doubt, or is it faith? Can you proclaim: He is risen indeed! If so, the next question is: Is Jesus risen in your heart?

John, the Gospel writer, made up a phrase that had never been used before. In Greek, you would say "I believe that," such as "I believe that God exists." But John made up the phrase "I believe *in*" something. And if you think about it, believing *in* Jesus isn't the same as believing *that* Jesus existed. You can believe that Jesus rose from the dead, but do you believe *in* Easter? Because if you really believe in the truth of Easter, it will change the way you look at everything. You won't be so worried about health or wealth or the little things. It doesn't mean you won't care about our world, terrorism and war and poverty and disease. You'll probably care about the world more because God cares about this world. But you will also have a peace in your heart that no events can shake. Like the Shunammite woman. Did you notice how everybody is asking her what is wrong, and she just says, "Shalom!" "Peace!" "It's all right!" (2 Kings) She has this desperate urgency to find help for the very real problem of her dead son…but she also has this unshakeable faith that it will all be ok.

That's why we say, when we pass the peace, may the peace of Christ be with you. It doesn't mean everything will always go ok in your life, but that no matter what happens, you will be able to say, Shalom! You might have doubts, you might have fears, but in the end, one side has to win. Can you proclaim with your whole heart, He is risen indeed!

And finally, if you believe that Christ is risen with your heart and your mind, then is Jesus risen in your life? When the disciples encountered the risen Lord, it changed everything. These ordinary fishermen and tax collectors gave up everything, went all over the world, shared everything they had, and spent the rest of their lives talking about Jesus. It got seven of them, seven of the faithful eleven, killed. Easter changed everything! And Easter doesn't really matter if it's just a long weekend. But if it's true, then it needs to be the central truth of your life that Jesus rose from the dead. If it is true, you must live differently! If He really was the Son of God who rose from the dead, and eternal life can be found in Him, then that will change everything you think and everything you say and everything you do. Romans 6:4 says, we will live new lives.

We are called to live as an Easter people every day, a changed people, a people of peace and faith, who by our actions proclaim that Christ is risen indeed. Every time an addict turns away from the bottle, He is risen. Every time a person wronged chooses to forgive, He is risen. Every time a Christian takes a risk for Christ, He is risen. Every time we choose love over fear, Christ is risen indeed!

Jesus did not rise from the dead so that you could eat ham this afternoon. He rose so that you and I could live new lives. So, Is Jesus risen in your life? He is risen indeed! So believe in Easter with all your heart, all your soul, and all your might; and let your life proclaim, "He is risen indeed!" every day.

In the name of the Father, and the Son, and the Holy Spirit, Amen.

Week Seventeen: Dynasty
1 Chronicles

1 and 2 Chronicles retells the stories of 1 and 2 Kings, the stories of the rise and fall of the kingdoms of Israel. Today's reading is part of the larger story of David's entry into Jerusalem. We have read how God created the earth, how humans turned away from God, and how God established a special relationship with a group of people, through whom He will bless all peoples of the earth. Now God is strengthening and protecting that people, creating a stable community so that His Word can be taught and learned. God establishes a monarchy through David, and a capital city, Jerusalem. Our reading today comes from the moment when David enters into Jerusalem, this climactic moment when God is fully present in the life of the nation.

David's Entry into Jerusalem:
David's Coronation (Ch. 11)
David Attempts to Carry the Ark (Ch. 13)
David Studies the Word (Ch. 14)
David Moves the Ark (Ch. 15)
David Prays (Ch. 16-17)
God Gives David a House (Ch. 17)
David Gives Thanks (Ch. 17)

David is crowned King of all Israel; but the coronation is almost a non-event, because David's first concern is to re-establish right worship of the Lord. Immediately after his military victories and coronation, David attempts to bring the Ark into Jerusalem. Saul has neglected the Ark for years (which is symbolic of Saul's failures to turn to God.) David wants to bring the Ark to his hometown, Jerusalem, to the place where Abraham was believed to have bound Isaac. But David doesn't consult God about any of this. Instead, he builds a little cart to carry the Ark, and posts some oxen to carry the Ark and some other guys to guide the oxen. Some of you have protested what happens to poor Uzzah, one of the ox-drivers. He reached out to steady the Ark on this cart, and God's power burst out of the Ark, almost like an electric current, and kills Uzzah. Not fair, you say. Why should God care about such a little thing as how the Ark is carried? And also, isn't this kind of weird, like the Ark is magic, or contains God in some way, when we know God is everywhere, and nothing can contain Him?

No, what happens to Uzzah is not fair. And life is not always fair. But David was performing a major operation—moving the place of worship from a temporary spot to a permanent one—without consulting God on whether or how to do it. As we have seen again and again, worship matters! David is trying to control the worship of God—to manage the worship of God in a way that makes sense to David. But David is thinking too small. The Ark is not his personal God-trophy, but a central part of the worship of the whole community. God cannot be contained by David's agenda; his power will burst forth from the Ark, just as it burst forth from the tomb, to show the world that God, not David, is in charge. So this is a message for us today, when we want to serve communion in a certain way or have a certain kind of music; we need to listen for what God wants. It's not my worship service or your worship service; it's God's.

So, David flips out a little bit, and sends the Ark to the home of a random guy who isn't even an Israelite—and that guys gets really blessed by God and has a whole bunch of kids, his stocks go up, all the plants in his yard get really green. And the Ark stays there for three months, while David prays and studies how to do this. And it turns out that this entry of the Ark is going to be a huge event. All the people are going to be involved, the priests and the Levites, there's going to be music, there's going to be crazy dancing, and lots of food. In fact, coming as this reading does on the heels of Holy Week and Easter, it's amazing when you look at just how many parallels there are between David's entry into Jerusalem and Christ's entry into Jerusalem.

The Coronation
David's Coronation: 1 Chronicles 11, "Then all Israel gathered together to David at Hebron and said, "See, we are your bone and flesh. For some time now, even while Saul was king, it was you who commanded the army of Israel. The Lord your God said to you: It is you who shall be shepherd of my people Israel, you who shall be ruler over my people Israel." So all the elders of Israel came to the king at Hebron, and David made a covenant with them at Hebron before the Lord. And they anointed David king over Israel, according to the word of the Lord by Samuel."

Christ's Coronation: John 19:2, "And the soldiers wove a crown of thorns and put it on his head, and they dressed him in a purple robe." Matthew 27:29, "and after twisting some thorns into a crown, they put it on his head. They put a reed in his right hand and knelt before him and mocked him, saying, 'Hail, King of the Jews!'"

Blessing the Lord
David's Psalm: 1 Chronicles 16:4-43, "He appointed certain of the Levites as ministers before the ark of the Lord, to invoke, to thank, and to praise the Lord, the God of Israel. Asaph was the chief, and second to him Zechariah, Jeiel, Shemiramoth, Jehiel, Mattithiah, Eliab, Benaiah, Obed-edom, and Jeiel,

with harps and lyres; Asaph was to sound the cymbals, and the priests Benaiah and Jahaziel were to blow trumpets regularly, before the ark of the covenant of God."

Christ's Prayers: John 17, "After Jesus had spoken these words, he looked up to heaven and said, 'Father, the hour has come; glorify your Son so that the Son may glorify you, since you have given him authority over all people, to give eternal life to all whom you have given him. And this is eternal life, that they may know you, the only true God, and Jesus Christ whom you have sent. I glorified you on earth by finishing the work that you gave me to do. So now, Father, glorify me in your own presence with the glory that I had in your presence before the world existed.

I have made your name known to those whom you gave me from the world. They were yours, and you gave them to me, and they have kept your word. Now they know that everything you have given me is from you; for the words that you gave to me I have given to them, and they have received them and know in truth that I came from you; and they have believed that you sent me. I am asking on their behalf; I am not asking on behalf of the world, but on behalf of those whom you gave me, because they are yours. All mine is yours, and yours are mine; and I have been glorified in them. And now I am no longer in the world, but they are in the world, and I am coming to you. Holy Father, protect them in your name that you have given me, so that they may be one, as we are one. While I was with them, I protected them in your name that you have given me. I guarded them, and not one of them was lost except the one destined to be lost, so that the scripture might be fulfilled. But now I am coming to you, and I speak these things in the world so that they may have my joy made complete in themselves. I have given them your word, and the world has hated them because they do not belong to the world, just as I do not belong to the world. I am not asking you to take them out of the world, but I ask you to protect them from the evil one. They do not belong to the world, just as I do not belong to the world. Sanctify them in the truth; your word is truth. As you have sent me into the world, so I have sent them into the world. And for their sakes I sanctify myself, so that they also may be sanctified in truth.

I ask not only on behalf of these, but also on behalf of those who will believe in me through their word, that they may all be one. As you, Father, are in me and I am in you, may they also be in us, so that the world may believe that you have sent me. The glory that you have given me I have given them, so that they may be one, as we are one, I in them and you in me, that they may become completely one, so that the world may know that you have sent me and have loved them even as you have loved me. Father, I desire that those also, whom you have given me, may be with me where I am, to see my glory, which you have given me because you loved me before the foundation of the world. Righteous Father, the world does not know you, but I know you; and these know that you have sent me. I made your name known to them, and I will make it known, so that the love with which you have loved me may be in them, and I in them.'"

Breaking the Bread
David Distributes Bread to the People 1 Chronicles 16:2-3, "When David had finished offering the burnt offerings and the offerings of well-being, he blessed the people in the name of the Lord; and he distributed to every person in Israel—man and woman alike—to each a loaf of bread, a portion of meat, and a cake of raisins."

Christ Institutes the Lord's Supper: Matthew 26:20-30, Mark 14:17-26 "When it was evening, he took his place with the twelve; and while they were eating, he said, 'Truly I tell you, one of you will betray me.' And they became greatly distressed and began to say to him one after another, 'Surely not I, Lord?' He answered, 'The one who has dipped his hand into the bowl with me will betray me. The Son of Man goes as it is written of him, but woe to that one by whom the Son of Man is betrayed! It would have been better for that one not to have been born.' Judas, who betrayed him, said, 'Surely not I, Rabbi?' He replied, 'You have said so.'"

Luke 22:14-20, "When the hour came, he took his place at the table, and the apostles with him. He said to them, 'I have eagerly desired to eat this Passover with you before I suffer; for I tell you, I will not eat it until it is fulfilled in the kingdom of God.' Then he took a cup, and after giving thanks he said, 'Take this and divide it among yourselves; for I tell you that from now on I will not drink of the fruit of the vine until the kingdom of God comes.' Then he took a loaf of bread, and when he had given thanks, he broke it and gave it to them, saying, 'This is my body, which is given for you. Do this in remembrance of me.' And he did the same with the cup after supper, saying, 'This cup that is poured out for you is the new covenant in my blood.'"

Bringing God's Presence
The Ark Enters God's House 1 Chronicles 15:15, "And the Levites carried the ark of God on their shoulders with the poles, as Moses had commanded according to the word of the Lord."

The Curtain is Torn - God's Presence Goes into the World: Matthew 27:52, "The tombs also were opened, and many bodies of the saints who had fallen asleep were raised."

Mark 15:38, Luke 23:45 "And the curtain of the temple was torn in two, from top to bottom."

David, now acting under God's guidance, has brought about this amazing moment of praise and worship, not just for himself, but for the whole nation. And he's so overwhelmed, he's on this spiritual mountaintop, and, like the disciples who witnessed the Transfiguration of Jesus, David just wants to stay on that mountaintop, and build a house there. So he calls Nathan, his prophet, and he says, you know, I really have a sweet house, but the Ark of the Covenant is here now, it's in the right place, but it's just sitting in a tent. What if we build a house for the Ark? And Nathan kind of hastily says, "Sounds good, Your Highness, whatever You want." But then God speaks to Nathan, and Nathan comes to David with a slightly revised proposal. Because even when we want to do something good for God, the road to hell might be paved with our good intentions.

"We should test our desires, even the highest and the holiness of them, by His will." ~G. Campbell Morgan

God doesn't want David, His anointed, beloved King, to build the Temple. But:

"Though the Lord refused to David the realization of his wish, he did it in the most gracious manner." ~Charles Spurgeon

When God gives us a no, he means to give us a yes to something better. It's the way we are with our children. We say no to the candy, because we know that the vegetables are better for them—and dessert will always have its place. Our son JP seems to constantly defy death. Why can't I run out in the street with the cars, Mommy? Because I want you to live long enough to get a driver's license.

David wanted to bless God by building this building. But God wanted something bigger and better: to bless David. David had to eat his vegetables, and wait for dessert, a dessert he wouldn't even get to eat himself. In fact, it's not until 1 Chronicles 22, many years later, that David even learns why he can't build the Ark. David had shed too much blood. The Temple must be built by a man of peace; Jerusalem is to be the city of peace. And isn't it like this with us, too? Sometimes God says no, and it's not until years later that we learn—that job opportunity was with a company about to close. Mr. Right turned out to be Mr. Oh So Wrong. God means to bless us, and sometimes it's an act of love to close the door and open the window.

How do we respond when God says, "Not this, but this"? David gives us the most beautiful response to God's gracious "No." He is humbled. He realizes that he is thinking too small.

1 Chronicles 17:16, "Then King David went in and sat before the Lord, and said, 'Who am I, O Lord God, and what is my house, that you have brought me thus far?'" He recognizes that he is so small in God's sight, and God's design is so much bigger than his desires. In verse 18, David, who gave this amazing Psalm prayer just one chapter earlier, recognizes that no words can express the greatness of God's grace.

1 Chronicles 17:20, "There is no one like you, O Lord, and there is no God besides you, according to all that we have heard with our ears." Humility is not thinking less of yourself; it's thinking of yourself less. Just as he did when he turned his attention from his own desire to move the Ark to God's design for moving the Ark, David here turns from considering himself, his own desire to be holy, toward simply marveling in God's greatness.

1 Chronicles 17:27, "therefore may it please you to bless the house of your servant, that it may continue forever before you. For you, O Lord, have blessed and are blessed forever." David recognizes that he's been thinking too small. He wanted to make a promise, a vow, to God. But we've seen that our vows to God can often get us into trouble—like Jephath's vow to sacrifice the first thing he saw to the Lord, which resulted in his own daughter being killed. Our minds are too small; our capacity to keep our vows is limited, because we are limited, we are sinful, we are mortal. Our promises to God are temporary. But God's promises are eternal. David is thinking too small. David is thinking about a building of wood and stone.

What's God thinking about? David is thinking about building a building; God is thinking about building a church. God is thinking about a family, a great family, that will stretch across the centuries and across the earth. God is thinking about Jesus. God is thinking about Peter and Paul, and Martin and Teresa and Francis and you and me. God is thinking about the thousands of cathedrals that are going to be built from David's faith, the billions of people who are going to be blessed through this man. Because David's descendants were not just the descendants of his body: through Christ, everyone who has accepted God's grace is a son of the King. When God says He will build David a house, God is not just thinking of a temple, not even thinking of a dynasty; God is thinking of the big, big house that He's preparing in heaven for David and his descendants, physical and spiritual, forever.

God's promise to David is ultimately His promise to us: that when we, like David, trust Him; listen to His word; pray before Him; and accept His love, that He will build us a house.

Jesus said, "my father's house has many rooms." John 14

Paul said, "We have a building from God, not made by human hands, an eternal house in heaven." 2 Corinthians 5:1

God was thinking so much bigger than David was. Are you thinking too small? Are you worried about your house, your physical home, or are you worried about this little tent you live in, this little body? It wasn't meant to house your soul. Not forever. Stop thinking small. Stop worrying about tents, about buildings. Instead, hear God's Word, because if you are a child of the King, they are words addressed not just to David, but to you: 1 Chronicles 17:13. "I will be Your father, and You will be my child. I will never take my love away from you."

In the name of the Father, and the Son, and the Holy Spirit, Amen.

Week Eighteen: Posers
2 Chronicles

Amy Cuddy who's a social psychologist, believes that the way we position our bodies can have a profound effect on our minds. Her TED Talk has over 15 million views on YouTube. And in this TED Talk, she describes something called Power Poses. The idea of the power pose is that by making your body bigger and confident-looking, you can make yourself feel powerful and strong, even when you don't really believe it. Cuddy says, "Body-mind approaches such as power posing rely on the body, which has a more primitive and direct link to the mind, to tell you you're confident." So, I hope you warmed up; we're going to do a little experiment. Let's see if this actually works.

Let's start with one you can do right where you're sitting: "the subway guy." Cuddy believes that if you're waking up in the morning curled up in a fetal position and just roll out of bed, you're doing it all wrong. Before you even get out of bed, you need to sit up and get into a position of relaxation but also taking up as much space as possible, like the guy on the subway who just stretches out, not caring that there's a ninety-year-old lady standing next to him holding onto a pole for dear life. Got it? Feeling confident yet? OK, let's try the CEO. President Lyndon Johnson actually consciously adopted this stance when he was in a difficult meeting, trying to strike a deal: his 6'4" frame would loom physically over the others in the room, and he would use the power of his presence to get the job done. So take a minute, rise from your seat, and lean forward. This is what you're supposed to do when you're in a meeting and you're trying to get someone to buy into your idea, you lean over the conference table like this. I don't actually know if it would work for me at 5'3". Probably, everyone would just have to bend down to try to see my face. OK, now the victor. This is my favorite. Stand up and throw your hands in the air. Cuddy says that when you go to a job interview, right before the interview, you should stand outside the interview room right before the interview and strike this pose and you will feel confident and like you've got this. Or, your potential employer might think you're crazy and call the police. It could go either way.

Alright, did it work? Are we feeling more confident? I don't know, but I tend to think there's probably something to it. We know that our bodies greatly influence our minds, and vice versa, so the physical positions we take, whether it's slouching or standing confidently, probably do influence our thinking.

But from a theological perspective, there's an issue with what Amy Cuddy is doing. It all goes into the American popular psychology—embrace power. Project confidence. Be in control of your own destiny. This way of thinking is how we're told we should think; it's how we achieve success, get things done. And it works, to a point. But there are some big problems to this power-based thinking—for one, it's all kind of based on a form of pride, isn't it? Power and control over other people. And the hard truth is, for each one of us, the moment will come when we're not in control.

King Solomon is at the height of his power in this moment in Second Chronicles. He's the unquestioned leader of the United Kingdom of Israel. He has legions of guards, servants, soldiers, workers at his beck and call. He had, according to 2 Chronicles 1, fourteen hundred chariots and twelve thousand horses. Israel is so powerful at this moment that 1 Chronicles 2 tells us Solomon had 153,000 workers brought in just to build the Temple. He is so powerful that he ordered kings of other nations to send him building materials as tribute. The author of 2 Chronicles eloquently writes, "the king made silver and gold as plentiful in Jerusalem as stones on the ground."

Not only that, but Solomon has just completed one of the greatest building projects in the history of the world. I found this video so you can get an idea of how incredible it must really have been…The Temple was massive and full of intricate artwork; four hundred bronze pomegranates, a hundred ceremonial bowls made of solid gold, an 18,000-gallon ceremonial pool called The Sea resting on twelve decorative iron bulls; inlaid with precious stones. This structure was an overwhelming display of the power of Israel and of Solomon its king.

So here the king stands, before the elders of Israel, all the chiefs, all the people; before 120 priests sounding trumpets, before choirs and musicians making loud and beautiful music; the whole nation come together, dressed in their finest. Solomon steps before the people, all ready to bow before him, to bend the knee. You can picture him, ready to make the ultimate power pose. And at this moment, cloud covers the entire temple. The fog is so great that the musicians can no longer play; all the sound stops. And this king, at the height of his power, falls to his knees. He is eclipsed by the power of God. God, who can overshadow the greatest of human achievements in a moment.

If Amy Cuddy teaches power posing, then Scripture teaches humility posing. Kneeling is not a position of power…it's a lowering of yourself, making yourself small; while sitting or crouching can allow you to get up quickly, if you're kneeling, you're at the mercy of your enemy, because you can no longer run away. Kneeling is the position a man takes when asking a woman to be his wife and the position a condemned man takes before the executioner swipes off his head. If you've ever had to kneel, you know that it's intrinsically uncomfortable. It hurts. You have to give up every semblance of dignity and power and comfort in order to kneel. And this is what Solomon does.

He kneels, and he raises his hands to heaven. When I first began praying with people, during my chaplaincy internship at Royal Oak Beaumont, I struggled with finding a position to pray. Somehow, I kind of slipped into praying with my hands lifted to heaven; perhaps it was the work of the Holy Spirit that moved me into this position, but it felt right. Sometimes I've wondered if people think I'm being showy when I pray like that, but truly, when I think about it now, that's not what it's about. It's a position of being open to God, directing your whole body to heaven; when I lift my hands and my eyes to heaven, to me, the prayer is not about me, it's about God. And I can tell you one thing, having prayed in this position many times, lifting the names of many, many people to heaven; it's physically demanding. And this is what Solomon does with his hands.

This is a position of humility, and it is a position of work. And prayer is work. Humble work. Solomon has a job to do here—to dedicate the Temple to God. When we think of 1 Corinthians, that Paul teaches us that our bodies are temples of the Holy Spirit, it's quite amazing that, as Solomon dedicates the Temple to God, he's dedicating his own body to the service of the Lord.

I have to admit, most of my prayers are sitting up or lying down, as though I just want to be relaxed; I think of my prayer time as kind of my "me" time. I don't want to be uncomfortable. But maybe part of prayer is being uncomfortable. Being humbled before God, physically as well as spiritually. Recognizing that we aren't powerful, that we're not in control, and dedicating our lives to the One who is, seeking His will for us in all things. That's the essence of Solomon's prayer. It's not so much asking that God would come down and bless the people; but asking that the people would rise up and bless God. He begins with praise:

2 Chronicles 6:14 NIV: "He said, O Lord, God of Israel, there is no God like you in heaven or on earth—you who keep your covenant of love with your servants who continue wholeheartedly in your way." Solomon praises God's power and God's love. He recognizes that even this Temple is far short of enough to give God glory:

2 Chronicles 6:18 NIV: "But will God really dwell on earth with men? The heavens, even the highest heavens, cannot contain you. How much less this temple I have built!" Solomon pleads with God to forgive the people and help them to repent to God. By one count, there are seven different petitions in this prayer; five are for forgiveness. Solomon prays:

2 Chronicles 6:27 NIV: "Then hear from heaven and forgive the sin of your servants, your people Israel. Teach them the right way to live and send rain on the land you gave your people for an inheritance." Amazingly, in this moment of intense national pride and the rising power of the monarchy, the king specifically prays for foreigners who will come to this Temple.

2 Chronicles 6:33 NIV: "Then hear from heaven, your dwelling place, and do whatever the foreigner asks of you, so that all peoples of the earth may know your name and fear you, as do your own people Israel, and you may know that this house that I have built bears your Name."

This prayer, much like the Lord's Prayer when you study it in depth, is really a prayer asking God to bring all things into alignment with his will and to work all things for his glory. It is a prayer of Thy Will Be Done, or what I have called a prayer of alignment. Do you ever think of prayer as a way of coming into alignment with God's will? We think so often of prayer as a checklist of requests for God. But many of these examples in Scripture are more about prayer as a way of communicating with God and bringing our lives into line with God's will for us.

When I was pregnant with our son JP, I suffered terrible sciatica. If you don't know what sciatica is, you're lucky, but it's this intense hip pain you get on one side that makes it hard to walk or sit or do anything. I remember having to carry my heavy bags of law school books and sit on hard classroom benches with that terrible pain. So, when I got pregnant with Charlie, I went to a doula, Margaret the Grosse Pointe Doula, who's someone who helps women with pregnancy and childbirth. She told me there was a chiropractor who would offer a discount to doulas referring their clients. I was somewhat skeptical, and I'd never been to a chiropractor in my life, but I asked her where the chiropractor was, and she said, well, it's all the way out in Royal Oak.

It turns out that this chiropractor was Optimal Wellness which is directly across the street from the church I could easily walk there, even very pregnant. So, I started going, and they showed me a scan of how my hips and my spine were out of alignment. They used this little adjuster which made funny clicking noises. I could barely feel it, and it was hard to believe it was doing anything. But, after I went, I would instantly feel more comfortable, lighter on my feet. After an adjustment, this child squirmed around a bit; I could actually feel him getting into a better position. And I have had no sciatica whatsoever. It turns out chiropractic services in pregnancy reduce basically every pregnancy-related problem. Women who use a chiropractor are more likely to deliver right on time and less likely to have a C-section.

If our physical lives can be so improved by being re-aligned, what do you think it would do to our emotions, our spirits, our souls to re-align with where they're supposed to be—which is within the will of God, God's dreams and desires for us? Prayer is God's gift to us to stop being a power poser, and instead just be honest, recognize that we don't have it all figured out, we don't have it all together, not even close.

This might sound like kind of a downer, I guess, in the eyes of the world; but nothing could be farther from the truth. In the end, I don't want to have all the power. I've seen what happens when I try to pretend that I have it all together—it's not a good situation. Just like the kings of Israel—soon after this moment of faith, Solomon himself fell away from God, and the kings that followed him were in it for their own power and glory. What happened? Israel descended into chaos and ruin; ultimately, they were conquered by Babylon. Their priests were murdered, their people led away in chains, and their beautiful temple burned to the ground. Sounds kind of like what my life has looked like at times. Here's the choice; I can have a messed-up, stressed-out, somewhat scatterbrained human-myself—steer the ship of my life; or I can hand it over to the creator of the Universe. What do you think is the rational choice here? Prayer is the process of letting God take the helm of your life and mine. And you know what? It's not sad. It's a relief; it's the path to peace; it's the gateway to joy.

Two things I know: there is a God, and I am not Him. Thanks be to God.

Week Nineteen: Rebuilding
Nehemiah 8

We live awash in words, more so than any previous generation. Words scream at us from social media, nag us from newspapers, bully us from billboards, and inundate our inboxes. And we go home at night to watch mindless chatter from TV, or incessant arguing as the political commentators interrupt one another so that you can barely understand what they're saying—which, of course, is the point. Text messaging is another convenient, urgent stream of words, as though we needed one more. Among all these urgent messages vying for our eyes, why should the millennia-old news of Scripture capture a moment of our attention?

For the returning exiles in Ezra and Nehemiah, the Word of God captures their attention not for a minute, or fifteen. They don't give an hour, or an hour and ten minutes, to hearing the Word of God. They stand for six hours to listen to the Torah read and proclaimed. And they don't fall asleep. Or check their email. Their eyes never focus on the light bulb in the sanctuary that needs changing. Nothing distracts them from the deep and eternal truths of God's justice and love.

They don't just listen either. This is not a morning's free entertainment. The people respond, immediately and bodily to the truth of Scripture. They stand out of respect for the Word. They raise their hands to heaven, and they fall on their faces. Not because this was what they did every Sunday at 10:30—this reading wasn't part of regular worship—it didn't even take place in the Temple. The people respond with body, mind, and spirit because they are overcome by the Word.

They weep. We don't know why they weep. Perhaps they are overcome by their failures to live up to God's commands. Perhaps they are so overcome by God's goodness; that, after all their sins, after their king had been captured, their priests murdered, the Ark of the Covenant destroyed, the Temple razed to the ground…God was still with them and had brought them home. Or perhaps the people weep because now, they finally recognized the beauty of God's Law. For the first time, the people saw God's Word not as a burden, but as a gift. They realize what God has been trying to tell them all along—that the idols aren't going to save them. That kings aren't going to rescue them; money and power and armies will all fail. They weep because they see how God has been trying to pull them to Him for hundreds of years; and they finally let Him.

Whether the people are weeping from great sorrow or great joy, Ezra, the priest's, response is the same: stop. "Do not mourn or weep." And Nehemiah, the governor, echoes him: "Get out of here and have yourselves a burger and a Coke. Sit down with your family and friends and stuff yourselves silly." "Do not grieve, for the joy of the Lord is your strength."

Religious people have done a great job of sucking the joy out of the Word of God. Do others think of us as a particularly happy people? Or is all they know about us that we don't drink, don't smoke, don't have sex, and that we seem to enjoy judging those who do?

Some of you grew up in a family that kept the Sabbath religiously. And what did that mean? It meant you had to sit in a chair, silently, in the living room, looking down solemnly at your Bible. It was, by no means, a day for laughter, or feasting, or joy.

God did not give us the Word to bring us down. He gave us His Word so that we could have life and have it abundantly. John 10:10 He gave us His Word to steer us away from those poor imitations of true joy that we can find in things like smoking, or drinking, or meaningless sex. He gave us His Word to decry us from those poor imitations of true strength we can find in money, or politics. He gave us His Word to explain to us why we were created, and how we can know true joy and true strength in this life and forevermore: basking in the love of God. As Nehemiah says so simply, "The joy of the Lord is your strength."

Nehemiah 8:10, "Then he said to them, 'Go your way, eat the fat and drink sweet wine and send portions of them to those for whom nothing is prepared, for this day is holy to our Lord; and do not be grieved, for the joy of the Lord is your strength.'" That is the truth of God's Word. And when we really hear that truth—we feast, we laugh, we sing, we dance, we rejoice. That's what God meant His Word to do—not to force us to live smaller, duller lives, but to inspire us to live fuller, brighter, richer lives of joy.

Olaudah Equiano was born in West Africa in the seventeen hundreds. He was kidnapped from his home at the age of eleven and put in chains. Eventually, he saved enough to buy his own freedom. Olaudah sought answers to why he had experienced so much suffering. He tried lots of churches, and even synagogues. But as far as he could see, none of them were practicing what they preached—none were doing half as well as the Muslims were at following the commandments. In despair, he stood one day on the prow of the ship, thinking about ending his life. Then he was led to Acts 4:12: Jesus is the only way—there is no name under Heaven by which we may be saved. He wrote: "The scriptures became an unsealed book…The word of God was sweet to my taste, yea sweeter than honey and the honeycomb." He even saw then how the evil wrought by human hands, tearing him away from his parents and into slavery, was used for his good. From then on, he devoted his life to sharing the Word of God and speaking out against slavery around the world. This is joy God wants for us.

Ravi Zacharias tells the story of a man named Hien Pham who served as an interpreter of Vietnamese for him. During the Vietnam War, Hien had worked as a translator for the American forces, and during that time had grown to believe in Christ. After the war, he was imprisoned by the Viet Cong, who fed him Communist propaganda and tried to convince him that Christianity was the corrupt tool of the West. Hien eventually started to believe them and resolved one day to stop praying and believing in God. The next morning, he was assigned the dreaded chore of cleaning the prison latrines. As he went about his task, he saw a piece of paper sitting on the toilet. That paper was a page from the Bible, Romans, Chapter 8: "And we know that in all things God works for the good of those who love Him…. for I am convinced that nothing shall be able to separate us from the love of God that is in Christ Jesus our Lord." It's what we would call a God sighting. Hien survived his time in prison, and eventually escaped to the United States, bringing with him four of the Viet Cong soldiers who had questioned him. This is the joy God wants for us.

When I was four years old, my mother explained to me who Jesus was, using the words and images of a child's picture book. He was a good man, a kind man, who healed the sick, and taught people about God's love. And then she turned the page, and she showed me what happened to Jesus; they killed him. I was so, so sad that people killed him; that He died. And then she turned the page. I still remember what that page looked like; the garden, the tomb…the stone rolled away. She explained to me, "He didn't stay dead! He woke up from the dead! And He never died! He is alive!" I danced. I danced, and I sang, the kind of songs four-year-olds make up in their heads. My little four-year-old self danced and danced and danced. This is the joy God wants for us.

When did we stop dancing?

If you aren't receiving joy from the Word, you aren't reading it right. If you aren't receiving joy from worship, please, go to another church. Because you aren't worshiping right. We were meant for joy. We were meant to be convicted, changed, transformed by the Word of God. We were meant to fall on our knees, to raise our hands to heaven, to dance. Because among all the torrent of words bombarding our day, what could be truer, more powerful, more worthy of our attention than these?

1 Corinthians 13:13, "And now faith, hope, and love abide, these three; and the greatest of these is love."

Galatians 5:22, "By contrast, the fruit of the Spirit is love, joy, peace, patience, kindness, generosity, faithfulness."

Psalm 118:24, "This is the day that the Lord has made; let us rejoice and be glad in it."

May you find in God's Word not guilt, but grace; may you be renewed daily by the power of His Word. Now go, and eat good food, and drink yummy drinks, and laugh and rejoice—that's how God wants us to respond to His Word. That's how God wants us to keep the Sabbath!

In the name of the Father, and of the Son, and of the Holy Spirit, Amen.

Week Twenty: Woman of Wisdom
Esther 4

Women are wise, and brave, and tough, and anyone who doesn't believe that has never read the book of Esther. The book of Esther stands next to Ezra and Nehemiah and tells a parallel story at the same time. Ezra and Nehemiah tell the story of the Jews who went back to the Holy Land and rebuilt it, but Esther tells the story of those Jews who stayed in Babylon, now part of Persia, and stayed faithful among an unbelieving culture. It's a story that really serves as inspiration for committed Christians today, who live as, I would argue, a religious minority in American culture. It's a story about how to live when you aren't in power, and that's why I think it's not a coincidence that a woman is the heroine of this story.

Women are good at making change without wielding power, at working behind the scenes; it's what we've always done. Men have written most of the great books of world history; but I submit to you, it's women who do most of the behind-the-scenes teaching of children. It's our mothers, grandmothers, and aunts who taught us the practical wisdom we use on a daily basis, like "eat your vegetables" and "treat others the way you want to be treated."

We're going to look at some of those pearls of wisdom from the example of Esther. Just as the nation of Israel felt orphaned by God during Exile, Esther is herself an orphan. She had been adopted by her cousin Mordecai, who worked at the palace, and she is selected to be part of the harem of King Xerxes. It's difficult for us to understand the compromises Esther and Mordecai make. At times, they hide their religion; they take on Persian dress and customs; Esther submits to a polygamous relationship with a Persian king. But part of being a wise woman is discernment.

Did your mother ever tell you: "There's a time and a place for everything."? Discernment is a fancy word for figuring out what to do when. Throughout history, women have had to discern and make compromises, because we were powerless to do otherwise. The story of Hagar is a great example. Remember back in Genesis, Hagar was Sarah's slave, and she ran away because Sarah was so cruel to her, but God urged her to go back into slavery, because without Abraham's protection her child would die. I think of Moses's mother surrendering her baby to the river, Bathsheba writing to the King, "I am pregnant."

Women do what it takes for the survival of themselves and their children, even when it means working within a broken system. In the same way, Esther learned to survive. While Vashti, Xerxes's prior wife, fought against Xerxes' commands and lost her crown, Esther learned to work within a less-than-ideal system. She kept her religion behind-the-scenes. But when she knew God was calling her to speak up, she stepped forward courageously.

Did your mother ever tell you: "Do what is right, not what is easy."? It's this attitude of courage that I think of when I think of the bravery of women. We often think of courage as a masculine virtue, but women have a quiet courage of their own. Anyone who has witnessed childbirth would testify that women, behind our smaller, weaker shells, can be extraordinarily brave.

Women are especially courageous when someone vulnerable is in danger. As a young girl, I used to go out on the paddleboat with my grandfather on the little lake behind his house. We came up to an island and I got off the paddleboat to explore, but as soon as I stepped foot on the island, I heard the most horrible honking sound, like a bullhorn straight in my ear. It was the biggest, scariest Canadian goose I had ever seen, atop her nest of eggs, and she told me in no uncertain terms to step off. We christened the island "Goose Island" and never dared to venture there again.

Another pastor described a similar experience as "getting shut down by Mother Goose." Women know to protect the most vulnerable among us. Esther is not a biological mother, but she is a mother to her people. She risks herself to save them. Haman, one of the king's officials, is angry that Esther's cousin, Mordecai, would not bow down to him. Mordecai, as a faithful Jew, would bow down to God alone. Haman angrily calls for the slaughter of all the Jewish people. Mordecai approaches Esther and tells her it is time now to work the system for the good of her people. She is afraid, since it's been a month that the king has even called for her, but Mordecai knows that God, like Esther, often works behind the scenes, and perhaps Esther has been placed in a position of power "for such a time as this." Esther 4:14. Esther then bravely declares that she will speak out for her people, "And if I perish, I perish." Esther 4:16. Like Mother Goose honking on her nest, Esther speaks up when the most vulnerable are threatened.

I think of other women who risked themselves to help the powerless. When you read the book of Esther, you cannot help but think of how history repeats itself; during the Holocaust, people like Haman tried to wipe out the Jewish people, and very nearly succeeded. A Christian woman, Corrie Ten Boom, hid many Jews in her own home during the Holocaust, becoming imprisoned in a concentration camp for her work. Of her own choice to endanger herself to help others, Ten Boom wrote, "Don't bother to give God instructions. Just report for duty." I think also of Rosa Parks, who refused to move to the back of the bus and became a catalyst for the Civil Rights movement. When thrown into prison, she said, "My feet are tired, but my soul is rested."

Women were at the center of the anti-slavery movement; women have worked to end abuse from human trafficking to drunk driving to child abuse prevention to animal welfare. Most of these women don't have millions of dollars or thousands of armies at their command. But their quiet bravery changes the world. They teach us to look out for the little ones, like Mother Goose. Esther, too, stands up for what is right; but she's also smart about it.

Women's wisdom is practical. Did your mother ever tell you: "Always wear clean underwear."? And why? "You never know when you could end up in the hospital." "Chew with your mouth shut." "Don't swim for half an hour after eating." This is the kind of practicality mothers teach. Esther has practical wisdom. Esther knows what her strength is; Xerxes doesn't want to hear her talk, he's not interested in her take on Persian politics or her religious musings. He wants her to look pretty and submit to his desires. That's how she got her position in the first place, working behind the scenes to find out what Xerxes likes, making friends with the people who run the harem. So Esther does what is right, but she also looks good doing it. She puts on her royal robes. Esther 5:1, "On the third day Esther put on her royal robes and stood in the inner court of the king's palace, opposite the king's hall. The king was sitting on his royal throne inside the palace opposite the entrance to the palace."

Not only did she look regal and lovely, but by wearing her royal robes, she was also subtly reminding Xerxes that he named her the queen, and it won't look good if he goes back on his word. So, the king lets Esther touch his royal scepter, and she makes a request of him. But it isn't the big request we're waiting for; she doesn't ask him to withdraw the decree. Instead, she just asks for a banquet. Esther 5:4. Xerxes must have thought, how sweet, the little wife wants to throw a tea party. Why did she hold off on her real request? Because she knows that if the king has a tasty side of beef and a good glass of wine, if she can spend some sitting next to him and pique his interest, she can get what she wants. It's not even until the second day of the banquet that she finally brings up her request. She's practical.

When I was looking for my first call, I had a lot of success when the churches looked at my resume and heard me on the phone interview, but not in person. My mother-in-law had a theory, and she sent me to the makeup counter at

Somerset Mall. I hadn't really worn much makeup before. She said to them, "Make this girl look older." She spent $300 on makeup for my next interview. I got the job. I think God was calling me; but she still swears it was the makeup. Women are practical; we have faith in God, we do what is right, but we also put on our makeup.

And finally, women are wise because we do trust God. Did your mother teach you your first prayer? I've wondered a lot why churches are mostly filled with women, seventy to eighty percent by most counts. I think it's because women have always known we are not in power. Even though women have made a lot of steps toward equality, we're still not there yet, even in this country, where I think women have greater freedom than anywhere in the world. Since we know we're not in charge, and have never suffered under that delusion, we learn that God is in charge, and we learn to trust Him.

Esther asks for all the Jews to fast and pray, not just for the customary one day fast, but for three days; and she directs her maids to pray with her, too. Esther 4:16, "Go, gather all the Jews to be found in Susa, and hold a fast on my behalf, and neither eat nor drink for three days, night or day. I and my maids will also fast as you do. After that I will go to the king, though it is against the law; and if I perish, I perish.". She puts the matter to God before she puts the matter to man. Women pass on the faith; fathers are extremely important in children's religious upbringing; but in most cases, it's mothers who teach us first about who God is.

The other day, I was praying with our daughter (Diana Mae), we prayed our nighttime prayer, the traditional "now I lay me down to sleep." She said, "Mommy, I know where you learned that prayer. It's the one your mother prayed with you. I know because I saw it on a pillow at her house." My mother taught me to trust God, and to see God at work; not always in dramatic, miraculous ways, but sometimes God works quietly, behind the scenes; guiding us, teaching us, helping us; like our mothers.

In the name of the Father, and the Son, and the Holy Spirit, Amen.

Week Twenty-one: A Weathered Faith
Job 2

Virginia Woolf once wrote to a friend: "I read the book of Job last night. I don't think God comes out of it well." What do we do with such a book, in which seems to allow Job's life to be destroyed so he can win a bet? What do we do with such a book, in which a purported man of faith curses the day of his birth (Job 3:1) and basically calls God a jerk, accusing God of laughing at the death of the innocent (Job 9:23)? What do we do with such a book, which questions the basic assumptions underlying most of the rest of the Bible?

Job's friend Eliphaz says, "God does great things too marvelous to understand. He performs countless miracles. He gives rain for the earth and water for the fields. He gives prosperity to the poor and protects those who suffer." Job 5:9-11. Couldn't those words be in any other book of the Bible, and we would accept them without question, embroider them on pillows? But the book of Job questions the idea that God does care for the earth or protect His people. God does not reward the righteous and punish the wicked, not always.

In the book of Job, God actually allows the exact opposite to happen; we know from the very first verse that Job is blameless, a man of complete integrity (Job 1:1), and yet God allows him to go through the most terrible suffering imaginable. The book of Job is so interesting because it's timeless; you can't really position the book of Job in any one time or even place. Job was from the land of Uz, a city mentioned nowhere else in the Bible. There's a hint that Job might have been written around the time of the Exile—Job 12:18-19 speaks of how kings are "led away with ropes around their waist" and "priests are stripped of their status." Job presents an extreme example of a man who was "blameless" whose riches, health, wife, and children are taken from him; and then, as though that were not enough, he experiences a terrible and painful disease and ends up on an ash heap, scratching at his sores with a broken piece of pottery. The Bible gives us this story to present to us the most difficult question ever asked of people of faith: how could a good God allow the suffering of the innocent?

And the book of Job is quite clear that God does allow the suffering of the innocent. As the story begins, God is sitting comfortably in heaven when his court comes in for their weekly staff meeting. Among God's apparent vice-presidents is Ha-Satan. Most translations call him Satan, but the book of Job always uses the article; Satan in Hebrew means Accuser, and Ha means "The." So, Satan here is simply "the accuser." His "job" appears to be to walk around the earth and accuse people of sin. What's disturbing about this exchange is that God and Satan appear to be working together. They kind of make a bet together! And it's God who brings up Job in the first place, bragging, "have you seen my servant Job? He's a pretty good guy." I mean, God, if you were in the mood for that sort of thing, couldn't you have just gone to the casino? (Not if he were a good Calvinist, I guess!) There's a movie called *Constantine* starring Keanu Reeves with a great line: "God's a kid with an ant farm, lady." This is, seemingly, the God of Job 1-2; God is willing to play around with human beings, allow them to experience great suffering, just to see what happens.

The book of Job, like Job himself, presents this disturbing picture of God, and I believe Job asks the hardest questions in order for us to respond with the deepest faith. The person of faith reads these chapters and cannot accept that God is playing around with Job; there's something more going on here. God is not just placing a bet in fun or playing around with humans like toys. God deeply cares about how we respond to situations of suffering. If there's one theme we have seen developing throughout Scripture, it's that God desires a relationship with us. God wants our love. And a relationship that's just built on transactions is not love.

God wants more than a business relationship.

This weekend I performed a wedding, and I thought, yet again, about the beauty of the traditional wedding vows. Today, many people want to write their own vows, and there's a certain value to thinking through your relationship and why you are choosing to marry. But, as Rick Warren points out, many of these self-written vows come out sounding like a middle-school love note. I love you because of your pretty hair and I promise to make you mango smoothies every day. The traditional vows don't focus on loving people when they are pretty and nice and everything is going well; instead, we promise to love and be faithful for richer or for poorer, in joy and in sorrow, for better or for worse. That's the kind of relationship God wants; a faith that does not depend on circumstances. God does not want fair-weather friends; God does not want a fair-weather faith.

God wants to find out who his friends are. The book of Job is a little like a country song—after all he's been through, we wouldn't be surprised if his truck broke down and his dog ran away—and there's a great old country song that goes, when you need a couch, need a floor, need a bus fare, "You find out who your friends are, Somebody's gonna drop everything, Run out and crank up their car, Hit the gas get there fast, Never stop to think 'what's in it for me?' or 'it's way too far.' They just show on up with their big old heart, you find out who your friends are."

God uses Satan, the accuser, and his weapons of illness, disaster, and death to learn whether Job is really his friend, whether Job really cares. It's easy enough to love God when all our prayers are answered. But God is not a vending machine. As Job says, Job 2:10, "But he said to her, 'You speak as any foolish woman would speak. Shall we receive the good at the hand of God, and not receive the bad?' In all this Job did not sin with his lips." If we love God because we think we can get whatever we want out of him, that kind of one-sided relationship isn't what God is looking for. He's not looking for a fair-weather faith.

Every morning, my daughter asks my husband, "Daddy, what's the weather going to be like?" My husband Dan is the designated news-watcher in our house; he keeps everybody else informed of when it's going to rain or the latest political scandals. Come to think of it, there should probably just be a "scandals" segment on the news, right after "weather," "traffic," and "violence." My daughter Diana wants to know the weather so she can pick out her clothes well for the day, but she also likes to know, I think, what to expect. But even though the weather guy can make a prediction, we never really know what to expect from the weather, just like we never really know what to expect from life.

This past week, it felt like July in May, and, being seven months pregnant, I have a newfound respect for every mother of a summer baby everywhere. Because I'm weaker overall, the weather is harder for me. It's like that with our faith, too; when our faith is weak, a small thing can damage it, cause us to live in fear and despair and stop trusting in God. But the more storms we have weathered in the past, the stronger our faith will become, the more honest, the more realistic, the more *real*. Faith is really faith in the storm, in the trials, in the tribulations of life, when we can't just spout off the easy answers. Like Job's first response: Job 1:21, "He said, 'Naked I came from my mother's womb, and naked shall I return there; the Lord gave, and the Lord has taken away; blessed be the name of the Lord.'"

Job never lets God off easy. As we will see, Job's faith is one that asks the hard questions, puts God on trial, challenges God, wrestles with doubt. He doesn't blame Satan, but instead lays the blame directly on God; the Lord gave me what I had, and the Lord has taken it away. Job is honest about who is in charge, and it's God. Job also doesn't discount the blessings he has had in this life. He does not take them for granted. I think of people whose marriage ends through a horrible divorce, but they are still able to look back and see the good years they had and the value of the marriage. Or the people who have lost a child, but still give thanks for the few brief years they were able to enjoy that beautiful life. This is the well-weathered faith. It's the ability to see life as a gift rather than an allowance. Job does not see his blessings as a reward, something he deserved, nor does he see his punishment as justice. Rather, he simply accepts both blessing and loss as coming from the hand of God, and, although he appears to have no real reason to do so, he says, "blessed be the name of the Lord." He doesn't bless God's name because God has done what he wants, or even because God has been fair or just. Job simply decides, through it all, to continue to have faith.

In my times of suffering, faith has been, for me, a decision. Not a feeling I have, not an emotional choice, not even a fully rational choice. I trust in God because He is the only one I can cling to amid the storms of life. A wonderful singer I know sings a song in church: "The anchor holds, Though the ship is battered, the anchor holds, Though the sails are torn; I have fallen on my knees as I face the raging seas; The anchor holds in spite of the storm." If I let go, the rains will drown me, the winds will carry me away; so I hold on in the storms even more than in fair winds. I'm still young, but my faith has gotten more weathered; now, rather than taking the calm for granted, I use that time to prepare for storms yet to come.

There's a saying that "wrinkles mean you laughed, gray hair means you learned, and scars mean you lived." I want a weathered faith. I want a wrinkled face. I want to bear the scars that show I lived. I want a real faith, a real relationship, and real relationships weather the storm, real faith holds on when it's hard, real love gives you scars. As His real love bore the scars for us. Real love stands firm even through the pain, and treachery, and brokenness, and suffering of life; and holds on through it all. When Christ rose from the dead, His hands still bore the scars, because they showed His love, and that love was beautiful. Your scars, your wrinkles, are the evidence of your well-weathered faith, the evidence that you held fast to God through all of the storms of life. And in His eyes, they make you all the more beautiful. So don't give up. When life hurts, when the waves crash around, when the Lord gives and takes away, when there is no justice to be found, and you are accused on every side, hold fast to your anchor, if for no other reason than it is all you have, and have the faith to say, "blessed be the name of the Lord."

In the name of the Father, and the Son, and the Holy Spirit, Amen.

Week Twenty-two: Where is God in Suffering?
Job 19

The other day our son JP asked me, "Can you play hide and seek with me?" What do you say? We went upstairs and I said, "OK, let's play hide and seek." And very excitedly he said, "Yay! We're playing hide and seek!" and just stood there. That's when I realized he had no idea how to actually play hide and seek and had probably just heard about it in a book somewhere. So I told him, "First, close your eyes. Then, count to ten and I'll hide. When you've finished counting to ten, come and find me." So he closed his eyes and counted, "One, two, three, four, seven, eight, nine, ten!' Because he's 2. I waited in the bedroom closet for a long time as he called out, "Mommy, where are you?" over and over. He didn't seem to be particularly worried, but it seemed to be taking him a long time, so I called out, "I'm right here, JP!" But he still said, "I can't find you!" So eventually I left the closet and found him standing in the hallway. When I saw him, I realized I had forgotten to include a crucial step in the hide-and-seek process: I forgot to tell him to open his eyes!

But what struck me was that, with the simple faith of the young, even though he couldn't see me, my son still trusted that I was there. In that way, he was very much like Job as we find him in Chapter 19. Job has undergone the most extreme suffering imaginable; he's lost his home, his livelihood, his family, and his health. He's calling out for God, like my son, calling, "Mommy, where are you?" But he doesn't see God anywhere. He says: Job 19:7—"Even when I cry out, 'Violence!' I am not answered; I call aloud, but there is no justice."

Job uses vivid images to describe how very alone he feels. He feels estranged from both his family and his friends. His wife finds his very breath repulsive: Job 19:17, "My breath is repulsive to my wife; I am loathsome to my own family." If your spouse is in need of Listerine, you might subtly write Job 19:17 on the bathroom mirror! Even Job's servants no longer listen to him.

We have seen firsthand how his so-called friends have failed him. Job's friends try to explain his suffering by pointing to the sovereignty of God; God is just, and there is a reason for your suffering you may not understand yet. In chapter 18, Bildad implies that Job has not just sinned, but that Job does not really know God at all; Job deserves this. That answer not acceptable to Job—and it shouldn't be acceptable to us, either. But we may have more in common with Zophar, Eliphaz, and Bildad than we would like to think. We need to recognize that most people think of Christians as pretty judgmental and holier-than-thou. And even if we don't spout the hate-filled speech that comes out of the mouths of some professing Christians, I for one find myself judging others so, so often. There's a reason God put the book of Job in the Bible; He knew that religious people would need it. We tend to think we've got things figured out. Recently, Dan said to me, "I think I understand Chronicles. When the people obey God, things go well for them. When they disobey, they get slammed." But the message of Job is not always. We can't be quick to judge others because they are suffering.

The philosophy of Job's friends is not just typical of religious people, it's typical of us as Americans as well. The phrase "God helps those who help themselves" comes from Ben Franklin's almanac, not from the Bible. Americans like to believe that anyone can be successful as long as they work hard and do what's right; this, after all, is the land of opportunity. The book of Job says, not so fast.

Job *can't* help himself, not anymore. He's totally friendless, totally alone. In verse 12, he says: "His troops come on together; they have thrown up siege works against me and encamp around my tent." He imagines himself on the battlefield, alone, with the entire army of God barricaded against him. And that's what life feels like sometimes. Sometimes, we don't sense any reason or justice to the world. If there is a God, He doesn't seem to be particularly kind or good. In the midst of natural disaster, extreme poverty, in the midst of senseless war, we can't see God. But in this moment, though Job can't see God, he still trusts that God is there. Job sees with the eyes of faith, sees beyond his situation, sees beyond history, sees beyond what he has been taught to think to what he knows in his heart:

Job 19:25-27, "I know that my Redeemer lives, and that at the last he will stand upon the earth; and after my skin has been thus destroyed, then in my flesh I shall see God, whom I shall see on my side, and my eyes shall behold, and not another."

Job opens his eyes to a vision of God the Redeemer. He sees an image of God different from anything he has been taught; God not as a divine judge, but a divine advocate. Not the God who is above us, but the God who stands beside us. Not God the Ruler, but God the Redeemer. As Christians, we believe, in essence, that Job saw the image of Christ. Christ who walked beside us, who suffered beside us, who died beside us. You see this word Redeemer, goal in Hebrew, was the person who would take care of your family in the event of your death. It was the person who would bail you out of jail, your emergency contact, your power of attorney. Usually it was your brother or next of kin.

There are a few times when we call someone "brother" or "sister" outside natural ties; one is in the church; another is in the military. As a child of the eighties, I cannot help but think of the song "Brothers in Arms" by Dire Straits, released in 1985. The song was released in response to the Falklands War and Dire Straits has used profits from the track to help soldiers with PTSD. The lyrics go as such:

Through these fields of destruction
Baptisms of fire
I've witnessed your suffering
As the battle raged higher
And though they did hurt me so bad
In the fear and alarm
You did not desert me
My brothers in arms

Job saw his Redeemer beside him, in the fields of destruction, in this baptism by fire. He believed that God witnessed his suffering and would never desert him, his brother in arms. Christ loved us enough to go into the battle with us, to stand beside us in our deepest suffering. He said, "Greater love has no man than this, to lay down his life for his friends."

Soldiers on the battlefield knew that kind of love, that kind of sacrifice, when their brothers lay down their lives for one another. On Memorial Day, we remember that sacrifice, dedicating ourselves to greater lives in the memory of those who laid down theirs. As Christians, God does not promise us we will not suffer in this life. But God does promise that we will not suffer alone. He promises us that he will go with us into the battle, into the deepest suffering that we will experience, and that he will not turn away even in death. And not only that, but we have a Redeemer who lives; because sacrifice that pure, that profound, is stronger even than death itself.

Whatever battles you face, whatever struggles stand in your way this week, you do not go into the battle alone. Open your eyes and see that your Redeemer lives; and when you meet your end, then in your flesh you shall see God; whom you will see on your side, whom your eyes shall behold, and not another.

In the name of the Father, and of the Son, and of the Holy Spirit, Amen.

Week Twenty-three: Advocate
Job 38

Have you felt what it is to be totally abandoned in your hour of need? When the higher-ups in your company devalue you and will not hear what you have to say; when the medical professionals talk down to you, as though you were a collection of organs instead of a human being; when the authorities stand in accusation against you, and you have no one to take up your cause.

Job feels as though he's been totally abandoned, with no one to take his case. The whole book of Job is rife with legal imagery. We know from Job 1 that it's really a courtroom confrontation between God and Satan; the issue is Job's faith, and the evidence will be Job's response to suffering. But Job wants to lodge a complaint against God.

Job 13:18, "I have indeed prepared my case; I know that I shall be vindicated." Yet Job feels as though he has no advocate, no one to fight for him. Who could contend for him against God?

Job 9:32, "For he is not a mortal, as I am, that I might answer him, that we should come to trial together." The disciples, too, were abandoned, and accused by those around them of the crimes of blasphemy, insurrection, and treason. In the words we heard read today from John 14, the words of the final discourse, Jesus seeks to prepare them for this trial. He says, John 14:16, "I am sending you an Advocate, to be with you forever, to always be within you, to abide with you."

This word advocate in Greek is *parakaleos*. Literally, it means "the called-out one;" the Spirit is the one you call. It can also be translated *the Comforter, the Encourager, the Backer, the Proponent, the Champion*. In Greek it had a legal meaning; the word for the Holy Spirit can be translated *Lawyer*. Jesus tells the disciples to lawyer up. Ultimately Job, as we have begun to see, also recognizes that there is Someone who will take his case before God, someone who will witness for him, and bail him out.

Job 16:19, "Even now, in fact, my witness is in heaven, and he that vouches for me is on high."

Job 19:25, "For I know that my Redeemer lives, and that at the last he will stand upon the earth."

The good news of the book of Job has always been, for me, that God shows up. It almost doesn't matter what God says in Job 38; the fact is that God comes to Job's side in the midst of his pain. God appears in the whirlwind: Job 38:1, "And God spoke to Job out of the whirlwind." The Holy Spirit is also a mighty, rushing wind; the Hebrew and Greek words for Spirit also mean "wind." So here, in Job, we see the presence of God the Spirit, the one you call. In the times when we feel most abandoned and accused, God has not left us without representation. God has sent His Spirit to fight for us, to stand up for us, and to witness on our behalf.

Many people are surprised to learn that, while my husband's family is full of legal types, my family of origin isn't in the slightest. My grandfather used to say, "What do you call a bus full of lawyers at the bottom of the ocean? A good start." But even he realized that when you need one, you need one. Any defense attorney, and any honest police officer, will tell you that when you are alone in that room with the cops, the only words you should say are "I need my lawyer." We all know how to Call Sam; but this Pentecost, I ask you, do we know how to call upon the called-out one, the greatest Advocate we can ever have—the Holy Spirit?

Do you ask the Holy Spirit, on a daily basis, for help, and guidance, and strength; to give you words, to share your faith, and tell others about our church, when you don't know what to say? To advise you in the right course in our daily living? To defend yourself when others attack our faith? Or do you and I ignore the Spirit? Do we rely on our own knowledge and strength? Do we, like the naïve suspect in the interrogation room, just start blabbing on, when we have an Advocate even better than Sam willing to take on our case—without charging 30%? And if we fail to draw upon the Holy Spirit, upon our zealous Advocate, our best defense against the accusers of this world, should we be surprised when people don't listen to Christians or take our case seriously?

That word, "zealous," I've been using to describe the Advocate, it's not just my word; the American Bar Association and the Model Rules use the word "zealous" to describe the obligation of a lawyer to his client. You're not due "competent" or "effective" representation; you are promised zealous representation.

I think of Atticus Finch in *To Kill a Mockingbird*. The patron saint of lawyers, Atticus Finch takes the case of a black man falsely accused of rape, and in so doing, he risks not only his livelihood, not only his reputation, but also his life. His family is ostracized, and spends Christmas with the black community, since they are welcome with no one else. His children sit in the "colored" section at the trial. And at one point, he faces down a lynch mob, armed only with a newspaper, narrowly escaping with his life.

In the same way, God advocates for us with zeal, sacrifices His own safety, and comfort, sacrifices even His life, for us. And we are called to advocate for those most alone, most abandoned, most in need of someone to stand in their corner. But we don't do it alone. We face our trials with the Creator of the Universe, the Sustainer of Life, the Redeemer of the World, by our side. So don't wait. Call Him today.

In the name of the Father, and the Son, and the Holy Spirit, Amen.

Week Twenty-four: Before and After
Psalm 30

When were you "saved"? Many Christians can point to a time when they were "born again," a moment when they accepted Christ, put away their sin, and began to live new lives. These people have experienced salvation in a profound way, and they separate their lives into "before" and "after." It reminds me of the many advertisements we see on television, featuring the overweight, ugly "before" photo, where the person is always frowning and dressed in something unflattering, and the thin, pretty "after" photo, all dressed up and smiling. For many born-again Christians, accepting Christ has meant putting aside addictions, sin, mean-spirited ways of living, and totally redefining their identity. So, they ask me, when were you saved? The classic Presbyterian answer to this question is this: *I was saved two thousand years ago, when Jesus died on the cross.*

For many Christians, including most Presbyterians, the language of getting "saved" or being "born again" doesn't quite fit our experience. For me, growing up in a Christian home, I can remember telling my friends about Jesus when I was five years old, hoping they would accept Him. I made time during kindergarten to pray. Does that mean I was saved sometime before I was five? Or that I never actually got saved? I don't have a great "before" photo; I don't have one moment I can point to as the turning point when I accepted Christ; I don't even have a memory of a time before I considered Jesus my Savior or trusted in God as the center of my life. Instead, I have something like a photo album; a long history of God working on me; many conversions, many moments when God keeps saving me over, and over, and over.

Here's the thing: I think both the born-again Christians and the lifelong believers have something to teach one another. For those of us who don't have that moment of salvation, we have to ask: is going to church, believing in Christ, following His Word just something we do, or is it who we are? Have we really allowed Christ to come in and change us—or do we just take it for granted that He will help us when we pray without unnecessary interference in the way we live our lives?

And for the born-again Christians—I've spent some time with newborn babies, and I can tell you that while babies are nice, moms feel a sigh of relief when they start growing up. I'm sure God feels the same way. Being "born again" is the beginning of the journey, not the end. I've met some Christians who confidently say they are sanctified—no drinking, no smoking, no sex outside of marriage. And I want to ask, yes, but do you covet? Do you judge? Does your mind wander during sermons? I want to say to them, John 3:3: You must be born again.

It's not the only verse about salvation. Psalm 30 is one Scripture few people talk about in terms of salvation. It's a psalm about healing, and it has a very special meaning for me because I feel as though I could have written it. And it's all right for us to read the psalms as our own words, our own prayers.

Psalm 30, like many psalms, is a psalm attributed to David, but it's also the psalm of the community. How do we know this? It's a song written for the dedication of the Temple.

Psalm 30,
"I will extol you, O Lord, for you have drawn me up,
  and did not let my foes rejoice over me.
O Lord my God, I cried to you for help,
  and you have healed me.
O Lord, you brought up my soul from Sheol,
  restored me to life from among those gone down to the Pit.
Sing praises to the Lord, O you his faithful ones,
  and give thanks to his holy name.
For his anger is but for a moment;
  his favor is for a lifetime.
Weeping may linger for the night,
  but joy comes with the morning.
As for me, I said in my prosperity,
  "I shall never be moved."
By your favor, O Lord,
  you had established me as a strong mountain;
you hid your face;
  I was dismayed.
To you, O Lord, I cried,
  and to the Lord I made supplication:
"What profit is there in my death,
  if I go down to the Pit?
Will the dust praise you?
  Will it tell of your faithfulness?
Hear, O Lord, and be gracious to me!
  O Lord, be my helper!"
You have turned my mourning into dancing;
  you have taken off my sackcloth
  and clothed me with joy,
so that my soul[b] may praise you and not be silent.

O Lord my God, I will give thanks to you forever."

What's wrong with that superscript? Well, remember, David wasn't there when the Temple was dedicated. David may have written the words, but it's also the Word of God, and it was meant to bring in the whole community, to speak to the experience of all people. When we're reading the psalms, we don't have to focus on the life of David; while we may learn something from considering his life, the ultimate purpose of the psalms is to speak to God's presence in your life and mine.

I first encountered Psalm 30 when I was recovering from a major depressive episode, during which I had experienced suicidal thoughts and been hospitalized. I've shared openly about my depression before for two reasons, first, because I believe it can help people, and second, because my story shows what God can do.

This Psalm is about healing, physical and spiritual. We in the West like to draw a hard line between physical and spiritual; medicine treats your body, prayers treat your soul. But the Bible doesn't draw that line, and depression is an illness that doesn't quite fit neatly into either category—at least, not according to me, as a depression survivor. Medicine, diet, and exercise can all help treat depression. Medicine helped save my life. Yet there was also a moment when God stepped in, and I could never have been healed without him.

Psalm 30:6: "I said in my prosperity, 'I shall never be moved.'"

Before major depression hit me like a ton of bricks, I thought I had it all together; everything figured out. Inside, I was a disaster; but to the world, it looked like I was an excellent student, a hard worker, a churchgoing Christian with a steady boyfriend. When I was in the hospital, dealing with suicidal thoughts, I was finally forced to admit that I needed help.

Psalm 30:2: "I cried to you for help, and you have healed me."

You have to admit that you aren't in control, or you can never be healed. If you say in your prosperity, you shall never be moved, you're sunk. You can't save yourself. You need God.

Psalm 30:3: "You brought up my soul from Sheol, restored me to life from among those gone down to the Pit."

God saved me in a very literal way. If God had not stepped in, I would have taken my own life. And even if I had not, life for me had become a living Sheol, a living hell. The demons, the thoughts inside my head, told me that I was worthless, a failure, that no one really loved me, that no one cared. I was sinking deeper and deeper into a downward spiral from which there was no recovery.

And then, there at the bottom, there was an element of choice, and the choice was whether to trust. To trust other people; to trust God. To trust that: Psalm 30:5, "Weeping may tarry for the night, but joy cometh in the morning." And so I chose to let go, and let God; and I began to experience joy. I'm not saying that it happened in a moment. The joy came little by little, the more I let go of my ego, my plans, my need to be in control and focused on daily life. It's still a process; people talk of themselves as recovering alcoholics; I think of myself as a recovering depressive. But when I let God in, he keeps restoring me to health; over, and over, and over.

Psalm 30:11, "You have turned my mourning into dancing; you have taken off my sackcloth and clothed me with joy, so that my soul may praise you and not be silent." When I experienced my calling to ministry, there were people in my life, and there still are, who couldn't accept it, people who pointed me to the words of Paul: *let the women keep silent in church*. When I read Psalm 30:12, I say: I cannot. My soul cannot keep silent. God gave me a story, and God gave me a message; and if I shut it up inside me, it is like a fire within my bones. I could be dead. I could be in a hospital somewhere. Instead, look what God has done! O Lord my God, I will give thanks to you forever and ever and ever, with every breath that is within me, with every opportunity you place in my life, let me praise your holy name.

That is one of my stories; those are some of the pictures in my album. But the book isn't finished yet. My family can tell you if you don't believe it—there are still parts that need healing, still parts that need saving. God is still working on the image in the picture. We are in need of salvation, in need of spiritual healing, every day. Sitting here, there is some part of you that God still wants to save. I don't know what it is—but you probably do. There's a part of you that's believing lies about yourself. There's a part of you that won't give up behaviors that hurt yourself and others. There's a part of you that refuses to let go and let God. Salvation isn't just an event; it's a process.

The salvation of John Newton, writer of Amazing Grace, is one of the great before and after stories. John Newton was a slave trader who accepted Christ, became a minister and an abolitionist. But it didn't happen overnight. Newton was born in 1725, and his father, a sea captain, began taking him on voyages at the age of 11. Newton ended up working in slaving vessels and becoming a slave trader. In 1748, when he was 23, Newton's ship got caught in a storm. He prayed to God, and the cargo miraculously shifted in such a way that it filled a hole in the hull and saved the vessel. Newton began taking an interest in the Bible, but in his memoirs, he wrote "I cannot consider myself a believer at that point." His faith grew, but he continued to sell slaves until his retirement from seafaring in 1754 at the age of 29. In 1764, he was ordained a minister at the age of 39, and also began to compose many hymns. At the age of 47, in 1772, he wrote Amazing Grace; I once was lost, but now am found, was blind, but now I see. Later, he began to reflect critically on his time in the slave trade, and in 1788, he wrote the pamphlet "Thoughts Upon the Slave Trade," and took up the cause of abolition at the age of 63. John Newton lived to see the slave trade abolished in 1807; he was 82. Salvation is a process. But it only happens as we let God change our ways of thinking and speaking and acting, we ask the self to step out of the way, and let the Spirit step in.

Psalm 30 is a psalm for dedication of the temple. In fact, it's the only Psalm written for the occasion. So perhaps it's surprising that there's nothing about community worship; nothing about Jerusalem; nothing about the House of the Lord; nothing about priests or sacrifice or the Ark. Instead, this is the personal praise song of someone who God has saved. And why is that? Perhaps because what God was getting at all along was the temple of the Holy Spirit; 1 Corinthians 6:19, "Or do you not know that your body is a temple of the Holy Spirit within you, which you have from God, and that you are not your own?"

What God really wants us to dedicate is not buildings, but lives. God wants us to dedicate our bodies, our hearts, our lives more and more to Him. And when we do that, God turns our whole lives into songs of praise. He turns our mourning into dancing. He takes off the sackcloth and clothes us with joy. He draws us up out of the hell we are living in and allows us to experience a little bit of heaven here on earth.

He begins to change us, change our ways of being in ways large and small, making us kinder, more trusting, more hopeful, more joyful, so that, as we turn the pages of the album, what shines from the page is less and less about me, me, me, and more and more, little by little, day by day, the image of Christ.

In the name of the Father, and the Son, and the Holy Spirit, Amen.

Week Twenty-five: What is Justice?
Psalm 72

What is justice, and whose job is it? We have a system of "justice" where we attempt to punish the guilty and restore the wronged. We have Supreme Court "Justices" whose job it is to fairly interpret and apply the law. But what is "justice," really?

First of all, justice is greater than fairness. My Granpap was the patriarch of the Smith family, and there's a great story about how he meted out justice; if two kids were playing with a toy, and there was fighting over the toy, the answer was simple—with a certain Solomonic harshness, he took the toy away. I'm sure the kids protested, "But that's not fair!" They wanted Granpap to figure out who the toy belonged to and give it to the correct party; that's fairness. But justice is greater than fairness. The children defined the problem differently than Granpap; they saw the problem as someone using the toy who shouldn't. He saw the problem as whiny, bickering children—the lack of peace in the family. By removing the source of the bickering and division, he created peace. If he had just given the toy to the kid who probably had it first, he would have taught the children to come to him whenever they had a fight, and there would be more whiny bickering. But because they knew he would take the toy away, he gave the kids an incentive to peacefully resolve their differences together. "Fairness" thinks about right and wrong; "justice" thinks about the greater good of the whole community, or what Jesus would call the kingdom of God.

Psalm 72 describes the kingdom of God. It's a unique Psalm, coming at the end of the second Book of Psalms. If you haven't noticed, the Psalms are divided into five books, with each one ending in either "Praise the Lord!" or "Amen, Amen."

1-41: Book One. Corresponds to Genesis ~ God's relation to humanity
42-72: Book Two: Corresponds to Exodus ~ Asking for deliverance
73-89: Book Three: Corresponds to Leviticus ~ Writings by Levitical musicians
90-106: Book Four: Corresponds to Numbers ~ Israel among the nations
107-150: Book Five: Corresponds to Deuteronomy ~ Celebrating God's Word

Psalm 72 ends the second book of Psalms with a song lifting up the ideal king. The people probably sang this song whenever a king was crowned. The psalmist, perhaps David or Solomon, describes what justice looks like under a godly king:

Justice (v.2): "May he judge your people with righteousness, and your poor with justice."

Prosperity for all (v. 3, 16): "May the mountains yield prosperity for the people, and the hills, in righteousness." "May there be abundance of grain in the land; may it wave on the tops of the mountains; may its fruit be like Lebanon; and may people blossom in the cities like the grass of the field."

The flourishing of all creation (v. 6, 16): "May he be like rain that falls on the mown grass, like showers that water the earth." "May there be abundance of grain in the land; may it wave on the tops of the mountains; may its fruit be like Lebanon; and may people blossom in the cities like the grass of the field."

Care for the poor, the weak, and the needy (v. 2, 4): "May he judge your people with righteousness, and your poor with justice." "May he defend the cause of the poor of the people, give deliverance to the needy, and crush the oppressor."

Freedom from oppression (v. 4, 12, 14): "May he defend the cause of the poor of the people, give deliverance to the needy, and crush the oppressor." "For he delivers the needy when they call, the poor and those who have no helper." "From oppression and violence he redeems their life; and precious is their blood in his sight."

First, justice means making judgments that promote the greater good. Verse 2 says, "May he judge your people with righteousness, and your poor with justice." Like my granpap taking the toy away, or like Solomon, when faced with two women bickering over a baby, who offered to cut the baby in half, the king will judge in such a divinely inspired way as to not just solve the immediate problem but create a better society.

Next, justice means everyone prospers. Verse 3 says, "May the mountains yield prosperity for the people, and the hills, in righteousness." If someone is not prospering, that is, if someone does not have a good and abundant living, then we have not yet achieved justice. This is contrary to our American way of thinking, that hard work yields prosperity; let he who works, eat. Psalm 72 says that abundance is God's gift in creation, so let everyone eat. Next, justice means all creation will flourish—verse 16 says, "May there be abundance of grain in the land; may it wave on the tops of the mountains; may its fruit be like Lebanon; and may people blossom in the cities like the grass of the field." Not only will the people prosper, but the land, the earth, will be flourishing as well. And justice especially means that life will improve for the poor, weak, and the needy.

Verses 12-14 say, "For he delivers the needy when they call, the poor and those who have no helper. He has pity on the weak and the needy and saves the lives of the needy. From oppression and violence he redeems their life; and precious is their blood in his sight."

The whole Bible, and it's especially clear in this Psalm, show that God has what is called "a preferential option for the poor." God has a special concern for the poorest, the weakest, the most hurting people in society. Justice happens when the rich and powerful stop oppressing the poor and weak.

Justice is greater than fairness. It's not about what's fair for one person; it's about the greater good of all people. And if we judge by the standard of Psalm 72, we can see that we have not quite achieved liberty and justice for all. We have not achieved prosperity when some people now have to work three jobs in order to make a living. We have not achieved the flourishing of creation when we poison our lands and seas, making the concrete jungle ever bigger, putting billboards where God put trees. We aren't caring for the poor and needy when our veterans and our mentally ill are housed in prisons or on the streets. We aren't ending oppression when we continue to exploit women and children, and the sex trafficking industry is such that some people estimate that the number of people living in slavery in the United States is as large or larger now than it was when slavery was legal. Somebody should do something about all this. But who?

Psalm 72 says that justice is the king's job. Psalm 72 is attributed as a Psalm of Solomon, the only Psalm attributed to the wise king. Yet at the end of the Psalm, it says "here the Psalms of David are ended." Which is strange because, first, we thought this was a Psalm of Solomon, and second, there's a lot more psalms of David to come. We can understand this as a Psalm which a father, David, wrote to his son, Solomon, or a Psalm which a son, Solomon, wrote to remember and honor his father, David. Either way, it's about a father teaching his son to be a good leader, a wise king.

We've proudly given up kings in this country, and eventually, they didn't work out for Israel either. But we still need leadership. We still need people to step forward and create justice, create prosperity, end oppression, make a better world. This Father's Day, we need men to step forward. When over 40% of children are born to single moms, when we see how men abuse women and children physically and sexually on TV and in real life, when we see a lot of men choosing drugs or gambling over their families, when so many of our churches are lacking men yet our prisons are full of them, I am so sad and so scared for our society.

One of the strongest impressions I have of my own teenage years was one day, when I was about thirteen, I came downstairs and my dad said, "Is that a skirt or a napkin? Go back upstairs and change." How many dads today would just look the other way? And I don't blame men; I blame all of us. I blame, in part, the church. In our church, we have men who step up to the plate; not only do they make sure everyone gets a bulletin every Sunday and a pancake on Easter, there's always a guy helping to install a refrigerator or change a lightbulb or flip the screen on the projector. And I think it's in large part because we have a great men's Bible study.

But overall, in the church, we haven't taught men how to be real men—men who are strong yet compassionate, men who work hard but aren't defined by work, men who know how to be good dads, men who will take away the toy. The church needs to show men how to be leaders, not just guys who can sit back and say, I've taken care of my family. The Bible says that's not enough. The Bible says the work of the leader is not done until there is justice for all.

One movie I always loved to watch with my dad was the George C. Scott version of "A Christmas Carol." George C. Scott was probably my dad's favorite actor, mostly because of "Patton" and "Dr. Strangelove: Or How I Learned to Stop Worrying and Love the Bomb." My dad's favorite line comes at the end of the movie; when Scrooge is sitting across from Bob Cratchit and chastising him for being five minutes late; and he says, "therefore…I will…double your salary!" Scrooge missed out on the chance to be a father himself; but to Tiny Tim, he becomes like a second father. He turns from thinking only of himself to becoming a father to all in need; and that is what leaders do. We in the church are called to be second fathers. We are called to look out for the Tiny Tims and the Bob Cratchits of this world, who are in need of someone to care for them, to defend their cause, to help them when they are in need, to teach them and guide them and help them to reach the abundant life. It's a great task—it's hard to know where to start—but we have a great Father to guide us.

God has promised to help us whenever we set our hearts to doing justice, and He has given us a great example. Christ was never a biological father either, but his life exemplifies what a real man should be, what a leader should look like, what it means to be a father to the fatherless. Psalm 72 points us, finally, to him; 72:17 NLT, "May the king's name endure forever; may it continue as long as the sun shines. May all nations be blessed through him and bring him praise."

When Christ came to earth, He could have had an easy, comfortable life; He could have been a king on a throne; had a beautiful wife, and lovely children and grandchildren. That would have been right; it would have been fair. Instead, He chose to give up comfort and ease in order to help us when we were most in need. He gave up all He had for the greater good of you and me. As Christ's body here on earth, we are called to continue His work. The church is called to father the fatherless, care for the poor, and keep working until there is justice on earth, as it is in heaven.

In the name of the Father, and the Son, and the Holy Spirit, Amen.

Week Twenty-six: Orientation
Psalm 119

"You shall not boil a calf in its mother's milk.", "You shall not touch the skin of a dead pig.", "A woman who gives birth to a daughter shall be unclean for sixty-six days." "Any woman who prays or prophesies with her head uncovered dishonors herself." People bring up these and other Scripture references, bizarre to our modern ears, to prove a point: Scripture has no relevance to us today. And it's a good question: why should something written thousands of years ago have any significance in this age, when Buzzfeed can tell you 15 Celebrity Tweets You Missed This Week?

Psalm 119 has plenty to answer to that. This Psalm is the longest single chapter of the Bible—176 verses, and they all say the same thing: "Lord, how I love your law!" The verse you might have heard the most is verse 105, "Thy Word is a lamp unto my feet and a light unto my path." This psalm is an acrostic. It goes through each of the 22 letters of the Hebrew alphabet, from Aleph to Taw, with eight verses beginning with each letter of the alphabet, all praising God's law. It's not an exciting Psalm to read; it's the same sentiment, one hundred seventy-six times. It doesn't even talk about what God's Law is. With only Psalm 119, we would know that the Bible is really super awesome, but we wouldn't have any idea what it says.

What is God's law? At the center is loving God and others; to love God and others, we have ten basic rules for living; and around that are all the other laws of the Bible, which seek to help us love God and others. That's it. That's how the Bible teaches us to live. And everything else—even the parts about dead pigs—points us back to those concepts.

Perhaps it's not as exciting as the Bill Cosby mistrial or the latest news on Beyonce's twins, but God's Word, the psalmist maintains, is the best information out there for living our lives. Psalm 119 says the same thing over, and over, and over…and over, because the psalmist is in love with God's Word—Jason Byassee writes that he's like a new convert, like someone newly in love, like a grandmother with her first grandchild (give me that baby!). He uses eight different synonyms for Scripture—and one of them is found in almost every verse of this Psalm. They are:

>*Dabar:* word
>*Torah:* law
>*Piqqudim:* orders
>*Miswah/Miswot:* commandments

Mishpat: judgment
Huqqim: boundaries
Edot: signs or reminders
Imrah: promise

We can see in these eight names for God's Word the many functions Scripture plays in our lives. In a way, these words are all synonyms; they all simply mean "law," "Scripture," the Word of God. But there is also much to learn from the meaning, or etymology of each word; that is, where it comes from. First, Scripture is the Word, or Dabar, of God. And what is a word? It's communication. Scripture is communication that comes from God.

When you look at your email, the first thing I see is who the email is from. If it's from Royal Caribbean Vacations, I don't even have to think about it; I just press "delete." But if it's from my husband, I don't even look at the subject line; I open it right away. What's the difference? The importance of the relationship. If your relationship with God is the most important relationship in your life—and I submit that it should be—you will open any communication that comes from Him right away. And His communication with you is Scripture.

Four of these names for God's Word have to do with God's authority in our life. Think about that word, "authority." God is the Author of life; He made it. Therefore, all of life is under His authority, and we obey His law or face the consequences; just as we pay the consequences from disobeying governmental law.

You might think that speed limits are stupid, when you see that cop out with his equipment on the highway, you slow down. In the same way, we are held accountable to God's law even when we don't like it. Like governmental law, God's law takes different forms; piqqudim and mitzvoth tell us what to do and not to do, like statutes or executive orders. God's law also takes the form of mishpatim, meaning judgments or decisions, applying the law to our everyday life, like judicial decisions that seek to interpret and apply the law. These four terms stress the authority of God, and thus remind us there are consequences even worse than speeding tickets for ignoring Scripture.

Three of these names for God's Word remind us that God's Word is ultimately there to help us. We talk a lot about boundaries today: healthy boundaries in relationships, in communication, in life.

In the 1960s, public schools experimented with an open-design concept; they built schools without walls to encourage children to have freedom and form relationships. Guess what? Fun in theory, impossible in practice. The same thing is going on in office spaces today; companies are removing walls and partitions. In order to get any work done, employees have to create boundaries in other ways; like by putting on headphones, even if you don't turn on any music. To create something of significance, you need to set boundaries. I think of the seventh commandment—the one against adultery. Not the most popular of commandments. But marriage can only develop into a meaningful and lasting relationship if you set boundaries around your marriage. Anyone can have fun for a day, or a week, or a month; but if you commit yourself to one person and one person alone for decades, you will learn about yourself, you will learn about life, you will learn about love, you will develop amazing patience, compassion, and character, and you will have a partner who truly knows you and loves you through it all. But none of it can happen without boundaries around that relationship. God's Word sets boundaries for our lives, tells us where we should not stray beyond, so we can create something of significance.

Another term for God's Word is edot, and one of the meanings of edot is warning signs or reminders. God's Word reminds us of what we already kind of know. Each of us has in our heart an understanding of right and wrong—it's what John Calvin described as "common grace," the sense of goodness we all have. Common grace is also just common sense—don't lie, don't steal, don't forget to call your mother on her birthday. We already know this stuff. That's why sometimes studying the Bible is boring. But sometimes, for me anyway, life could use a little less excitement and a little more common sense. The Bible is here to help us remember what we already know. And remembering is important.

I once heard a Muslim speaker talk about the sin of forgetfulness. In his "Mac Daddy days," as he called them, he met a beautiful woman at a nightclub. He bothered her until she gave him her number. But he never called. When he saw her again the next week, she wouldn't have anything to do with him. "But I just forgot!" He whined. And he never forgot what she said. She said, "There's no such thing as just forgetting. When you forgot, it was as though, in your mind, I did not exist." When we forget God's Word, it's like denying God's existence, God's importance to our lives. God's Word is a signpost, a reminder, a pop-up warning on the iPhone, there to remind you of what you need to do, because there's no such thing as "just forgetting."

Finally, the last way of describing God's Word is imah, or the promise. And this word is in the singular throughout Psalm 119. We often talk about standing on the promises of God. But this Psalm reminds us that there is just one promise—and that is to love us. God's love is at the center of everything.

In fact, it's because God loves us that He gives us the law, that He gives us Scripture, He gives us His Word.

My daughter has a friend named Dalina, and sometimes I feel like every sentence she speaks begins with "Me and Dalina." And it drives me nuts, because I like rules. I guess I'm a good Calvinist. So every time she says, "me and Dalina," I say—and I try to say it without sounding annoyed—"Dalina and I." I figured if she heard it a thousand times, eventually, it would stick inside her brain—and one day, when she is taking the SAT, she'll hear my voice saying "Dalina and I." Perhaps that's how God feels—if he tells us something a thousand different times, we might get annoyed at him—but one day, when we need it, we'll hear His voice. He loves us, and He's promised to love us. His Word is a reminder of that promise.

Eight names for God's Word, repeated in eight-verse sections for every letter of the alphabet. Eight is a number of completion. Mark Thronveit writes, "In mathematics, 8 is the first cubed number (2x2x2). In Chinese thought, the number eight represents the totality of the universe." Biblically speaking, eight represents the day after the seven days of creation. When babies are circumcised on the eighth day of life, it represents the totality of creation, and a new beginning.

God's Word is complete, it's total, it's everything we need—and it's a new beginning. Have you ever read Scripture, and it's as though God is speaking just to you? He is. He wants to help you, and He's given you a resource. Many of us, especially, might I say, some of the guys, when we open a kid's toy, or a new appliance, like to have some fun trying to figure out how to put it together, how to make it work, all on our own. But eventually, what was fun becomes frustrating. At some point, we all have to give up our pride and read the directions. God's Word gives us direction. There is a message for you today—a message for a better life, better relationships, better health, better ways of living. It's your purpose for today and your promise for tomorrow. So put the remote down, put the iPhone away, stop the constant flow of junk into your brain, and take a moment today to drink deeply from God's Word.

In the name of the Father, and of the Son, and of the Holy Spirit, Amen.

Week Twenty-seven: Pledge
Psalm 146

When I was a child, school days always began with the words: "I pledge allegiance to the flag of the United States of America…" we recited the Pledge, and always a few snarky kids would add "Amen" at the end. The pledge, after all, felt something like a prayer. But we giggled, because we knew pledging is different from praying. We pledge our "allegiance," but "allegiance" is not the same as "faith." The words "under God" stress that the nation itself is under God's authority.

The distinction between nation and God is important to the author of Psalm 146. Psalm 146 falls into the final collection of six psalms of praise at the very end of the book of Psalms, and this Psalm uses the poetic technique of the inclusio to contrast the power of princes with the power of God. An inclusio is a technique that parallels one concept with another around a central idea.

- Hallelujah!
  - Vow to praise "my" God
    - Princes are perishable and do not help
      - Creator God
        - Who keeps faith forever
      - Sustainer God
    - God is imperishable and our only help
  - Confession of the Lord "your" God
- Hallelujah!

The psalm begins and ends with the word "hallelujah," which simply means "Praise the Lord." Then the psalmist proclaims his personal faith in my God. The psalmist finishes by calling the people to trust in "your God." So, the psalm persuades the hearer to make "my God," "your God."

Today, it seems sometimes that the latest political or social slogans, whether "Black Lives Matter" or "Make America Great Again" are more interesting to people than the time-honored message of faith. Christians shouldn't disengage from the political process; as the study of this Psalm will show, God calls us to do quite the opposite. But these political movements, and even love of our country itself, are human endeavors, and should not command the full devotion due only to God. And I think we are seeing people become more passionate about, and more argumentative and divisive about, their political affiliations because those affiliations take the place of God, the ultimate good. C.S. Lewis said that the greatest things, like love of family, love of country, love of justice, are the most popular idols because they are so close to who God is. That is why love of country, patriotism, political affiliation so easily takes the place of God in our lives.

This is nothing new. The psalmist exhorts the people not to place their trust in princes, not to place their trust in governments, in leaders, in celebrities, because that is exactly what people were doing then as now. Princes are mortals and they cannot help. In Hebrew, man or humanity is "adam" and the earth or dirt is "adamah". So in the second chapter of Genesis, Adam is nothing more than dust, into which God has breathed the breath of life. This psalm echoes those words, adam and adamah, to remind us that, whether you are the poorest and weakest person on the planet or the richest and most powerful, we are all simply dust, on our way to the grave. And if you put your faith in dust, what do you expect? Princes and politicians are but dust, and they have broken their promises forever. Like all of us, they are prone to make choices based on their own narrow self-interest rather than the common good. But the Psalmist tells us who does keep every promise: Psalm 146:6, "He keeps every promise forever." That's the central message of the psalm.

Ultimately, the movements, the causes, the governments, even the churches cannot help what ails us, which is sin and death. But God can. This is our message to the world. This is how "my God" becomes "your God." Tell the world of all the promises he has kept in Scripture, in history, in your own life. Proclaim with the psalmist that where princes have failed you, you can trust in the Prince of Peace. Psalm 146:7-9, "He gives justice to the oppressed and food to the hungry. The Lord frees the prisoners. The Lord opens the eyes of the blind. The Lord lifts up those who are weighed down. The Lord loves the godly. The Lord protects the foreigners among us. He cares for the orphans and widows, but he frustrates the plans of the wicked."

The psalmist tells us who it is that gives justice to the oppressed and food to the hungry; God alone. The only prince in whom we, as Christians, can place our trust is the Prince of Peace. Christ echoed the message of Psalm 146 when he spoke to the synagogue at Nazareth: Luke 4:18-19, 21, "The Spirit of the Lord is upon me, because he has anointed me to bring good news to the poor. He has sent me to proclaim release to the captives and recovery of sight to the blind, to let the oppressed go free, to proclaim the year of the Lord's favor." The eyes of all in the synagogue were fixed on him. [21] Then he began to say to them, "Today this scripture has been fulfilled in your hearing."

If governments, churches, or other human institutions help the poor, it is because they are following God's direction and putting to good use to the resources with which God has blessed the land. If we take Scripture seriously, it is clear that God demands care for the widows, for the orphans, for foreigners; God demands us to look out for the poor and oppressed. We in the church are called to speak for God, to hold governments, to hold princes accountable to the higher ideal expressed in Psalm 146, and to share God's Word so that more and more people will support governments based on the ideals of Scripture rather than narrow self-interest.

We can and should pledge our allegiance to our country this Independence Day. We should celebrate our heritage, and our continued commitment to work until we have truly achieved liberty and justice for all. We pledge our allegiance to the United States of America, but we pledge our faith and place our trust in God alone.

Many people know about Dietrich Bonhoeffer, the Lutheran pastor who spoke out against Naziism and lost his life in a German concentration camp. Fewer have heard of the Barmen declaration, in which a group of Calvinist pastors and teachers decried Naziism—not because they knew the depravities of the Holocaust, because like many Germans they did not recognize the extent of the crimes of the German state. They decried Naziism because they saw in it the cardinal sin of idolatry, because Naziism gave the German nation the praise due only to God.

The declaration stated, "We believe that we have been given a common message to utter in a time of common need and temptation. Jesus Christ is God's assurance of the forgiveness of all our sins…he is also God's mighty claim upon our whole life." These pastors and teachers signed the proclamation with the full knowledge that they faced death at the hands of the most powerful prince of that time, because they were accountable not to him, not even to their country, but to their God.

When we come to the communion table today, we are acknowledging that we are weak, that we are dust, that we need nourishment, which can only come from God. We acknowledge that we are weak, we are poor, we are oppressed until Christ sets us free. We humbly place our trust in Him. So this holiday weekend, let us pledge our allegiance to our nation, and renew our dedication to the ideals of justice, freedom, and peace for which she stands. But let us pledge our faith in God alone, and in his Son Jesus Christ, in whom true hope is found, and in whose service, we find perfect freedom.

In the name of the Father, and of the Son, and of the Holy Spirit, Amen.

Week Twenty-eight: Cricket's the Name
Proverbs 1

The movie *Pinocchio* was very important to my childhood. In 1984, when I was three years old, the movie was released onto VHS for the first time, and it was one of the first videos we owned. Pinocchio is the only movie to receive a 100% "fresh" rating on Rottentomatoes.com. It's a movie that resonates, in part, because it is full of spiritual truth. It draws from the story of Jonah and has themes of prayer, repentance, and redemption. Even the name Jiminy Cricket is a minced-oath version of Jesus Christ. Geppetto is a woodcarver who has spent his whole life making children smile, but he's all alone, and one night, kneeling, hands clasped as though in prayer, he wishes upon a star that his wooden puppet Pinocchio might be a real boy. As Geppetto sleeps, the blue fairy comes to him like an angel, and she grants his wish and animates Pinocchio. The Blue Fairy explains that Pinocchio must help his father, always tell the truth, and let his conscience be his guide. And Pinocchio asks, "What's a conscience?" Jiminy Cricket spouts, "A conscience is that still small voice people won't listen to." And that, there, is Proverbs 1, except Wisdom is not a still small voice people won't listen to. She's the loud, terrifying, inescapable voice people won't listen to.

Jiminy is dubbed Pinocchio's conscience, Lord High Keeper of the Knowledge of Right and Wrong, and guide along the straight and narrow path. Can you imagine such words coming out of the movies today? We seem to have lost our belief that there really is such a thing as right and wrong, a straight and narrow path. Rather, we teach people that there are many paths, and they are all good. But that's just not true. CS Lewis writes, "If anyone will take the trouble to compare the moral teaching of, say, the ancient Egyptians, Babylonians, Hindus, Chinese, Greeks and Romans, what will really strike them will be how very like they are to each other and to our own. Whenever you find a man who says he does not believe in a real Right and Wrong, you will find that same man going back on it a moment later. Human beings, all over the earth, have this curious idea that they ought to behave in a certain way, and cannot really get rid of it… (what's amazing is) that they do not in fact behave in that way."

This week Dan was listening to one of the podcasts we like, Freakonomics Radio. And Freakonomics was looking at some very interesting research, that marriage rates have decreased nationwide, and today only 60% of children are born into a marriage. It used to be that social scientists believed marriage rates had gone down because men are less financially able to marry. But a recent study of communities where, because of fracking, men have been able to get good, steady jobs has demonstrated that those men who get good jobs do not become any more likely to marry. Yet marriage has great benefits to men—longer lifespan, less disease, higher income. Marriage has even greater benefits to children. Children have better life outcomes in a home with two people who are married than with two people who have cohabitated for many years. There is a difference. Even the economists on Freakonomics recognized the benefits of marriage—and they asked, bewildered, so why aren't people getting married?

The Christian hears this and wants to bang his or her head against a wall. Because we believe that, Jiminy Cricket, the answers are easy. They're there all along, in the simple message of Christ, in the Scriptures. The answer is the central message of Proverbs—the fear of the Lord is the beginning of knowledge. Trust in the Lord with all your heart and lean not on your own understanding. In all your ways acknowledge him, and he will direct your paths. We believe that the problems come in when we ignore the Wisdom that's inside us, and we believe that another name for Wisdom is God. Or as Jiminy would say, always let your conscience be your guide.

Proverbs is the most practical book of the Bible, and it's a book of common sense…what we generally already know, because God has put it into our hearts from the beginning. Think before you speak, Proverbs 10:19. Discipline your kids, Proverbs 13:24. Don't get into debt, Proverbs 22:7. Be faithful to your wife, Proverbs 5:15. Don't get too much wine and get drunk, don't eat too much food and get fat. Proverbs 23:20. Work hard and save for the future. Proverbs 10:4-5. This is not rocket science. We know who wisdom is. She's not hiding. She's out on the street corner yelling her head off. The problem is, there's only one Wisdom, and there are so, so many other voices out there pulling us away from the straight and narrow—Proverbs calls them the mockers, the simpletons, the fools, and they are so, so popular. They call Pinocchio, as they call us today, to a place called Pleasure Island where you can do whatever you please. And everyone goes.

Wisdom is unpopular. Can't you just picture her in your mind? She probably looks like your mom. In Proverbs, there are two figures: a father figure, educating his son, and a mother figure, wisdom. In Hebrew, Wisdom is Chokmat; in Greek, Wisdom is Sophia. In Christian tradition, she is also a figure of Christ. She is a feminine image of God, of the mothering Spirit of the Lord that nurtures and guides us. Did you, as a child, ever lean back in your chair at the dinner table, only to have your mom say, "don't lean your chair back like that, you'll fall and hurt yourself?" Is there any child on the planet who never leaned back in your chair at the dinner table? Why is that behavior so irresistible? And is there any one of us who did not, eventually, fall down on our butts? Wisdom is saying, there are laws to the universe. Like gravity. And if you ignore them, you'll fall on your butt. And when you do, I will laugh at you.

Proverbs 1:20-33 is structured chiastically; it's a structure we studied last week in Psalm 146. Everything is paralleled around a central idea. And the central idea here is in verses 26-28: "I called you so often, but you wouldn't come. I reached out to you, but you paid no attention. You ignored my advice and rejected the correction I offered. So I will laugh when you are in trouble! I will mock you when disaster overtakes you—when calamity overtakes you like a storm, when disaster engulfs you like a cyclone, and anguish and distress overwhelm you." Now maybe you read these verses this week and thought calamity will overtake you like a storm, disaster will engulf you like a cyclone, I will mock you to your face, OK, on to chapter two. These verses are not meant to be taken lightly. Preacher Derek Neider opined, these verses are there to literally scare the hell out of you. Wisdom is a tough teacher—almost a cruel teacher. When calamity strikes, Wisdom will laugh at your distress? I see this as a depiction of the honest frustration God experiences when we repeatedly ignore His voice.

There are physical laws to the universe, like gravity. If you lean back on a chair, you'll fall down. There are also spiritual laws to the universe, spiritual gravity. The law of spiritual gravity is this: Trust in the Lord with all your heart and lean not on your own understanding. Don't lean away and you won't fall. It doesn't mean we won't ever suffer. It's not a guarantee that our lives will be easy. But what God does promise us is that, when we lean on Him, we will have greater peace, greater hope, greater joy. I think back to Job, how, with all the physical suffering in his life, he was able to praise God, and even to deepen his faith to the point where he saw the image of Christ: "I know that my Redeemer lives, and at last he shall stand upon the earth, and then in my flesh I shall see God." God is wiser, God is stronger, God is greater, God is the solid rock at the center of the universe—and so when we lean on him, we cannot be moved. No matter what trouble may come, what disaster or calamity may strike us, we will stand firm in the Spirit.

There are temptations around you, mockers, simpletons, and fools, and temptations within you, calling you to unhealthy habits, selfish ways, unhelpful thoughts, mean-spirited words. I know my own temptations; I can only guess at yours. But what I know is that if you listen to them, if you lean away from the table, lean away from God, if you ignore that screeching voice inside your head, Jiminy Cricket, you will fall. So lean on the Lord. Follow the simple, common-sense path of Wisdom. And always let your conscience be your guide.

In the name of the Father, and of the Son, and of the Holy Spirit, Amen.

Week Twenty-nine: Hobbits, Dogs, and the Meaning of Time
Ecclesiastes 3

There are dog people and there are the rest of people. My family of origin is dog people. My brother and his wife married almost three years ago, and my brother gave a beautiful speech describing his love for his beautiful and talented wife Alexx, but also his love for his dog Chicco, whom he met on the same day he met Alexx, which, I think, was not a coincidence. Chicco, of course, was ring bearer, and kind of co-officiated with me in the ceremony, giving his own benediction (he started howling right after I pronounced them husband and wife!)

Dogs can teach us a great deal about life. What is remarkable about a dog is that they are completely transparent. Here is a photo of my dog Rosie with her birthday bone.

I can tell you right now that the only thing Rosie is thinking about is her rawhide bone. She has no sense of past, or future, or any reality apart from the existence of that, $2 piece of dehydrated meat. She has no idea that the bone has anything to do with her birthday, or that she even has a birthday.

You and I, on the other hand, are both blessed and cursed by our ever-present sense of past and the future. You could be sitting down stuffing your face with a delicious, moist, chocolate birthday cake covered in homemade buttercream icing, and thinking about the presentation you have at work on Monday, or the fact that the kitchen chandelier needs dusting, or that you wish your uncle had been able to make it to the party.

Ecclesiastes puts it this way (NIV): "I have seen the burden God has laid on men. He has made everything beautiful in its time. He has also set eternity in the hearts of men; yet they cannot fathom what God has done from beginning to end." Ecclesiastes scholar Roland Murphy wrote that this verse is a fantastic statement of divine sabotage. God has placed us in this catch-22. We are mortal; we are limited; our time here is brief, and yet we, alone out of all creatures, have a sense of limitlessness, of eternity. We have a sense of past and future, yet we are also cursed with the understanding that we were not part of that past and will not be part of that future. It all goes back to the trees in the Garden of Eden. Remember them? There was the tree of life, and the tree of knowledge. We ate from the tree of knowledge when we weren't supposed to, and that act cut us off from the tree of life. So humans have the knowledge of eternity, but we won't live forever.

What's the solution? How do we then live? Eat the birthday cake. Live in the moment. The author of Ecclesiastes, traditionally Solomon, tells us: embrace the season you are in. Even hard things, even suffering. Be where you are. Or as Christ told us: Matthew 6:34: "So don't be anxious about tomorrow. God will take care of your tomorrow too. Live one day at a time."

The author tells us there is a time for everything, a time for every season under heaven. He begins with our beginning; a time to be born, there is also a time to die. He gives us these sets of opposites, telling us, showing us, that even difficult things have their season in God's design. Our task is to constantly be reminded our mortality, our limitation, and to live totally and fully in the moment, trusting in God to take care of the past and the future.

This means accepting our death, and the death of our loved ones. This passage spends a lot of time talking about grieving and how to give it a proper time. Not only does the author say that there's a time to be born and a time to die, he also says there is a time to weep and a time to laugh, a time to mourn and a time to dance. He also says: Ecclesiastes 3:7, "A time to tear, and a time to mend." In that culture, when you grieved, you tore your clothing as a sign of your grief. The author is saying there's a time for that, and there's a time to take those torn shreds of cloth and piece them back together.

I've noticed that in American culture, we expect people to "get over" their grief very quickly. You might get three days off work for the death of a parent or a sibling. This is unique in all the cultures of the world, where people wear black for a year. The fact is that everyone grieves differently, and we can't expect people to be happy right away. And it's also okay if some people grieve differently or more quickly than others. I've seen in families so much difficulty surrounding grief. People get worried because someone in the family grieves differently. Some men, for example, don't cry, they just get angry and difficult. But that is their way, and it's what they need to do. The fact is that everyone does it differently, and the time for you to grieve, or the way that you grieve, might be different from the way that I grieve.

The problem comes in when you never sew your clothes back together. When you never dance again. When your grief from one death is holding you back from the births that are surrounding you. One person I care about described grief this way; there's a hole in your heart. And it will always be there. But over time, new things begin to grow in around the hole. They don't take it away, but they make it beautiful, they make it livable. So dance. Let new things grow.

Another important point to the author of Ecclesiastes is that there is a time for working and a time for resting. When the author says, Ecclesiastes 3:5, "A time to scatter stones, and a time to gather them." He is talking about the rocky fields of the Holy Land, and the task of preparing a field for crops. At one time, you would throw those stones out of the field so you could plant crops. There were also times when you might gather stones to build a wall or a building. The point that the author is making is that you're really just shuffling stones. In the end, the stones will still be there. The walls you build will one day be scattered. So do your work, but don't think it will last forever.

In American culture, many of us live to work, instead of working to live. We place a lot of value on what we do, instead of how we live, as though our accomplishments will universally live on. But the reality is, we are all little drops in a great ocean. The presentation you have to give on Monday? It won't change the world. Ecclesiastes spends a lot of time reminding us that everything is meaningless. You may have heard it translated as vanity. In Hebrew, the word is *hevel*, meaning wind, nothingness, meaninglessness. It doesn't seem like a very religious sentiment—everything is meaningless. But what the author wants to get across is that our little lives, in and of themselves, are nothing; we are called to place our trust not in our own accomplishments, not in what we are doing, but in what God has done.

Ancient people shuffled stones; you and I might shuffle paper, or install plumbing, or restock shelves. All these things need to be done, and there is a time for them; but the paper will get unshuffled, the plumbing will one day give out, the shelves will need restocking. The stones will be scattered. So, work like a dog. Work for your treat, and then lie down and enjoy it. Don't stress about the jobs you have to do. Do your work, and then rest. The goal of life is not to finish with an empty inbox.

So, is it all really meaningless? Yes, and no. The author reflects, Ecclesiastes 3:12-13, "I know that there is nothing better for men than to be happy and do good while they live. That everyone may eat and drink and find satisfaction in his toil"—this is the gift of God. The divine sabotage, the catch-22, the curse and the blessing, is that we are caught in a time, and that we are aware of eternity, aware of God, aware that we have this gift not to be wasted. Our awareness of our own mortality means that nothing matters—and also, that everything matters.

That's actually the title of a book I read once, a strange and beautiful book, about a young man named Junior who was born with the awareness that a meteor would hit the earth at an exact day and time, destroying all life on earth and making this planet unlivable. He was also, in this novel, a scientific genius. And he was presented with a choice. He could tell all the scientists, all the governments, help them prepare the world for this catastrophe. He could head up a team to try to quickly colonize the moon and choose a few select people to go there so the human race would live on. He could watch as the world tore itself apart fighting over who would get to go on that ship. He could live through the fighting and the chaos and the pain. Or, he could live his life. He could marry, have a child. He could put his genius to work improving life for the few years that life would be a reality. He could invent underground pumps that would provide whole communities with fresh, clean water. He could, in the end, wait with everyone else, for the end, surrounded by his family, surrounded by love. And that was what he did.

At one point in his life, he went to a television interview about his brother, a famous professional baseball player, and his daughter, a famous activist for world peace. And his brother said, "What I'm doing is so small, so unimportant, compared to what my niece is doing." And only Junior knew that statement was not true. Because everything matters, baseball, and world peace, would both bring people joy in the short time they had under the sun. Our life has meaning because of our death. Life has meaning because we are caught in time. And we only are able to understand that meaning because we have a sense of the eternal. So perhaps God has not cursed us after all. Perhaps God has created, in us, someone who can get a sense of the great, great gift that we have: the gift this passage begins with in verse 1, a time to be born.

Ecclesiastes 3:8 says there is a time for war, and a time for peace. Ecclesiastes 3:1-8 begins with birth, and it ends with peace. At the very end, just after mention of war, the most terrible reality humans can know, comes peace, and that is where we end. Our lives are a short flurry of joy and suffering bookended by the reality of God, the reality of life, the reality of love, the reality of peace. But where would we be without all that comes in between? The fever, the story, the joy and suffering of life, gives that peace so much more meaning.

My family is dog people; we are also movie people. I tend to judge movies by the way they end, by the last scene. My family could recite for you my lecture on how *The Dark Night Rises* should really have the same ending as *Monsters, Inc.* But perhaps my favorite ending is in Return of the King by the Christian author J.R.R. Tolkien. Tolkien begins his epic Lord of the Rings series (the book version, now) by describing to you the Shire, the little home of the Hobbits. "Hobbits are an unobtrusive but very ancient people…they love peace and quiet and good tilled earth." From this ordinary beginning, Tolkien catapults us into enormous world events, weapons of mass destruction, death and sacrifice and pain and love and war. Frodo, the little Hobbit from the Squire, and his friends, are at the center of it all. When the world has been saved, Frodo finds himself searching for peace, unable to forget the great drama of his story, and so he leaves the Shire to find peace in the Undying Lands. But he must say goodbye to his friends, including his friend Sam, who was his companion through all his adventures, who carried him when he could not go on, who was with him in the deepest part of the earth, when life and death and all things hung in the balance, and the little hobbit was called upon to make the great sacrifice.

Frodo leaves; but I love this scene because it doesn't end there. It ends when Sam comes home, to his simple hobbit-hole, half hidden in a grassy hill; to his little wife, and their little children, and the stones that must be gathered together another day. And they run and embrace him; and in that moment, as he stands there, holding them, he looks out. And I think in that moment he sees, the vast and terrible story, the horrors of war; all the suffering, the great sacrifice, that has allowed him this moment to hold these people in his arms. He looks out and sees that everything matters. And he goes into his little house. And he shuts the door.

Without the story, we would see nothing more than a man, coming home to his family. It's only because we know the story that this moment is filled with meaning. Because we now know that it all matters, the Shire, the children, the stones, it all matters so much. It is all part of this greater story. It's because of everything in between that we can see the beauty of this moment of peace.

We, as Christians, are called to be like Sam. We know the pain and the sacrifice that has given us the gift of this peace—the greatest sacrifice of love, demonstrated in the life and death of Jesus Christ. We know the story, and so for us, the peace and joy of everyday living is endowed with greater purpose. We, like Sam, are called to look out, and see the vast and beautiful meaning of this simple life, because we know what it cost. We know, then, that everything matters. We are called to share that knowledge with the world, so that others may experience the depth of God's love and the power of His peace.

Ecclesiastes 3:12-13, "I know that there is nothing better for men than to be happy and do good while they live. That everyone may eat and drink and find satisfaction in all his toil—this is the gift of God." May you embrace each season in its time. May you eat, and drink, and find satisfaction in your toil. And, every once in a while, may you look out, and see the beauty of your story, of our story, of The Story, made beautiful because it ends; and may you and then rest our little stories in the midst of the great eternal peace; and, gently, close the door.

In the name of the Father, and the Son, and the Holy Spirit, Amen.

Week Thirty: Who You Gonna Call?
Isaiah 7

My family recently introduced my son to the movie *Ghostbusters* and presented him with one of his new favorite toys, The Stay-Puft Marshmallow Man. He likes to show it to me over and over throughout the day, and every time he shows me, he repeats the Ghostbusters tagline—"Mommy, who are you going to call?" And of course, my daughter Diana, the snarky one, says, "JP, you're supposed to say it fast, who you gonna call?" The question presented to King Ahaz in Isaiah 7 is—*who you gonna call?*

Ahaz is the king of the southern kingdom, Judah—remember, God's people split centuries earlier into the northern kingdom, Israel, and the southern kingdom, Judah. Judah is not the superpower of the ancient Mediterranean world. The top dog right now is Assyria, and Assyria is threatening all the other kingdoms in the area, forcing them to pay tribute, and all the nations are terrified. Israel is terrified, and so the Israeli king, Pekah, has come up with a solution: why not form an alternative alliance with Judah and Damascus, and together they can stand up to the Assyrian bully. Except Judah wants no part in this alliance. So Pekah and the king of Damascus, Rezin, say, Okay, let's go down there and just take over Judah, install a puppet king who will join our alliance, and on the way let's kill a bunch of people and take their stuff. It'll be great.

Ahaz and the people of Judah are quaking in their boots at the thought of this invading army. Isaiah 7 literally says Judah is shaking like a leaf. There is something strange in the neighborhood. Who are they going to call? Faced with this situation, Ahaz does just about the stupidest thing he can do. He calls on Assyria, the superpower, the big dog, the kingpin of the ancient Mediterranean, and says, hey, can you help us? Now this would be like saying, hmmm, these summer mosquitoes seem to be sucking me dry. I need someone who can help me with this problem. Hey, Count Dracula, can you take a look at this?

Isaiah has an alternative solution. He calls on King Ahaz to trust God, rather than the Assyrian army. Who you gonna call? Isaiah says, call on the Lord. Isaiah, remember, has just been granted this vision of the vast glory of the heavenly kingdom in Isaiah 6. So he isn't scared of King Pekah or King Rezin. He isn't even scared of the Assyrian superpower. He knows that there is a much greater king at work. And Isaiah is right. In fact, both King Rezin and King Pekah are going to be dead within two years.

It's easy for us to be critical of King Ahaz—but who do we call on? In our time of financial need, do we turn to God to help us through—or do we turn to banks and creditors to help us? When we look at the state of affairs of our communities and our government, do we turn to charismatic politicians—or do we seek God's will? When our lives become stressful, confusing, and chaotic, do we turn to the glass of wine, to the bucket of ice cream, to drugs, to sex or romance to help us cope—or do we turn to God in prayer? Who you gonna call?

Ahaz has given up on God. But God hasn't given up on Ahaz. Isaiah says, God will give you a sign. And he is speaking both to Ahaz, and to all the people of Israel. Isaiah says that a maiden will give birth to a son. A lot of exegetical ink has been spilled on the word "maiden," or "virgin," or "young woman" here. The Hebrew word is Almah, and it referred to a woman's age rather than her sexual status, but in that culture to be a young woman was also to be a virgin. It was so important that a woman be a virgin on her wedding night that there were proofs and tests of her virginity. But the point here is not so much the sexual status of the young woman—it's the name of the child. Because this is a new name, a unique name, pregnant with meaning that will not be fully borne until the birth of the Messiah. The name is this: Immanuel, God is with us.

It is not until Christ is born that the fullness of Isaiah's prophecy will come to fruition, when a virgin will give birth to a son, and God will show us that He is with us in everything—that He will take on our flesh, take on our life, take on our pain and even our death, and will never let us go. He will show us that we are not alone against the big dogs and the big bullies that have us quaking in our boots. He will show us that we are not alone even in those moments when we cannot sense him, when we cry out, "My God, my God, why have you forsaken me?" That God himself knows and has entered that pain and fear and conquered it forever.

What God did in Christ is the profoundest form of love: to be with someone in their suffering. Sometimes, when a person is hurting, the most important thing we can do is simply to be with them, to reach out to them physically, emotionally, and spiritually, to be present, as God was fully present with us. Like many people, I have some things that make me squeamish, and one thing I never liked, when I was younger, was going to viewings, because I never understood the point of touching a corpse. It creeped me out. So when I was at Beaumont hospital doing my clinical pastoral education, I would come to the room whenever someone died, and it was my rotation to cover pastoral care. I would pray for the family and leave and would avoid actually touching the body.

Well of course God was having none of that. Partway into the summer, I was called to my first situation of the death of a child. It was a twelve-year-old girl, and she had died of AIDS, which she had contracted from her mother in utero. The father had lost both his wife and his child and was visibly broken as his little girl lay on the bed, gone from him forever. And I held his hand, and I prayed with him, and stayed with him for some time. And then I got ready to leave. But he grabbed me, and he said, "it's ok. You can touch her."

And in that split second, it came to me all that that poor little girl had suffered in her short life. All the people who had shrunk at her touch. The girls who must have whispered about her in the bathroom stalls. The pain of her short life, with too many needles and not enough hugs. And I heard God saying, you are my representative to this place, to this father. So you get over this and you get over it right now. And I laid my hands, and my mouth, and my body all over that child. I can guarantee you that father today remembers not a single thing that I said. All he can remember is that I touched her. That I was with her. That God was with her.

As God is with you. What are you afraid of? What kings, what conquerors, what invading army? Are you going to be defined by your fear, or by God's love? 1 John 4 says that perfect love casts out fear. I have come to believe that the opposite of love is not hate, but fear. Fear is our enemy, and leads us into bad choices, that will define us long after the thing that initially caused the fear is gone. Like Ahaz. He creates this unholy alliance with Assyria in order to shake off these two little kings. Does he think Assyria won't expect anything in return? Our fears cause us to run from our faith and make bad choices that define us forever. So don't choose fear. Choose faith. I saw a video about fear that I just can't shake. Will Smith was on a talk-show, talking to the host about his skydiving experience. This is the transcript:

"You take a drink with your friends, and somebody says, 'Yeah, we should go skydiving tomorrow!' You go, 'Yeah, we'll go skydiving tomorrow!' 'Yeah! Yeah!' Everybody goes, 'Yeah!' Then that night, you're lying in your bed and you just keep, 'Uh, uh.' You're terrified. You keep imagining over and over again jumping out of an airplane, and you can't figure out why you would do that. You wake up the next day, and you go down where you said you were going to meet, and everybody's there. You get in the van and be like, 'Oh my God. Oh my God.' Your stomach is terrible. You can't eat and everything, but you don't want to be the only punk who doesn't jump out of this airplane. You fly, and you go up, you go up, you go up, and you go up to 14,000 feet."

"Somebody opens the door, and in that moment, you realize you've never been in a freaking airplane with the door open. You're looking out down to death. They say, 'On three,' and they say, 'One, two,' and he pushes you on two because people grab on three. You go, 'Ahhh.' You fall out of the airplane. In one second, you realize that it's the most blissful experience of your life. You're flying. There's zero fear. You realize at the point of maximum danger is the point of minimum fear. It's bliss. Why were you scared in your bed the night before? What do you need that fear for? Everything up to the stepping point, there's actually no reason to be scared. It only just ruins your day. **The best things in life are on the other side of terror, on the other side of your maximum fear, are all of the best things in life."**

In a day, in a week, in a year, that thing you're afraid of, that unbearable situation—it will be over and done with. How will you spend your time until then? In the end, there are only two choices: fear, and faith. Trusting God and trusting anyone else. I don't know what armies stand against you this week. But I do know that armies of angels stand at your back. You can choose fear, or you can choose faith. Who are you going to call?

In the name of the Father, and the Son, and the Holy Spirit, Amen.

Week Thirty-one: The Suffering Servant
Isaiah 53

When Dan and I were first married, we had a little dispute as to whether a star or an angel goes on the Christmas tree. I maintained that a star should go on the tree because the wise men followed the star. Dan argued that an angel goes on the tree because the angel told the shepherds of Christ's birth. We used to walk by the tree and actually change what was on the top. In the end, we compromised; and that's how we became the strange family with a cross on the Christmas tree.

We told everyone it was because Christ is our peace. But when my brothers saw it, they said—what does Jesus think about this? "Thanks guys. Way to remind me of that on my birthday!" Or, as Jeremy Clarkson called it on *The Grand Tour*, the "spoiler alert" Christmas tree.

But Christmas cannot be understood without the cross. To be sure, a baby born of a virgin is not something you hear about every day. While miraculous, the virgin birth would just be a footnote of history, an odd anomaly, without the cross and the empty tomb.

The world celebrates Christmas, and all is joy and warmth and light. But as Christians, we celebrate Christmas always with Good Friday in mind, always with Easter in mind. We remember that Jesus was born to die and born to rise again; we proclaim that his birth matters not just for a pretty picture of a baby in a stable, but for work God began in that manger—the work of redeeming the world.

Today we begin a look back at the prophets and see how prophecy is fulfilled in Christ. When we study the Old Testament, we take it in its context. Here, the context of Isaiah is a security threat; Isaiah is preaching to a people who are threatened by the Assyrian Empire and afraid for their survival as a nation. Yet we read these texts and, because of our faith, cannot help but hear prophecy of Jesus Christ, who speaks to a greater security threat; sin and death itself.

For example, Isaiah 53:2: "My servant grew up in the LORD's presence like a tender green shoot, like a root in dry ground." The servant is a "tender green shoot," not a strong, solid tree of life, but a young, tender, vulnerable seedling. The Savior is born a totally vulnerable baby; the Son of God is utterly dependent on his parents for everything. And as though to emphasize His weakness, God chooses to be born in a stable, among animals, poor and unprotected. This passage reminds me of *A Charlie Brown Christmas*.

Charlie Brown, as you remember, chose a Christmas tree that was tiny, weak, and skinny. The children mocked his tree, but eventually came to see how it was perfect for the message of Christmas; that what appears small and weak to the world is actually possessed of the greatest power of all.

When we read these words of Isaiah, we hear how the shoot grew out of the dry ground. And here, too, is great meaning; like a seed that bursts forth life where it has no business growing, brought life out of death, a baby from a virgin womb, resurrection from the ignominious cross. For, Isaiah 53:5 "He was pierced for our rebellion, crushed for our sins. He was beaten so we could be whole. He was whipped so we could be healed."

It's so easy to read past these words and not hear the deeper meaning within. But notice that the Hebrew here is châlal, which means "to bore through," "to pierce." For us, the image of the nails boring through Christ's hands is unmistakable. This is not the only place in which the Old Testament speaks of being pierced; Psalm 22 and Zechariah 12 also describe the death in this way.

What is the meaning of Christ dying by being pierced, as opposed to poisoned, or drowned, or some other death? Perhaps there is no deeper meaning, but I tend to think of the holes in Christ's hands, feet, and side as reminding us of the emptiness in our own lives. He experienced that crushing emptiness that we know, what has been called a God-shaped hole in us that represents our need for God, our longing for the Holy One. When he was pierced, Christ experienced that need, that separation from God, so that He could heal it once and for all. Do you feel an emptiness in your life?

That's why I'm comforted by the truth that the Christmas story, the real Christmas story, is not without suffering. Mary and Joseph suffer the shame of pregnancy out of wedlock. They suffer the inhospitality of a foreign city. Mary gives birth in the straw and dirt of a stable. And as soon as the new child is born, they are on the run from those who seek already to kill him. It's not a pretty or a perfect story, but one in which God enters into our pain, brokenness, and emptiness, and brings new life even here. So, if you come through this Christmas with longing, or pain, or emptiness, know that you are not alone. Christ didn't come to make everything perfect. Remember, the resurrected Christ still bore the nail marks. He came to enter into our emptiness and help us to heal.

Isaiah 53:9, "He had done no wrong and had never deceived anyone. But he was buried like a criminal; he was put in a rich man's grave." The suffering servant died with criminals and laid in a rich man's grave. This is true of Christ, who died amongst thieves, and was buried in the tomb provided by Joseph of Arimathea:

Matthew 27:57-58: "As evening approached, Joseph, a rich man from Arimathea who had become a follower of Jesus, went to Pilate and asked for Jesus' body. And Pilate issued an order to release it to him."

We look at all of these prophecies that are fulfilled by Christ and it gives us reassurance; it brings us security. Just as the original hearers of Isaiah were reassured by God's promise that He would help and comfort His people, we are reassured by God's promise that He will free us from death through Christ. If God has fulfilled all of His promises so far, will He not fulfill them in the life to come?

Professor Peter Stoner calculated the probability of eight Old Testament prophecies being fulfilled in one man's life as being 1 in 1,017. He illustrated the meaning of this number by asking the reader to imagine filling the entire State of Texas knee deep in silver dollars. Include in this huge number one silver dollar with a black check mark on it. Then, turn a blindfolded person loose in this sea of silver dollars. The odds that the first coin he would pick up would be the one with the black check mark are the same as 8 prophecies being fulfilled accidentally in the life of Jesus.

God has fulfilled not just eight, but, by one count, over three hundred prophecies by the life of Jesus. So we can and should believe that He will fulfill all His promises to us, that he will fill all the empty places, heal all the wounds, mend all the brokenness in our lives.

Today I made promises to raise my new child in the Christian faith, to teach him to receive Christ's love for him and live as one whom God has claimed. I don't have control over whether my new child will accept that love, that claim, or not, but I have promised to give him the opportunity. Now, you all know by now that I am far from a perfect person. I'm flawed, I'm weak, I'm human. And so is my new child's father. But do you doubt that we will fulfill our promise to show newborn son Charlie the love of Christ?

And if we, who are weak, can be trusted to keep our promise to this child, cannot God be trusted to keep His promises to us? We have this evidence: a baby. A miracle of life coming where it has no business being. As I preach today on the miracle of this birth, I am so thankful for the miraculous life of my son, Charles Dante.

I am so busy these days running around taking care of three kids, worrying about laundry, exhausted by the endless diapers, that I can be forgetful that this child is a miracle I never expected to have. How many of the miracles of life do we take for granted?

We so often dismiss, forget, or minimize the miracle of Christ. Perhaps this story deserves a second look, this man should be considered anew. This after all, is the great and beautiful story, ringing with eternal truth; that life should enter in where it had no business coming; that God should love us so much to enter into our messy world; that, in the midst of our emptiness, and woundedness, and pain, love should find a home among us.

In the name of the Father, and of the Son, and of the Holy Spirit, Amen.

Week Thirty-two: Lighthouse
Isaiah 60

"Therefore justice is far from us, and righteousness does not reach us; we wait for light, and lo! there is darkness; and for brightness, but we walk in gloom. We grope like the blind along a wall, groping like those who have no eyes; we stumble at noon as in the twilight, among the vigorous as though we were dead."

Every year, around January, I begin to wonder why it is that I live in Michigan. Winter in Michigan seems to hit us like a ton of icy-cold bricks. "Everyone talks about the cold like they couldn't see it coming. Our state is literally shaped like a piece of winter apparel."

In January, in Michigan, you have to get motivated to go outside to take out the trash, let alone brave going to the grocery store. And we wonder why we don't live in someplace like Georgia, or Florida instead—but of course, sometimes it snows there, too, we tell ourselves. (Yeah, like one inch.)

But the worst part of winter in Michigan, to me, is the lack of sunlight. Thrillist recently rated Michigan winters the second worst in the country, after an intensive period of research of every state in the country (but the website also rated Michigan the #1 best state in the country!) This is the website's explanation of why we have the second worst winters:

"Winter in Michigan begins well before Thanksgiving and stretches far past Easter, which makes for four-to-six wearisome months of always-gray, always-cold, always-drizzly, but-rarely-snowy-in-a-good-way misery. Some other states may see colder temps or more snow, but Michigan winters are unrivaled for their utter lack of sunshine. The ceaseless cloud cover begins in October, and envelopes the state in a daily sense of gloom that only worsens when the apathetic sun slouches below the horizon at quarter-to-five.

For the Michigander, this is winter: you leave work at 5 or 6, already in the dead of night, and fight your way down 94 or 96 or 75 or whatever Godforsaken stretch of highway. You can't even tell if it is drizzling rain or snow, because the brown salt sludge that sprays up off the road coats your windshield more completely than anything that falls from the sky. Overnight, the road freezes. In the morning you wake up and it is still dark."

Isaiah's audience was living in physical sunlight, but political darkness. Overshadowed by the empires of Egypt, then Assyria, then Babylon, forced to pay tribute to pagan kings, it became hard for God's people to believe God really was with them. What about God's promise to give them a land of milk and honey? What about God's promise to give them a king who would provide them with safety, power, and strength to defeat all their enemies? Where was God? Where was the light?

This passage comes right at the end of the bleak midwinter of Isaiah 59, "Therefore justice is far from us, and righteous does not reach us; we wait for light, and lo! There is darkness, and for brightness, but we walk in gloom. We grope like the blind along a wall, groping like those who have no eyes; we stumble at noon as in the twilight, among the vigorous as though we were dead."

Amidst this background of darkness, the light comes as though from nowhere, a shock, like a lightning bolt stunning God's people with its power and brilliance. Isaiah 60:1, "Arise, Jerusalem! Let your light shine for all to see. For the glory of the LORD rises to shine on you." The glory of the Lord comes as a great, shining light; reminding us that the first thing God says in all of Scripture is: Let there be light!

On Epiphany, we celebrate God's light coming into the darkness of our lives as Christ is born and revealed among us. We say we have an "epiphany" when we finally see something for what it is, when a light bulb goes on in our heads, and epiphany is when we finally realize that Jesus is the King of King, the Lord of Lords, Immanuel, God with us, and in him is light and life and truth and our salvation. This is what the magi realized, and why they traveled so far to lay their treasures before him. A miracle has occurred; light has broken into our darkness; life in the bleak midwinter.

But the miracle is not just the act of God, but also a call for us to act. The words of Isaiah 60 are in the imperative—the text doesn't say, arise! God is shining! But rather, You! Yes, you! Get up! Start shining! The Message paraphrase captures the sense of the text. Isaiah 60: 1-2, "Get out of bed, Jerusalem! Wake up. Put your face in the sunlight. GOD's bright glory has risen for you. The whole earth is wrapped in darkness, all people sunk in deep darkness, But GOD rises on you, his sunrise glory breaks over you. Nations will come to your light, kings to your sunburst brightness. Look up! Look around!"

We are called to be the light, even in the midst of darkness, to shine for others to see. As Christians, we are called to be a beacon of hope for others living in this frozen tundra, to shine for them, and bring them hope. This is why our church provides the warming shelter ministry—not only to help people in body, but also, hopefully, to help them in spirit, by providing a bright smile, a cheery word, a little moment of light in what must be dark and difficult days.

Today's woes are tomorrow's witness. Whatever struggle you are facing, whatever hill you have to climb, whatever darkness covers you—shine through it. Isaiah 60:3 "Nations shall come to your light, and kings to the brightness of your dawn."

Isaiah 6:6 "A multitude of camels shall cover you, and young camels of Midian and Ephah; all those from Sheba shall come. They shall bring gold and frankincense and shall proclaim the praise of the Lord."

When I think of the magi, and their gifts, prophesied here in Isaiah, it strikes me that when the Magi set out, they weren't sure what light they were going to find. They brought their gifts, not knowing who the king would be, or where they would find him. They had to arise even before the light had shone upon them; they had to have faith before they had seen Jesus for themselves. Why do we remember these wise men? Because they got up, they did something, and they witnessed to the light.

Will someone remember that you got up, that you did something, that you witnessed to the light that has arisen upon you? Would someone point to you and say, Jesus is shining through that person? Now is the time. There is no other. Take the bushel off and let God's light shine. In the bleak midwinter, who can you shine on today? How can you share the light of the world?

You and I are here to shine, like Michigan's iconic lighthouses, in the middle of winter; to bring hope, to guide others with the light, to share the message that life is a gift, that God is real, that the light has shined among us, and, if we are looking for it, a star still shines.

In the name of the Father, and of the Son, and of the Holy Spirit, Amen.

Week Thirty-three: Written on Your Heart
Jeremiah 31

"Covenant" is not a word we tend to use today. We might hear it in the name of a hospital, or a nursing home, but if asked, most people wouldn't really have any idea what the word means. The sole reference that many people might remember is Indiana Jones seeking the Ark of the Covenant in Raiders of the Lost Ark, so they might have some understanding that the covenant refers to the Ten Commandments, but that's it.

Today, the closest thing we have to a covenant is a contract, when one party gives a promise in exchange for another party's promise or action. If one person breaks the contract, the other doesn't have to perform. For example, you sign a contract with a farmer to pay ten thousand dollars in exchange for a shipment of…what? We're going healthy, so let's say brussels sprouts. But the farmer never delivers the brussels sprouts. Of course, nothing binds you to pay the ten thousand dollars. That's a contract.

By contrast, ancient covenants were generally unconditional. Each party commits to a certain action, regardless of whether the other party keeps the covenant. So, even though the farmer never delivered the brussels sprouts, I still have to pay him the ten thousand dollars.

The unconditional nature of the covenant is clear in God's covenant with us. We don't keep to the covenant. We never have, not fully, not entirely. But God keeps his promises regardless. We see this in Jeremiah 31, "The day is coming," says the LORD, "when I will make a new covenant with the people of Israel and Judah. This covenant will not be like the one I made with their ancestors when I took them by the hand and brought them out of the land of Egypt. They broke that covenant, though I loved them as a husband loves his wife," says the LORD.

The children of Israel had a covenant relationship with God, a love relationship, as intimate as that between a husband and wife. Yet the children of Israel were unfaithful to God; they broke covenant with Him by worshiping idols, by breaking the commandments, and by failing to live into God's vision of justice and righteousness. Yet God does not break His covenant with them; rather, He expands that relationship into a new covenant. Rather than give up on humankind, he offers us more—more love, more grace, more of His own self.

God describes the situation in verses 29 and 30, "The people will no longer quote this proverb: 'The parents have eaten sour grapes, but their children's mouths pucker at the taste.' All people will die for their own sins—those who eat the sour grapes will be the ones whose mouths will pucker."

This is a really vivid image: one person eats the grapes, but another person's mouth puckers. It's like that trick where one person puts his arms through another person's sleeves and tries to eat. One person's doing an action, but another person feels the effects. That's the old covenant: children were punished for the sins of their parents. God says, that's all changing. From here on out, everyone will reap the punishment of their own sins. At first, we think this is good news. It sounds fair, doesn't it? Every one of us gets the payback for our own sins. But then we think about it some more. Every one of us gets the payback for our own sins. Every little lie you've told, every uncharitable thought, coming back to you. Or worse. The lying, the cheating, the stealing; every time you've hurt someone else, coming back onto you. You can't ring up debt and then expect our children or our grandchildren to pay it off.

Thank God that God is not that fair. Would you make the deal that God makes with us? If your husband, if your wife, were unfaithful to you…would you take them back? And let's say it went beyond that. Let's say she racked up a debt, a huge debt. Would you take her back, and pay off her debt? Or what if it went beyond that? What if her debt could only be paid in blood? Would you die for her, this lying, cheating spouse? Would you take on his bad debts? Would you pay them off? And what will happen, when he gets into trouble again? Will you keep bailing him out, when he disappoints you, again, and again, and again? God did.

Here in Jeremiah, we have a promise, a prophecy, of a new covenant, or sometimes it's translated new testament—this is where we get the title of the New Testament. And the offer, the contract, the covenant with God's people is this: I will cancel your debt. I will forgive your wickedness. I will take you back.

Like all ancient covenants, this is sealed with a sacrifice. The meaning of a sacrifice in an ancient covenant was this: if I break my promise to you, may it be with me as the fate of this poor creature. So, when God makes His great sacrifice, it is the sacrifice of His only Son, Christ, who laid Himself down for our sins there on the cross. And with that sacrifice, He is saying: I would give my very life out of love for you.

And what is called for from us? What is our end of the deal? It is only what these new members of our church have done today, what this soul offering herself for baptism has done in your hearing: to say, "I do."

I accept. That's all we are called to do. And when we do, God promises to do even more for us. The water of baptism washes us not only once, but throughout our whole lives. The water of baptism seeps into our very pores, soaks into our bones and sinews so that our whole life is infused with grace, and we are changed.

Verse 33, "But this is the new covenant I will make with the people of Israel after those days," says the LORD. "I will put my instructions deep within them, and I will write them on their hearts. I will be their God, and they will be my people. And they will not need to teach their neighbors, nor will they need to teach their relatives, saying, 'You should know the LORD.' For everyone, from the least to the greatest, will know me already," says the LORD. "And I will forgive their wickedness, and I will never again remember their sins." Written on our hearts; God's law becomes internal, not external. Here's what it looks like when a desire becomes internal.

Our son is locked in a war with us over dinner, because this momma refuses to make two different dinners; you eat what's on your plate and that's it. Our son fights it, and we end up negotiating: four more bites, JP. OK, three more. Two more. One more. OK just get out of here. Until Dan, in a stroke of brilliance, asked him, JP, do you want to be in the clean plate club? Now you or I, being adults, would have had dozens of questions. What is this clean plate club? Where does it meet? Who else is a member? Are there any dues? But to a three-year-old, any club is a fun club. And now we don't have to count four bites, we don't have to negotiate, because the motivation is internal. Miraculously, our son has an appetite.

When God's law is written in our hearts, the motivation is internal.

When you were young, many of you, your parents had to beg you to go to church. When you got older, perhaps you came because you liked going. That's where some of you are; you're in church to get a good message. So, you come when you want to. And that's a good place to be. But here's what it looks like when it's written on your heart; you come to church because that is who you are. It's at the very essence of what defines who you are. And you come not so much for yourself, but for the person next to you, and the person next to them; you want worship to be beautiful, not so you can get something out of it, but in order to make a joyful noise to God, in order to reach a world in desperate need.

And when God's Word is written on your heart, now you are the ark of the covenant. You are the holy place in which God's Word is stored. One more reason to take care of your body, for watching over your life.

The new covenant isn't about rules. It isn't about punishments and rewards, heaven and hell, not really. It's about a new way of being. A new way of living in this world. That's what Jeremiah prophesied, and that's what Jesus died for; for a new relationship between humanity and its creator, in which we do good not because we have to, not even because we want to, or because it feels good, but because doing good has become who we are; and in time, our hearts begin to beat with the beat of God's own heart.

In the name of the Father, and of the Son, and of the Holy Spirit, Amen.

Week Thirty-four: A Strange God
Ezekiel 1

How do you picture God? Most of us picture God as an old white man, something like Santa Claus. Perhaps the most famous depiction of God is The Sistine Chapel. Generally we see in our heads a kind of grandfatherly figure on a throne; a kind of sky-judge, but also someone we can relate to, no more imposing, really, than Albus Dumbledore or Gandalf the Grey.

Ezekiel doesn't see Gandalf. What he sees is, to be honest, totally freaky weird. We wonder if Ezekiel might have eaten some really bad hummus there by the river Chebar. It's also a really weird time to have a vision of God. What was Ezekiel doing, taking a bath? This is a seemingly random time, and a seemingly random place, to encounter the holy.

The children of Israel are at a low point when Ezekiel encounters the Almighty. The book of Ezekiel begins with these words, Ezekiel 1:1 "On July 31 of my thirtieth year, while I was with the Judean exiles beside the Kebar River in Babylon, the heavens were opened, and I saw visions of God."

Now already things are weird; they are not as they should be. Why? Because it's Ezekiel's thirtieth year, and in the Jewish religion, when a man of the priestly family turned thirty, that was when he was supposed to assume his duties as a priest. Ezekiel's in a priestly family, but he can't assume his duties as a priest—why? Because he's in Babylon. He's in Exile. Things are not as they should be. But God breaks into this weird place.

And it's a weird image of God. Perhaps it's blasphemous of me to say that God is weird in Ezekiel, but I can't think of any other words to describe Ezekiel's vision. Wheels within wheels? Creatures with four faces? And why does it matter that their legs are straight?

As I consider this passage, it seems to me that this is one of those passages of the Bible that's rife with symbolism. I believe the Bible is the Word of God; but I also believe that the Word of God contains some things that can't be contained in words. That's why, in this passage of Ezekiel, as in the book of Revelation, we hear the words "something like," repeated over and over. The vision of God is so otherworldly that the things we've seen and the words we have to describe them can't encapsulate the experience. It's too, well, weird to us. Strange, supernatural.

And I also don't believe that the Creator of the Universe is really a man on a wheeled cart pushed by four really freaky monsters. That's why I think that even Ezekiel's vision doesn't encompass who God is, not fully. No vision could. Rather, Ezekiel's vision is meant to symbolically show us in words who God is. And that's where it gets really interesting.

One thing Ezekiel's vision teaches us is that God is a living God. There's a scene in The Chronicles of Narnia when winter is turning into spring, and one of the characters says, "Aslan is on the move." You see those words spark joy in the faces of all. God is on the move in Ezekiel's vision.

Ezekiel 1: 16-20: "The wheels sparkled as if made of beryl. All four wheels looked alike and were made the same; each wheel had a second wheel turning crosswise within it. 17 The beings could move in any of the four directions they faced, without turning as they moved. 18 The rims of the four wheels were tall and frightening, and they were covered with eyes all around. When the living beings moved, the wheels moved with them. When they flew upward, the wheels went up, too. 20 The spirit of the living beings was in the wheels. So wherever the spirit went, the wheels and the living beings also went."

Why does Ezekiel spend so much time describing the wheels? Why is the spirit of the living beings in the wheels? Why are the wheels covered with eyes? I think it's because it's meant to teach us that God is on the move. God is alive, active, moving throughout His creation.

This is different from how we tend to see God. We think of God as stable, unmoving, old, historic even. Maybe that's why our Bibles get dusty, or why we want everything in our churches to be the same as it always was. It's better if God just stays in one place, unmoving, traditional, solid.

But that's not who God is. God is on the move. God is doing new things all around us, speaking in new ways. But I love verse 40: the beings could move in any of the four directions, without turning as they moved. God moves among us, yet God never turns; God never changes. He is the same yesterday, and today, and forever; and yet, we understand Him in new ways. In Ezekiel's time, that meant that even in Exile, God was still at work; even when the king was in captivity, even when the people were cast out of the Promised Land, even when the Temple was destroyed, God was doing a new thing. Today, the church is in a kind of Exile. We've been cast out of our privileged place in society. Christianity no longer influences society the way it once did; our churches are sparsely populated, mostly with older folks, and the young people feel that church is irrelevant, God is unimportant to how they live their lives. So we're forced to reconsider the way we do church. Why? Because God is doing a new thing. And maybe it's not about societal power and influence. Maybe it's not about numbers and big budgets. Maybe it's about being something real, something true in a society that feels increasingly false.

Maybe we're being burned away. Another captivating aspect of Ezekiel's vision is that it's full of fire. Ezekiel 1: 4: "As I looked, I saw a great storm coming from the north, driving before it a huge cloud that flashed with lightning and shone with brilliant light. There was fire inside the cloud, and in the middle of the fire glowed something like gleaming amber." Or Ezekiel 1:13: "The living beings looked like bright coals of fire or brilliant torches, and lightning seemed to flash back and forth among them." Or Ezekiel 1:27: "From what appeared to be his waist up, he looked like gleaming amber, flickering like a fire. And from his waist down, he looked like a burning flame, shining with splendor."

What is all this fire about? Remember that in Old Testament Judaism, fire was used in sacrifice. Fire is an agent of purification; you use fire to purify metals in a crucible. Fire burns away impurities; fire makes something pure and holy. So, all this fire means that God is holy, and God also makes us holy. Ezekiel's vision and prophecies were aimed at purifying the people. Ezekiel's message was that the people had to become holy again, to burn away their sin and idolatry, to return to God, so that God would return them to the Promised Land. I think of my son going into time-out, where he seems to be a lot lately. Exile was kind of a time-out for Israel, a time to think and reflect on what God really wants and how they are meant to live. That's why so much of the Bible comes from that time in exile. In the same way, perhaps, this time in the church's history is meant to be a time of purification; a time when we stop trying to be something we're not, a social club or a political group or a form of entertainment, and be who we are meant to be: the body of Christ, sharing His love and His message with all. It's a time when we must be honest with ourselves and one another about our failure to live up to our calling, or put another way, our sin, and seek each other's forgiveness and God's.

But I see something more than judgement in Ezekiel's vision, something more than holiness. And it's because I am a Christian that I see in this vision a message of infinite power and also infinite grace. Where do I see this? First, here, Ezekiel 1:10: "Each had a human face in the front, the face of a lion on the right side, the face of an ox on the left side, and the face of an eagle at the back."

Because I am a Christian, I believe that Ezekiel's vision was supernatural. I believe his vision taught of the Gospel. The four gospel writers are often compared to the four faces of Ezekiel's vision. Matthew is the human face; Matthew shows us Christ's human nature, steeped in Jewish tradition. Mark is the lion – a figure of courage, who shows us Christ working miracles and conquering death. Luke is the ox – showing us Christ the servant of all. And finally, John is the eagle – showing us the eagle's eye vision of what God is doing through Christ. These living creatures, with their four faces, to me show us that God can be encountered in different ways. Each of the Gospels is different, and yet they are all included in Scripture, because God recognizes that we come to meet Him in different ways. Through the Gospels, God meets us where we are—just as God met Ezekiel and his people where they were, far from the Temple, far from the Promised Land.

Finally, I look to the one seated on the throne: a figure like a man. Ezekiel 1:26: "Above this surface was something that looked like a throne made of blue lapis lazuli. And on this throne high above was a figure whose appearance resembled a man." Why should the Creator of the Universe look like a man? As a Christian, I believe that God came to us in human form because of His grace and love; that God meets us where we are. God shows us Himself in a way that is both awesome and otherworldly, but also something we can understand. God comes to us both as a purifying fire, and also as a loving Father.

Ezekiel's vision is strange; it is weird; it is otherworldly and supernatural. It's also the message Ezekiel needed to hear. That God was on the move; that God desired to purify His people; that God was willing to meet them where they were and show them grace. It's weird, but in a way, it's also wonderful.

And encountering God is always kind of weird. Why? Because God is fundamentally other than who we are, and who we want Him to be. God isn't a white man who shows up once a year or so and gives us what we want. That, again, would be Santa. God shows up in unexpected places, does unexpected things, through unexpected people. He's unpredictable; He's frightening; He's untamable. And yet, He's more amazing than the gods we create for ourselves.

I've heard God speak through the mouths of the poor and homeless; I've seen God act in psych wards and on street corners; I've witnessed Him in the midst of great pain and suffering, with rape victims and drug addicts, as much as within the walls of any church. This week, I sat with a young, homeless black man and asked him what he wanted prayer for. Rather than pray for himself, someone who surely had a laundry list of needs, his prayer was for the world, for peace, and he prayed for our enemies, even for terrorists and criminals. I heard God through that young man's words more than the piles of words of the theological scholars and preachers I combed through, looking for truth in Ezekiel. But that's what God does; he shows up in strange and unexpected ways. He's not a tame God; he's not a God we can contain or understand. He's not Morgan Freeman or Santa Claus. Instead, he's greater, more mysterious, and yet accessible to even us. He's not the God we want; he's scary, he's strange, he's dangerous; but He's the one true God, the one hard, true thing in this world of so many soft, easy lies; and, the more we encounter Him, the more we recognize He's the God we truly need.

In the name of the Father, and the Son, and the Holy Spirit, Amen.

Week Thirty-five: The Good Shepherd and Good Sheep
Ezekiel 34

Everybody is familiar with the image of Christ the good shepherd. But the thing is, nobody really wants to be a sheep. We are bad sheep. We hold up our noses at those who blindly follow directions like sheep do. We would rather be independent, follow our own path, than be guided, be herded.

Let me give you an example. Have you ever been to the security checkpoint at an airport? This is the ultimate sheep experience. You have to be part of the herd. You've got to wait in line, stay in your place, listen to directions. People are horrible at this. They get to the line, and it's like they've never been through security before. Take off my shoes? Really? For some reason, people wear the *most elaborate* shoes the day they go to the airport. Maybe it's a small act of defiance. Like, forget you, Mr. Big Government, I refuse to wear slip on shoes to the airport. Take that. Your own private revolutionary war in the form of difficult-to-remove footwear. And no one has their ID ready. You get to the front of the line, and it's like, really? I'm going to need a photo ID and a boarding pass? It doesn't matter how they tell you: they can have signs up, a voice over the loudspeaker, a TSA agent whose sole job it is to remind you to get out your photo ID: some people will get to the front of the line, and it's like it comes as a total shock. Wait, you want to know who I am? We are bad sheep. We stink at being herd animals.

As a youth pastor, I probably spent a hundred hours designing, ordering, and distributing matching T shirts for youth trips. Have you ever seen a group of kids at the airport wearing matching T shirts, and you automatically know they're on a mission trip? Let me explain to you why we do this. Teenagers all of a sudden develop teaspoon-size bladders at this moment. Everybody needs to go to the bathroom. The point of the T shirt has nothing to do with group unity or representing Christ to the community. The mission trip T shirt is about making sure you don't leave a kid in an airport bathroom when you change planes in Atlanta.

We are bad sheep. Looking for commentary on Ezekiel 34, I found a ton of stuff about good shepherds and bad shepherds. And Ezekiel does spend the first half of the chapter talking about the bad shepherds of Israel, the poor leaders who have led the flock astray, and don't care for their needs. But the second half of the chapter describes the people not as shepherds, but as sheep. And we're pretty bad sheep. Think of all the times you've heard preaching on the 23rd Psalm. We are quite comfortable with the image of

Christ the good shepherd. But ourselves as sheep? Nobody wants to be a sheep. It sounds weak and stupid to just go around getting herded, getting poked around with that rod and staff. It's almost insulting to be thought of as a dumb herd animal.

But we need the guidance and care only the shepherd can provide. We need to be good sheep. I don't know about you, but whenever I try to find my own way, I get lost. Left to my own devices, I'll pick the wrong path, every time. I'll choose the job that makes more money but doesn't feed my soul. I'll eat the junk food that promises a moment of joy but a lifetime of bad health. I'll say the words of sarcasm and bitterness instead of the words of thoughtfulness and encouragement. I need the rod and the staff. I need to be a good sheep.

As I read Ezekiel, there are three things a good sheep needs to do: first, a good sheep needs to find the shepherd. Verse 12 "As shepherds seek out their flocks when they are among their scattered sheep, so I will seek out my sheep. I will rescue them from all the places to which they have been scattered on a day of clouds and thick darkness."

We tend to wander into the clouds, into the darkness, into places where it's hard to even see the shepherd, let alone follow him. A lot of people feel like God is absent during difficult times in their lives. And I ask them, how much time do you spend in prayer? How much Bible study are you doing? Been attending church? If you feel far from God, guess who moved?

We are bad sheep. The good news is that Christ is the good shepherd, and he seeks us out. We don't have to find him; he finds us and drags us back to the flock. Do you know the popular poem "Footprints?" Where a man looks back on his life, and he sees a path of footprints, his own, next to a second set of footprints, which belong to Jesus? But during the difficult points in his life, there's just one set of footprints. And Jesus says, it was during those times that I carried you. Well, my life would look like a set of footprints next to a deep groove: where Jesus had to drag me along, kicking and screaming!

Christ seeks us out and rescues us from all the places we've wandered off. He drags us along sometimes, kicking and screaming, into the herd. Like a youth pastor who finds her kids shopping in the TravelMart instead of going through security. And do you know how I found them? Matching T shirts, that's how. For Ezekiel, God sought him out in distant Babylon, in the strangest of places, beside the river Chebar. The people had wandered far from God; they ran after idols, after Baal and the gods of their neighbors. But God sought them out and brought them back. Christ seeks us out, in all the cloudy, dark places we wander, and brings us back, even if he has to drag us back into the herd.

So the first thing the sheep has to do is to find the shepherd. The second thing a good sheep needs to do is to graze. Verses 14-15, "I will feed them with good pasture, and the mountain heights of Israel shall be their pasture; there they shall lie down in good grazing land, and they shall feed on rich pasture on the mountains of Israel. I myself will be the shepherd of my sheep, and I will make them lie down, says the Lord GOD."

For a sheep, eating takes time. Looking into some basic information for ranchers, sheep need to rest and ruminate more than cattle. Sheep need to graze seven to ten hours a day, whereas cattle can get away with four hours. For sheep, eating isn't just about consuming food; it's about having time to chew on it, to rest with it, to lie down in green pastures. It's grazing; it's taking quality time in the green grass.

And that's what we're called to do in our walk with Christ. To feast on His Word; to take time in His presence. Not to come to church as one more thing on our to do list, to get our worship checked off before brunch. Not to speed through our devotions, to finish up with God before we get our coffee. But rather, to spend time with God throughout the day. To seek Him in the little moments of our day, in traffic, at the gym, in the office; to lift up prayers and to call upon Scripture throughout the day, to chew on His Word for hours and hours instead of just minutes.

So the sheep are called to find the shepherd, and to graze, and also to be part of the flock. And this is the part that Israel was doing a really bad job at. Verses 20-22, "Therefore, thus says the Lord God to them: I myself will judge between the fat sheep and the lean sheep. Because you pushed with flank and shoulder and butted at all the weak animals with your horns until you scattered them far and wide, I will save my flock, and they shall no longer be ravaged; and I will judge between sheep and sheep."

Are you a fat sheep, or a lean sheep? This is not really a passage about weight loss—it's about being gluttonous. It's about whether we take more than our fair share or whether we think of others. In Ezekiel's time, the rich were exploiting the poor. The leaders of the people were gluttonously, selfishly building up wealth, while the poor suffered. And not much has changed today.

Many times throughout the week I get phone calls from people wanting to drop off clothing for the homeless. I can tell you that I've never gotten a call from someone asking what the homeless actually need. Rather, we're trapped in these patterns of consumption where we buy, buy, buy, and then we use for a little while, and then we give it away or throw it out. That pattern of using and giving away reminds me of this passage: Verses 18-19 "Is it not enough for you to feed on the good pasture, but you must tread down with your feet the rest of your pasture? When you drink of clear water, must you foul the rest with your feet? And must my sheep eat what you have trodden with your feet, and drink what you have fouled with your feet?"

Why do we give people in need our leftovers, instead of our best? Why don't people call up and ask, what do homeless people need? Because it may not be your used clothing. It may be your precious time. It may be time that's difficult for you to spare, such as the night of the Super Bowl when everybody would rather be in a comfy chair watching the game. But the question is: are you going to get fat while others in the flock are starving? Sheep aren't meant to live alone. They are meant to be part of the flock. And the problem with many Christians today is that we want to go it alone. We don't want to be part of a church and do the uncomfortable work of loving others, of thinking of the needs of others, of sharing the pasture. But it's how we are meant to live. We're meant to share the pasture, to live together as one flock under one shepherd.

So, seek the shepherd; take time to graze. But don't forget about the rest of your flock. Don't be the fat sheep. Because guess what happens to the fat sheep? Instead, share some of those green pastures, share some of those still waters. Lead others back to the Good Shepherd, back into the flock where life is found. I want you to take a moment and think of the person who led you back when you were in a time of need. Who encouraged you to graze, to take in the nourishment you needed at a difficult time, who led you back to the Good Shepherd. Someone needs you to help them back. Someone needs you to show them the green pastures, to nudge them over to the still waters. Someone needs you to share. Will you share? The Good Shepherd is calling. Will you be a good sheep?

In the name of the Father, and the Son, and the Holy Spirit, Amen.

Week Thirty-six: Kings of Industry
Daniel 7

As you'll know from hearing my sermons, I am not a big fan of the news cycle. It's not that I don't believe in being well informed, it's just that I believe there's a difference between being informed and being obsessed, and in our current culture, some people know and care more about the latest political or celebrity hijinks than about their own families and neighbors. But Christians also need to speak truth to what is happening around us. And what I see happening around me desperately needs a word of truth.

The movement that started with the exposure of Harvey Weinstein, then Matt Lauer, Roy Moore, John Conyers, Al Franken…the list goes on and on—the #metoo movement has shown us that these kings of industry, these political titans, these economic gods among men, are, in fact, pigs. And not just pigs, but beasts; sexual harassers and abusers.

And my question is—why are we shocked? Why are we outraged? Why do we expect anything more? This is nothing new. People have been sinning for thousands of years. Men have been abusing their power for thousands of years. And God has been telling us for thousands of years not to trust the kings of industry, not to trust the political titans, not to trust the economic gods among men. It's here in Daniel 7.

In order to understand our reading today in Daniel 7, you've got to look at it in context. Daniel, like Ezekiel, was active during the time of the Babylonian Exile, and he prophesied about the coming kings.

First in 7:4 is the lion with Eagle's wings. The Old Testament prophets called Babylon a lion. A lion with eagle's wings was a prominent symbol on Babylonian coins and on Babylon's walls.

Second in 7:5 is a bear with three ribs in its mouth, representing the Medo-Persian Empire. When the Medes and Persians overthrew Babylon, they also conquered Lydia and Egypt. The three ribs in the bear's mouth represent these three nations—Babylon, Lydia, and Egypt.

Third, in 7:6, the leopard represents Alexander the Great's empire, Greece. The Greek king conquered with the swiftness of a leopard flying with eagle's wings. Why does this leopard have four heads? When Alexander died in a drunken stupor at age thirty-three, his four generals—Cassander, Lysimachus, Seleucus, and Ptolemy—divided up the empire.

And fourth, in 7:7, the Roman empire, a terrifying beast with iron teeth. Rome brought on the Iron Age and conquered the world in 168 B.C. by defeating the Greeks at the Battle of Pynda. Bible prophecy is incredibly accurate.

But what does this all mean? Amy Merrill Willis observes that Daniel depicts "these kingdoms as wild, fierce, and predatory animals with unnatural features. They have too many heads, or too many wings, or too many horns." There's something wrong with them. These kings are cruel, power-hungry, abusive, unnatural. They are beasts. But another king is coming. Daniel 7:11: "I kept watching until the fourth beast was killed and its body was destroyed by fire."

Daniel 7: 13-14: "As my vision continued that night, I saw someone like a son of man coming with the clouds of heaven. He approached the Ancient One and was led into his presence. He was given authority, honor, and sovereignty over all the nations of the world, so that people of every race and nation and language would obey him. His rule is eternal—it will never end. His kingdom will never be destroyed."

While the kings of this world are cruel beasts, the coming King is the Son of Man—that is, he represents what humanity can be, what we should be. He is our redemption. He represents all that is good and just and right and true. And his kingdom will never end. All the kings, all the cruel beasts of this world, will and must bow before him.

As Christians, we see this Son of Man, this perfection of what humankind was meant to be, in Jesus. In Jesus who said, Matthew 5:27-30, "You have heard that it was said, 'You shall not commit adultery.' But I say to you that everyone who looks at a woman with lust has already committed adultery with her in his heart. If your right eye causes you to sin, tear it out and throw it away; it is better for you to lose one of your members than for your whole body to be thrown into hell."

The truth is that within ourselves, all of us have a moral compass that, at some point, when objectifying glances become harassing words and then assaultive touch, that we see sin as sin. We recognize that there's a right way to be, a right way to act, a right way to live. And if you study Jesus, you will find that it's all there, in his life, in his words, in his death, in his resurrection, Jesus embodies all that humankind was meant to be.

So, thank God that we don't have to place our faith in the kings of industry or in the political titans; that we don't have to look for our salvation in princes or presidents; that we look to a King who is more. If we raised our sons to emulate Him, to live His simple teachings, and not what they see on television, we wouldn't have a problem with sexual harassment or assault.

We cannot trust the kings of this world, the powerful men of our society. We know they are beasts. Instead, we must trust and believe the Word of prophecy; that kings and kingdoms will all pass away, but Jesus will reign forever; and one day, every knee shall bow, and every tongue confess that He is Lord.

History is moving toward something greater, something more beautiful; toward a better King, the Son of Man. His self-sacrificial love represents the pinnacle of what humanity can achieve. Why give your allegiance, your time, your money, to any lesser king, any lesser god? Instead, fix your eyes upon Him; bend your knee to Him; let your life be one of service to this King.

Come and be humbled. Admit that you need Christ. Receive Him into your heart, and your body, and your life. Is there an aspect of your life, your finances, your relationships, your words, maybe even your sexuality, in which you need to let Christ rule? Come and let Him rule in your heart today.

In the name of the Father, and of the Son, and of the Holy Spirit, Amen.

Week Thirty-seven: Brokenhearted God
Hosea 11

If you're wondering how the transition of baby Charlie's arrival has been for me, I will be honest with you and tell you it's a challenge going from two to three. J.P. is particularly upset with the change, and he's acting out—throwing food, hitting his sister, etc. We're doing a lot of time outs at the Grano house. He knows exactly what he's doing, too. The other day, he was kicking me as I tried to put on his clothes, and he asked, "Mom, am I being difficult?"

Well, parenting is difficult. Period. Parenting small children is hard work, but in some ways, it only gets harder as they grow up; as they become teenagers and destructive choices become available to them. One of my deepest fears as a parent is the opioid epidemic that's sweeping our country. I see what is happening to parents that I know—and I know there are even people here today who have watched a child, your own or another child you love, slip down into the nightmare, the hell of addiction. Recently in Harper Woods, Michigan, a group of five young adults all overdosed, one of whom was the child of a friend of our family. He was in the ICU and nearly died, but through many prayers made it out and into rehab—only to walk out of rehab and back to the needle days later. You hear stories like this, and you think, how could a child do that to their parent? He's volunteering for his own destruction. It's heartbreaking.

I don't offer easy answers to this crisis, I can only say that God's heart is broken, too. Hosea literally tells us that God's heart is caving in on itself, as he watches Israel, his child, walk down the path of self-destruction: Hosea 11:8: "My heart is torn within me, and my compassion overflows."

Throughout Hosea, God likens himself to a husband betrayed by an unfaithful wife. In the most disturbing and vivid example of divine enactment in all the prophets, Hosea marries a prostitute, who continues with the world's oldest profession after she marries him. Hosea has children with her that may or may not be his biological children, and God tells Hosea what to name these children: Jezreel, or "scattered," Lo-Ruhamah, or "not-pitied," and Lo-Ammi, "not-my-people." Hosea's own life, and the lives of his children, realize God's pain and suffering at being betrayed by the unfaithful people. For an interesting love story based on the prophet Hosea, I recommend the novel "Redeeming Love," by Francine Rivers.

Imagining what Hosea and the children went through is devastating. How could God order him to subject himself and his children to this life of abandonment and betrayal? Well, how could we subject God to the abandonment and betrayal God experiences?

You might say, God is all-powerful. God can't experience abandonment and betrayal. But there's no other way to read Hosea. Indeed, there's no other way to read the Old Testament. God experiences emotion—particularly, God gets angry. He is watching his children make terrible choices, choices that will result in their own self-destruction. I loved you, God says. Why do you choose idols? I will protect you, God says. Why do you turn to Egypt and Assyria? We just got out of Egypt! Why did you go back? Why walk out of rehab?

Like any parent, when God looks at the rebellious Israel, addicted to self-destructive idol worship, looking for love in all the wrong places, and God sees, not the young adult Israel has become, but the innocent infant Israel once was. "Mom, am I being difficult?"

Hosea 11:3-4 says: "I myself taught Israel how to walk, leading him along by the hand. But he doesn't know or even care that it was I who took care of him. I led Israel along with my ropes of kindness and love. I lifted the yoke from his neck, and I myself stooped to feed him."

The NRSV translation says: Hosea 11:4 "I was to them like those who lift infants to their cheeks. I bent down to them and fed them."

Here God compares the act of leading the people out of Egypt, and feeding them manna and quail, honey from the rock, to a mother intimately nursing her child and teaching him to walk. Isn't it blasphemy to think of the all-powerful God in this way? It's not blasphemy, it's biblical. It's the message of the story of the Prodigal Son, and the message of the incarnation. God loves us enough to limit his own power, to have an intimate relationship with us. That's why God came to us in human form in Jesus Christ, and that's why God let himself love Israel, knowing that they would break his heart. That's also why God feels such wrath against Israel:

Hosea 11:9, "I will not execute my fierce anger; I will not again destroy Ephraim; for I am God and no mortal, the Holy One in your midst, and I will not come in wrath." God has to remind himself that he is not human, that he can't give in to his anger. He destroyed Israel once, but he will not do it again.

Scholar Richard Nysse reminds us that we can't pass by that word "again." It's actually left out of the NLT translation, but the NRSV translation here is more literal. Because the kingdom of Israel was completely erased by the Assyrian invasion. If you took anything from reading these prophets, you can't have missed the fact that God chose to, and did, allow the utter destruction of Israel, recorded in 2 Kings 17:6, and later Judah, in 2 Kings 24:2. Israel and Judah are not on life support, they are dead. The temple has been razed to the ground. The ark of the covenant is nowhere to be found. The priests have been slaughtered. Children are lying dead in the streets. The king's line is wiped out.

And maybe there's a message for us here. That sometimes, you can't intervene. If only for your own survival, you have to step back and let the child do what he will do, even if it means his own death. It's a hard truth: but if you've lived with an addict, you know it's a real truth. Sometimes you have to let them hit rock bottom. You have to let go and let God. If there is hope, it's not in resuscitation, it's in resurrection. Good thing our God is in the resurrection business.

Hosea 11: 10-11, "For someday the people will follow me. I, the LORD, will roar like a lion. And when I roar, my people will return trembling from the west. Like a flock of birds, they will come from Egypt. Trembling like doves, they will return from Assyria. And I will bring them home again,' says the LORD."

We look at our children, we look at our nation, we look at our world and we see destruction and death. The hurricanes that have swept our country are devastating, but to me the spiritual, emotional, and physical illnesses that are sweeping us are more devastating still. When I hear about what young people are doing to themselves, when I think that my children are growing up around these temptations, my heart, like God's, breaks within me. What can we tell the mother, the father, who has watched her child, his child, fall into utter destruction? We can tell them, Hosea 11:11, "I will bring them home again, says the Lord." We can tell them God is in the resurrection business. We can tell them that God is the God of the cross and the empty tomb. We can tell them that God's message is the same in Genesis 3 and Hosea 11 and Mark 14 and Revelation 22: "I am making all things new."

You ask for proof? Well, Assyria is no more, Babylon is long gone, Egypt has never risen to its former glory—but God's people, the Jewish nation, Israel, have survived. We have the cross, we have the empty tomb. But maybe the proof is not that abstract. Maybe it's here in our hearts.

Because I ask you—whatever that child has done, to himself, to you, to us—when he steals from you, when he walks out of rehab, when he runs back to that terrible woman, when he abandons his own kid—when he breaks your heart—do you still love him?

And if you, who are mortal, can put aside your anger, your heartbreak, your sadness, and keep loving, how much more will your heavenly Father keep loving us, even when we destroy ourselves, even when we break His heart? Asked another way: when we break God's heart, what flows out?

Hosea 11:8 tells us the answer: "My heart is broken, and my compassion overflows." When God's heart was broken, compassion flowed out. When God's body was broken, in Christ's body on the cross, love flowed out. When God's life was broken, love lived on. When all else is lost, hope remains. So don't stop hoping. Don't stop caring. Don't stop loving. You might have to let go—but don't forget to let God. And don't give up.

God won't give up—so don't you give up either.

In the name of the Father, and the Son, and the Holy Spirit, Amen.

Week Thirty-eight: Ice Princess
Obadiah

If I said the names Anna and Elsa, would they mean anything to you? If not, you have not been in my kids' bedrooms. Anna and Elsa are the two main characters in the Disney movie "Frozen," and their faces are plastered all over my daughter Diana's sheets, clothes, and playthings. JP is not immune either and has been seen playing with Anna and Elsa dolls. We own the movie, and Anna's boot is currently sitting on my kitchen counter, for some mysterious reason.

"Frozen" is based loosely on Hans Christian Anderson's story "The Snow Queen." The older sister, Princess Elsa, has cryokinetic powers, that is, she can make stuff freeze. But Elsa has a little sister, Anna, who doesn't have powers—and who's kind of accident prone. When Elsa and Anna were young princesses, they used to have fun with her powers, building snowmen and skating around, but after Elsa got hurt, Anna had to hide her powers away from everyone. But then Anna, who's kind of a klutz in life and in love, comes to Elsa with her plans to marry a guy she's met like 15 minutes ago, and Elsa goes ballistic and starts freezing things. Now that her secret is revealed, she flees from society and builds herself an ice palace, high in the sky where no one can touch her—although unbeknownst to Elsa, she has plunged her sister Anna and the entire kingdom into an eternal winter. And since this is a Disney movie, she does it while singing a catchy song that has become an international phenomenon—"Let It Go."

Preacher Darren Larsen remarks that, although we don't have any evidence that Hans Christian Anderson is reading Obadiah, Elsa is very much like Edom:

> *The Lord says to Edom,*
> *"I will cut you down to size among the nations;*
>   *you will be greatly despised.*
> *You have been deceived by your own pride*
>   *because you live in a rock fortress*
>   *and make your home high in the mountains.*
> *'Who can ever reach us way up here?'*
>   *you ask boastfully.*
> *But even if you soar as high as eagles*
>   *and build your nest among the stars,*
> *I will bring you crashing down,"*
>   *says the Lord.*

Elsa is the very picture of pride. Like Edom, she makes herself "a rock fortress" "high in the mountains." She declares, "No right, no wrong, no rules for me." She has overinflated ideas of herself: "I am one with the wind and sky." And she proudly proclaims that no one can hurt her: "You'll never see me cry." Just like Edom: "Who can reach us way up here?" What does it say about Americans that "Let It Go" became such a hit, and people everywhere identified with Elsa in her moment of prideful independence? Of course, Anna, the needy one, finds Elsa in her ice castle, and pleads with her to come to her aid. But Elsa refuses to help, sending a frozen bolt straight into Anna's heart.

Edom, too, wants to be separated from her sister state, Israel, in her moment of need. Edom comes from Esau, the big brother, whereas Israel descends from Jacob, the little brother. We first met these twins wrestling in Rebekah's womb back in Genesis 25. They have always been rivals, but during Jacob's lifetime they were able to achieve peace. Now, however, Edom scoffs at Israel's destruction.

> *"Because of the violence you did*
> *   to your close relatives in Israel,*
> *you will be filled with shame*
> *   and destroyed forever.*
> *When they were invaded,*
> *   you stood aloof, refusing to help them.*
> *Foreign invaders carried off their wealth*
> *   and cast lots to divide up Jerusalem,*
> *but you acted like one of Israel's enemies.*
>
> *"You should not have gloated*
> *   when they exiled your relatives to distant lands.*
> *You should not have rejoiced*
> *   when the people of Judah suffered such misfortune.*
> *You should not have spoken arrogantly*
> *   in that terrible time of trouble.*

Who among us does not have an Anna—a kind of klutzy relative, the little sister, lacking in power and strength—the black sheep, the poor relation, the one who seems to always be in therapy? Everyone has a sister, a brother, a cousin, a nephew who is constantly in need—out of a job, needing a place to stay, needing to talk about his or her difficulties—needing love. There's a "black sheep" in every family. There's a needy, powerless, Princess Anna in every family, and when you see her on caller ID, sometimes you are tempted not to answer. Actually, sometimes you want to go off into an ice palace and live alone sometimes.

But here's the thing: you might be thinking of that person in your family who's always needing help—but was there a time when you were the black sheep? When you were the Princess Anna, always getting into trouble and needing to be bailed out? Elsa finds herself defenseless against the evil Prince Hans, and it turns out that it's her sister's love that saves her. The message of "Frozen" is that Elsa's pride is destructive, and her powers can only be rightly used when she uses her powers in love and stops trying to live in prideful isolation.

Families are tough. The ice palace is tempting. But God places us in families for a reason. Rick Warren says that the only thing you will take to heaven is your character. So God uses people in our lives to build our character.

1 Timothy 5:8, "Those who won't care for their relatives, especially those in their own household, have denied the true faith. Such people are worse than unbelievers." It's true that some people really, really build our character. It's also true that sometimes you have to place boundaries around abusive people for your own protection. But you also have to ask—are you being loving, or are you reacting out of your own pride? If you're calling her harsh and rude—have you ever been harsh and rude? If you say he's whiny and irresponsible—have you ever been whiny or irresponsible? Remember that when you point your finger, four fingers point back to you.

And I have to say that it's the same in the church. What is the church but a family of faith? Today we ordain our clerk of Session, Rick We are so thankful, Rick, that you have been called to this important role. This church is a family, and as the clerk of Session and chair of Personnel, you have the calling, as I do, and the Session does—not an easy task—of helping us to be a loving family. Are some people challenging for us to deal with? Of course they are. But let us not be like Edom, cutting ourselves off from others who might be hurting, might be dealing with struggles we don't even know about. Let us not be Elsa, running away to an ice palace crying "Let It Go." Instead, let us run toward the black sheep, to embrace him and bring him back in the fold—remembering that the Good Shepherd would leave the ninety-nine to run after that one sheep who has fallen astray—remembering that the Good Shepherd would even give his life for the sheep—remembering that we are called to love as Christ loves—remembering that, at times, the lost sheep is none other than you and me.

In the name of the Father, and the Son, and the Holy Spirit, Amen.

Week Thirty-nine: Glory
Haggai

When I was a kid, if you had a birthday party, you wanted to go to Chuck E. Cheese. Chuck E. Cheese was a magical land of amazing games, prizes, the world's greatest foods: Pizza and ice cream, and a magical band of animals that played rock music. It was the Valhalla of kiddom.

A few years ago Diana went to a birthday party at Chuck E. Cheese. I hadn't been there in years, and when I drove to the storefront in a mini-mall, next to a Burlington Coat Factory and an Ace Hardware, I was first struck by how small the place actually was. In my memory, Chuck E Cheese was approximately the size of the Taj Mahal. Inside, about half the rides were broken. Children screamed to receive candy from a costumed mouse. And for the first time, I realized that the mechanical band's mouths moved at times seemingly completely unrelated to the piped-in covers of sweatin-to-the-oldies. The review on yelp covered it just about right: "Same cardboard pizza, mechanical rat, and tired game consoles from when I was a kid."

But my disappointment in the faded glory of Chuck E Cheese is just a shadow compared to the deep gloom the people of Israel felt returning from Exile to the holy city, taking in the partly-completed repairs to the broken foundations, the mended curtains, the furnishings. The sad reality of the situation is expressed in the very first words of our reading:

Haggai 1:15, "In the second year of King Darius." This would be a little like if I said in the second year of President Vladmir Putin. The Israelites are under foreign control.

Haggai 2:2, "Speak to Zerubbabel son of Shealtiel, governor of Judah, to Joshua son of Jehozadak, the high priest, and to the remnant of the people." After the Temple was destroyed, and the king's line cut down, people were allowed to return under governor Zerubbabel, but there would be less of them, only a remnant, and no Israelite king, no great Davidic monarchy. This meant a loss of power and wealth. Temple ornaments that were once silver and gold would now have to be replaced with wood and brass. And amidst this backdrop, the people have to keep going.

Haggai 2:1, "On the twenty-first day of the seventh month, the word of the Lord came through the prophet Haggai." That day would have been the seventh day in the eight-day festival of booths. Now remember, the festival of booths was an autumn festival in which the people of Israel had to live in tents, a little like camping, to recall the days of wandering in the wilderness and give thanks for what God had done. Something like our American feast of Thanksgiving. This is ironic because the people are not feeling very Thanksgiving-y.

Haggai 2:3, "Who of you is left who saw this house in its former glory? How does it look to you now? Does it not seem like nothing?"

Rather than giving thanks for the new project underway, the people are unimpressed by the work that's going on, instead gloomily remembering the good old days. Does any of this sound familiar? Do you remember when your building was new and state-of-the art, when the pews were full of worshipers dressed in their Sunday best, when the Sunday school rooms were teeming with children, and there was a wedding every week? It must seem like nothing to you now. The church is but a shadow of its former glory.

Or is it? Maybe it's all in how we define "glory." In Hebrew, the word is *Cavod*, and it can be defined by appearance, impressiveness, and magnificence. But the root of the word has to do with weight. So "glorious" really means "weighty" or "heavy." We hear the word again in verses 6-9:

Haggai 2:6-9, "This is what the Lord Almighty says, in a little while I will once more shake the heavens and the earth, the sea and the dry land. I will shake all nations, and the desired of all nations will come, and I will fill this house with glory, says the Lord Almighty. The silver is mine and the gold is mine, declares the Lord Almighty. The glory of this present house will be greater than the glory of the former house, says the Lord Almighty. And in this place, I will grant peace."

Have you ever heard someone say something and you just go, woah, that's heavy? Like Diana says to me the other day, "Just because you're breathing doesn't mean you're really living." That's heavy, or maybe we would say, that's deep. But that's what God means by glorious; cavod, heavy. The meaning to us might be impressive, or beautiful, or shiny; but to God it means, weighty, deep, fundamentally important. The things of God are glorious. Not because they are pretty; not because the pews are filled up, or the children wear their Sunday best, or because we have a shiny new pipe organ. The church, like the Temple, is glorious to the extent that Jesus is here. God says, the silver is mine and the gold is mine. God is saying, do you think it matters how fancy things look? How shiny? Whether we have a pipe organ or new carpeting or an electronic sign? Do you think it matters whether children are here in fancy dresses, or homeless people dressed in whatever they happened to find? That's not what makes the church glorious! The silver is mine and the gold is mine, says the Lord. It's not whether we present a shiny package to the world. It's whether Jesus is here. And why do I say that? Because Haggai says:

Haggai 2:7, "I will shake all nations, and the desired of all nations will come, and I will fill this house with glory, says the Lord Almighty." What was God talking about? Was he talking about the end times? I don't think so. God is talking about the time when all nations will come into the temple. And when is that? What is the moment when the earth shakes, and the curtain of the Temple was torn in two, because the glory of God could no longer be contained in a little room in a little temple in little occupied Palestine?

Matthew 27:50-51, "Then Jesus cried again with a loud voice and breathed his last. At that moment the curtain of the temple was torn in two, from top to bottom. The earth shook, and the rocks were split." The moment Christ died for our sins was the moment when the glory of God filled the earth, and all nations were called to come into right relationship with God the Father, through the sacrifice of His only Son. That moment was the moment of greatest glory, the heaviest, deepest, truest moment the universe has ever known. And you and I and the church are glorious not to the extent that we look good, that we have a nice fancy budget, even that we have people in the pews—we are glorious to the extent that we reflect that moment, of Christ's sacrificial love, to the world.

Are lives being changed here? Are people on fire with the Holy Spirit? Are we going deeper into relationship with God? Are we doing our daily devotionals and Bible reading, really making time for God as though He is the most important thing in our lives? Are we sharing the Good News? Are we repenting from sin? Are we serving the poor and needy? Are we working for peace and justice? Are we putting Christ, more and more, in the center of our lives? When we are doing the weighty things, the fundamental things, we are what God calls glorious.

If you want to see God's glory in the church, don't just talk about the good old days. Because if we're honest, for many years, not just in the church but in America, there was some, not all, but some, people going to church as a matter of habit, not a matter of faith. And God isn't looking for empty ritual. God is looking for lives in which Christ is fully present. God is not looking for a pretty picture or a nice building; God is looking for the kind of earth-shaking glory that changes hearts and minds and families and nations.

This is a greater mission than keeping the building clean or having a nice coffee hour. This is great, weighty, deep work, and it is not easy. We have great work to do, but we have a great God to help us do it.

Haggai 2:4, "Be strong, all you people of the land, declares the Lord; and work, for I am with you, declares the Lord Almighty." In this season of fall, we give thanks that God is in this place. We might not have our former glory as the world sees it. But I see lives being changed, I see hearts being brought closer to God. I look out and I see people—not hundreds, but a few—who have come to this church in the last few years after being estranged from the church for decades. I see people who have come to know Christ because of the message that is being shared in this place.

Thanks be to God—we're getting heavier! And I know we are not alone, that we have a companion in this great work, and He will not rest until it is brought to completion.

During my maternity leave I worshiped at a big church with a budget about ten times ours. When I would go out into the sanctuary rocking Charlie, I was surrounded by beautiful stained-glass windows. The floor is decorated in beautiful patterned tile, angels adorn the chancel, and the baptismal font was carved from marble by a commissioned artisan. By contrast, in our church we don't have angels in the chancel, just a plain wooden cross; the floor is decorated with plain, brown carpet, purchased by the faithful savings of the members of the church; and the font was carved by hand from ordinary wood by George, or as we know him, "military George". But you know what? They are more beautiful to me. Because the cross; the carpet; the font; I know they were given out of simple faith, sacrificial faith, not out of a desire for window-dressing. They're not silver or gold, but they are glorious, because Christ is in our church.

So, don't lie around complaining about the glory days. Don't sit around saying somebody should do something about that. Somebody should restart this ministry. Somebody should start an evangelism campaign. Somebody should start doing mission work. Instead, be the somebody. Be the hands and feet of Christ as you and I are called to be. Be strong, and work. Get heavier. For I am with you, declares the Lord Almighty. Do the weighty things, the fundamental, ordinary work of showing Christ to the world? Because that is how God shows forth his glory.

In the name of the Father, and of the Son, and of the Holy Spirit, Amen.

Week Forty: Company's Coming
Malachi

A few years ago, a friend of mine came by unannounced. She seemed disappointed when she came through the door. We were good enough friends that she could tell me: "I was hoping to see what your house is really like. But it looks perfect." This was before I had three kids, a dog, and a cat (and a husband). Now, if you are coming to my house, I prefer at least three days' notice. If Jesus were coming back today, what would you to clean up? Is your spiritual house in order? Because I have news for you…Jesus is coming today. Today we finally begin the New Testament. So this is another opportunity for those who have fallen behind. You have an opportunity to return to the Bible in a year project and read the entire New Testament this fall.

We have been longing for Christ, as we read through Leviticus, and Chronicles, and Jeremiah. When we read of God's judgment, when we read God's exacting law, we longed for Christ, God coming with love and grace to save us, to be merciful unto us. But there can be no mercy without judgment. There can be no grace without law. There can be no salvation without sacrifice. And there can be no redemption without repentance. We want Christ to come as the baby in a manger; as the feeder of the five thousand; as the loving Messiah who took children on his knee. But do we want the Christ who made a whip and cast moneychangers out of the Temple? Do we want the Christ who said if your eye causes you to sin, cut it out; if your hand causes you to sin, cut it off?

Because Christ came to reveal God's judgment, just as he will come again to judge you and me.

Malachi 3:5 tells us what God will find when he comes: "I will draw near to you for judgment; I will be swift to bear witness against the sorcerers." Perhaps you don't practice sorcery. But the real problem with sorcery is trusting in any power other than God to deliver you. Do you believe in good luck? Do you place your faith in a politician or a talk show host? Do you believe medical science can save you, a new drug, a miracle treatment? Christ is coming to judge you and me.

against the adulterers,
Christ said that even to look at another person with lustful intent was the same as committing the sin of adultery. Let he who is without sin cast the

first stone. I would venture to guess that no one here above the age of fifteen has a stone to throw. Christ is coming to judge you and me.

against those who swear falsely,
Ever lie? Ever stretch the truth when telling a story to make yourself look better? Ever tell a half-truth because it sounded better than the full story? Christ is coming to judge you and me.

against those who oppress the hired workers in their wages,
Ever buy anything made in China? That worker most likely made a dollar a day. But if we were to buy products from workers paid a living wage, well, we wouldn't be able to buy as much stuff. And what we want, what we need, is more stuff. Isn't it? Christ is coming to judge you and me.

the widow and the orphan,
Ever ignore people who are weak or poor because they can't do as much for you as the rich and powerful? Ever turn away from the kids in foster care who need a loving home? Ever fail to visit the elderly who need someone to care? Christ is coming to judge you and me.

against those who thrust aside the alien,
All the Republicans, who really liked it when I was condemning adultery, are unhappy now. God says we need to treat newcomers and strangers in the land with the care and love we would show to Christ himself. Christ is coming to judge you and me.

Malachi 3:2 says "who can endure the day of his coming? Who can stand when he appears?" Who indeed? Christ is coming to judge you and me.

Malachi 3:1 tells us: "See, I am sending my messenger to prepare the way before me." When we come to the Gospels, we come seeking the love of Christ, but we are hit with John the Baptist, who uses these very words from Malachi…prepare the way. "My messenger" is the meaning of the word "Malachi." He brought a message for the priests and the people of the returned nation of Israel, who were falling into their old bad habits of sin. But Christians believe Malachi saw beyond his own time to the coming day.

Malachi 3:1, "and the Lord whom you seek will suddenly come to his temple." We hear that God himself is coming to his temple. We believe this prophecy refers to Christ, whose presence will fill not only the temple, when he comes in person to purify God's house, but the personal temple of every person who receives him. So we see the prophecy: first a messenger shouting "prepare the way," then God himself will come to the people. Malachi 3:1,

"The messenger of the covenant in whom you delight—indeed, he is coming, says the Lord of hosts." Christ is coming both to judge and to bring delight, to bring joy.

Malachi 3:2-3, "For he is like a refiner's fire and fuller's soap; he will sit as a refiner and purifier of silver, and he will purify the descendants of Levi and refine them like gold and silver, until they present offerings to the Lord in righteousness." John the Baptist said, I baptize you with water, but he will baptize with fire and the Holy Spirit.

A refiner's fire takes gold and silver and removes all the impurities so that it could shine like it was meant to shine. You see, all the sin you are holding onto, all the bad habits and tired ways of being, they are preventing you from shining the way you are meant to shine. But the process of refinement is not easy for the gold; it requires going through the fire.

Recently I went running with Diana, and she wanted to stop every time her chest or her belly hurt. I had to explain to her that when you run, you're working your heart and lungs more than they've ever been worked, and it hurts. You get cramps, and sometimes your chest feels a rawness, a tightness, even in your throat there's a rawness just from breathing so fast and so hard. But you can't just stop and walk when you cramp up, because the cramp will start right back up again as soon as you start running. The only way to get rid of the pain is to go through it, expand your heart and lungs greater than they were before, and get stronger.

Spiritually, it's the same concept. When we become stronger, it hurts. The experiences that purify us—experiencing pain and loss, going through doubt and fear, turning away from sinful habits, reading the Bible in a year—they are sometimes painful experiences. But they are refining you like gold. The only thing you will take into heaven is your character; not your wealth, not your prized possessions, not even your body. So, God is interested in refining you, in making you shine the way you were meant to shine.

But even with all our hard work, we know we won't be perfectly shining on that day. We won't go through all the purification we need to do. We will fail to become everything God wants. Thanks be to God, that God takes on the worst of the purifying pain unto himself. Malachi 3:4 says,

Malachi 3:4, "Then the offering of Judah and Jerusalem will be pleasing to the Lord as in the days of old and as in former years." We believe that the offering that is pleasing to the Lord is not the animals people brought to the Temple. Because nothing changed following the prophecies of Malachi.

People kept bringing their imperfect offerings, their half-hearted attempts at purification. What happened was that, in the fullness of time, God came to bring a perfect offering, an offering pleasing to the Lord; Christ. And he purified us not through our own actions or offerings, but by his blood; by his work on the cross, which cleansed us from sin beyond our own power, even beyond our own belief.

The entire Gospel, then, is laid out for us in these verses in Malachi, written five hundred years before Christ; from John the Baptist to the cross and the empty tomb, it is all here. Malachi probably went to his grave doubting the Word that God gave him, because he never got to see Christ in the flesh, and know that, five hundred years later, his words would be fulfilled in a greater way than he even dreamed possible. But we know what he could not.

In the same way, you and I might doubt the work we are doing. We might doubt the message of God's return. We might doubt that company really is coming, that Christ will come to restore and redeem this messed-up world. But what if Malachi had doubted himself so much that he never did God's work? Do the work God has given you. Tidy up. Get ready. Because one day it will become as clear to our spiritual descendants as it is to us, reading Malachi over two thousand years later: God has a greater plan. He is looking beyond our small situation to the work of centuries. Company's coming. So get your house in order.

In the name of the Father, and of the Son, and of the Holy Spirit, Amen.

Week Forty-one: God Gives Handouts
Matthew 5

Who knows the end of the quote: "A good lawyer knows the law. A great lawyer knows…"?

The answer is: the judge. A good lawyer knows the law. A great lawyer knows the judge.

The old joke is funny because it's true. In the battle between rules and relationships, relationships win every time. A Christian in name knows the rules. A Christian in deed knows the Ruler.

Jesus's sermon on the mount moves us from the rules to the ruler, from rules to relationship.

I've done this before but it bears repeating. Can I get a volunteer from the congregation?

Stand back to back with me. Now, follow me. Anywhere I go, you need to go exactly that way.

This is life without the law. You don't know where to go. You're blindly wandering through life.

And this is the way many people live today. They don't know the Ten Commandments. They are without a Law, without a standard to follow. You need to know the law. Now, stay here; you're on the hook for a while.

Jesus in Matthew says, I came not to abolish the Law, but to fulfill it. Dan commented to me that Matthew is a little like the Old Testament. We begin Matthew by reading through that list of genealogy…and it's so different when you've just read the entire Old Testament. It's like paging through a family album. You see how Jesus is descended from this incredible line of people who trusted God…. you see that the story of God is not one story in the Old Testament and another in the New, but one continuous, unfolding drama of God's love in relationship with humankind. Matthew is a little like the Old Testament. Matthew depicts Jesus as the new Moses, the great Law-Giver, the great teacher. It's in Matthew that Jesus gives the Sermon on the Mount, just as Moses received the law on a mountaintop—Mount Sinai.

Matthew is also divided into five books, just as the five books of Moses. It's hypothesized that Matthew's audience was a synagogue of Jewish Christians in the Holy Land. Matthew emphasizes that Jesus did not come to abolish the law, but to fulfill it. Now turn around. We need to know the Law. We need to know the Five Books of Moses, the Torah, the Ten Commandments and all the rest. Without them, we're blind.

Now my volunteer is following the movements of my hands. But is he following them perfectly? No. And Jesus says: Matthew 5:48, "You are to be perfect, even as your Father in heaven is perfect." How can this be? How can we be perfect? Isn't perfectionism a bad thing? It is if you are talking about rules. Have you ever met one of those "perfect" believers? People caught up with trying to live squeaky-clean lives, instead of letting Christ's forgiveness wash over them? These are people who seem always anxious, always saying "I wish I could do this," or "I need to do that," people continually frustrated with themselves for not being perfect. Do you know one of these people, living like this? Is it you?

I think of a South African preacher, described by Philip Yancey in *What's So Amazing About Grace*, an anti-gay crusader, whose theology was all law and no grace. Turns out the guy was a prolific child pornographer. I think of the fictional character Javert in Les Misérables, the cop who would rather see the evil in others than the good, and when he encounters a criminal who is truly a good man, he can't handle the paradox and takes his own life. I think of Judas. What drove Judas to turn Christ in? Perhaps money, but I think it was the extravagance of Christ's grace; Judas couldn't get over the fundamental unfairness of God's love, and he came to believe Christ was an imposter. When he realized his error, he couldn't accept God's love, couldn't accept grace. In his quest for rules, he missed the ruler. It's good to know the rules—but it's better to know the Ruler.

What is the only way to be perfect? It's not in the constant quest for perfection. That's a test we are doomed to fail. This fall, we celebrate five hundred years since Martin Luther nailed his 95 theses to the church house door. People have asked about the 95 Theses. They are a celebration of grace, and a rebuke to church authorities who say grace can be bought by money, rather than by true repentance. Martin Luther was a monk who beat himself, worked, strove to eradicate sin and came to the conclusion that we can never achieve perfection on our own. The fourth thesis is: "The penalty [of sin], therefore, continues so long as hatred of self continues; for this is the true inward repentance, and continues until our entrance into the kingdom of heaven." Luther finally recognized that he could never achieve perfection on his own; like St. Paul, he said, "thy grace is sufficient for me."

What is the only way that he can follow my hands perfectly? By taking me by the hand.

See? Now he is following me perfectly. And he's not anxious. He's not working hard. He's just letting me lead him. That's what God wants! It's good to know the rules; but it's better to know the Ruler. And that's what the Sermon on the Mount is all about. We have seen how, from the Garden of Eden, God is striving for this relationship with humanity. So, he changes strategy—he focuses on one part of the human family, the people of Israel, that by them he may bless all nations. He teaches them the law, he teaches them about grace and forgiveness, power and love. But now the time has come to share the message beyond this nation. The time has come for God's arms to open wide on the cross, reaching out to embrace the world. Jesus comes to help the people see beyond the rules to the Ruler, beyond rules to relationship. It's not about the letter of the law, it's about the Spirit. And that's what we read today.

Matthew 5:38, "You have heard the law that says the punishment must match the injury: An eye for an eye, and a tooth for a tooth." Jesus is quoting Exodus 21:22-25, Leviticus 24:20, and Deuteronomy 19:21 all at the same time. But he goes beyond the rule to the Ruler; he goes beyond the rule to the relationship. The point of the rule is not to escalate injury; to let the hurting stop with you; to live in justice and love. Notice that Jesus isn't talking about the dramatic injuries that won't often happen in our lifetime. He's talking about the smaller hurts that we so often dramatize as though they were murders—insults, lawsuits, someone stealing your tunic, someone borrowing money without repaying it. When, in verse 41, Jesus talks about soldiers: Matthew 5:41, "If a soldier demands that you carry his gear for a mile, carry it two miles."

Soldiers in Jesus's time were the hated Roman occupying troops, who raped and murdered the Jewish people. The same Roman soldiers who would be responsible for Jesus's death. He says, carry their gear for them! Do even more than they ask of you! This would be like, to us, saying "If a North Korean bomber stops at your airport asking for a tank of gas for his plane, refill it with premium!" How could Jesus ask this of us? It's shocking! But Jesus says we must overcome evil with good.

I've heard it said this way: If someone is hurting you, try walking a mile in their shoes. Because you'll be a mile away from them—and you'll have their shoes. Jesus says, don't resist that. Turn the other cheek. Let them hurt you—overcome evil with good. And that is exactly what He did. He didn't overcome violence and hate with violence and hate. He overcame it by his love, bleeding out on the cross. If Jesus can say "Father, forgive them" to the people who crucified him, can you maybe give the benefit of the doubt to that co-worker, that sister-in-law, that friend, who hurt you? Can you turn the other cheek? Because the rules might allow you to exact punishment—but it's not about rules, it's about relationships.

Matthew 5:43, "You have heard the law that says, 'love your neighbor and hate your enemy.' But I say, love your enemies! Pray for those who persecute you! In that way, you will be acting as true children of your Father in heaven. For he gives his sunlight to both the evil and the good, and he sends rain on the just and the unjust alike."

When we're in relationship with God, we can't help but be unfair to people, because God is unfair to people. What, you say? God can't be unfair! But He is. Grace is the very essence of unfairness. God gives people the gift of life, sun and rain and gladness and wealth, whether they deserve it or not. He allows us the freedom to choose, even though He knows we will choose sin. It's not fair, but it is good. God is love, and He calls us to love, even people who don't deserve it. Because God knows, none of us deserve it. None of us is worthy of the great gifts God has given us. But it's not about rules—it's about relationship. When you are in relationship with Christ, in relationship with His Son, he counts you worthy of every good thing.

Do you need this relationship in your life? Are you tired of striving after perfection? Would you like to receive His healing and His grace? Is there a part of your life, of your body, in need of God's healing, physical or spiritual? A member of the church has asked that after the service today, I remain in the chancel to pray with all those in need of a relationship with Christ. If you need Jesus today, if you need healing, if you need to take God by the hand again, please come up to the chancel after the service. God's hands are reaching out to you from the east to the west. Come, take Him by the hand. You may not be perfect in this life, but you are perfectly loved.

In the name of the Father, and of the Son, and of the Holy Spirit, Amen.

Week Forty-two: Jump
Mark 9

About five years ago, I went to Manresa conference center for a silent retreat. Almost everybody else was a monk or a nun, and I was the youngest person there. And at the end of the retreat, I saw a sign that there would be a healing service. At first, I didn't really feel the need to go to the healing retreat. After all, I am pretty healthy. I didn't feel that I needed healing. But then I thought, perhaps God wants me to do the healing. So I went. And when I got there, it was a very simple service. There was a brief Bible reading and sermon on what healing was all about; that healing is about Christ coming into your heart and your life. Then we were invited to come forward; and when we arrived at the front of the chancel, we would turn around, and whoever was behind us would be our partner. We would lay hands on one another and pray. Just us, ordinary people, not flashy preachers—we were supposed to pray for one another, and somehow, this would heal us.

Mark's gospel is a gospel of healing. It's the action Gospel, where Jesus is moving immediately from one place to another, and everyone is asking—who is this man, who performs these signs and wonders? In this passage, a big crowd has gathered in order to receive Jesus's healing.

Mark 9:14, "When they returned to the other disciples, they saw a large crowd surrounding them, and some teachers of religious law were arguing with them." There's such a big crowd that other teachers have come to take advantage of Jesus's popularity and share their own messages. It's like the Goodyear blimp—you're not there to hear about Goodyear, you're there to root for the Tigers. The people were there to see Jesus—and the teachers have this blimp up, "Love God? Join the Pharisees! Handy rules for every situation!" But the teachers aren't doing a good job with the situation, because they're arguing with the crowd. We don't know the details of this argument—but it seems like it has to do with the best way to heal a little boy. We know that the disciples are trying to heal him:

Mark 9:28, "Afterward, when Jesus was alone in the house with his disciples, they asked him, 'Why couldn't we cast out that evil spirit?' Jesus replied, 'This kind can only be cast out through prayer.'" So picture this situation. Everyone is standing around, trying to figure out how to heal this boy, arguing about what's really wrong with him, and nobody's praying. How could they be so silly?

Well, today's Bible commentators aren't much better. A lot of ink has been spilled over the question: what is really wrong with this boy? When we read the description: Mark 9:18, "Whenever this spirit seizes him, it throws him violently to the ground. Then he foams at the mouth and grinds his teeth and becomes rigid." We ask, is this really an evil spirit, or is this a medical condition? Is this epilepsy or a demon?

And it's the same way with the problems that we face today. We look at the mass shooting in Las Vegas which took place recently. And everyone's arguing about how to fix the situation. Mental illness certainly played into this situation. And this mentally ill person had access to weapons that could kill a lot of people very quickly. So, we are talking about bump stocks, and we are talking about mental illness. And I'm not saying that those are not issues that have to be dealt with. Just like I'm not saying that the boy did not have epilepsy. What I'm saying is that while we're all standing around arguing—did everybody forget to pray? Did everybody forget to let Jesus in? Did everybody forget that the ultimate healing is found not when we heal the body, but when we heal the spirit?

Ultimately, there is really no medical cure for epilepsy. But you can help people to spiritually deal with it—to learn to control the heart, the emotions, the spirit and the attacks will become less. The spiritual healing is as important as the physical. This kind can only be driven out through prayer.

When we argue and focus on the problems, we don't get anywhere. But when we pray and turn to Jesus, he changes everything. I never learned to perform exorcism, but I have learned that the goal of an exorcism is not to focus on the demon or the evil spirit. It's not to drive the demon out; it's for Christ to come in. If you focus on the problems, on the demons, on arguing about the problem, you fail to see that what we really need is Christ. What we really need is spiritual healing. After all, if someone truly allows the love of Christ in their heart, you want to take all anger, all impulses to hurt others, even to insult other people out of your life. Violence is so far from your heart when Christ steps in.

Look what happens when Jesus shows up here. Mark 9:15, "When the crowd saw Jesus, they were overwhelmed with awe, and they ran to greet him." When Jesus arrives, we are so overwhelmed with love, we run to greet him, and we run away from everything else, every other fear and pain and illness and evil spirit that plagues us. We even run away from our doubt. Because the father doubted. One of the reasons this story doesn't make it into the lectionary is probably verse 24: Mark 9:24, "I do believe, but help me overcome my unbelief!"

He cried I believe! Help my unbelief! This year is the five hundredth anniversary of the Reformation. Part of our tradition as Protestants is that salvation is not about our deeds, but about our faith; sola fide, by faith alone. How can we Protestants, founded on the tradition of Martin Luther and John Calvin, how can we speak of doubt? But we all experience doubt. Some of us have experienced great doubts even reading through the Bible. How could God pass judgment in the violent and terrible ways we see in the Old Testament? Why is God so angry? And maybe there's nothing that I've said this whole year that can help you understand the judgment, the wrath of God. Maybe the Old Testament causes you to doubt. And what this Scripture has to say to you is that that's all right.

John Calvin writes, "there is none of us that does not experience both of them [doubt and faith] in himself. As our *faith* is never perfect, it follows that we are partly *unbelievers;* but God forgives us, and exercises such forbearance towards us, as to reckon us believers on account of a small portion of faith."

Let me explain it to you this way. Here is everything I can prove. And here is the belief that God created the universe. That the Bible is true. That Jesus rose from the dead. For every one of us, there is some gap between what we can prove and what we can believe. The question is not how big that gap is. The question is whether we jump. Some of us wrestle with a lot of doubt. Some of us wrestle with a little. But do you believe despite your doubts? Do you go out and pray, and trust, and work for God? Do you jump? Because when we jump, we are healed.

Mother Teresa spent most of her life in spiritual darkness. *Come Be My Light* is the title of a book published of Mother Teresa's writings, writings she never wanted anyone to see; the records of her personal journey. It turns out that while mother Teresa was tending the dying and the hurting among the forgotten people of India and while she was speaking and writing words that showed millions the undying presence of a loving God, she herself spent the majority of her life experiencing a profound sense of God's terrible, overwhelming absence. She wrote, "the silence and the emptiness are so great that I look and do not see, listen and do not hear."

But Mother Teresa jumped. She based a life on following Christ, and in that life she showed countless persons depths of love and justice and grace and truth. And that is all that matters. Mother Teresa performed miracles. She healed people physically and spiritually. The person in India who was healed by her doesn't care how much she had to struggle to do what she did, doesn't care about the nights of doubt, doesn't care that she very nearly lost her faith; he cares that she didn't.

And no matter what the official Catholic Church says, you know, and I know that Mother Teresa was a saint. No matter what can be proved, we believe she was God's saint. God used her to heal people, through medicine and through faith. God used her to work miracles. It doesn't matter that she doubted. What matters is that she jumped.

It doesn't matter that I struggled to go to the healing service; it matters that I went. I walked up to the chancel, and I turned around. And looking at me was this sour, old nun. I had watched her all week and didn't particularly like her, and I suddenly had no idea what I was doing, the lone Protestant in this sea of Catholics, a Presbyterian caught in some kind of Catholic healing ritual, about to lay hands on a nun and pray for a miracle.

But this kind can only be driven out through prayer. So I jumped, and I prayed. I didn't know what to pray. So I just let God open my mouth. And I don't remember everything I said, but I remember that I prayed for this woman's coming retirement, and since it was a silent retreat, we had never spoken. I do remember what she prayed for me: she prayed, Father, help Marianne to be a light to young people, and help her to balance her work and her family. God knew what needed to be healed in me, even if I did not. The evil spirits plaguing me could only be cast out by prayer—the prayer that trusts God, runs toward Jesus, and in so doing leaves everything else behind. The prayer that jumps is the prayer that makes us saints.

When the father brought his boy to Jesus, he took the leap of faith. And nothing else mattered. "I believe! Help my unbelief!" It is enough for God. And it was enough for Jesus. Jesus invites us to come to him as we are; Jesus invites our doubts and our fears and our questions; Jesus invites us to take them and jump. Just jump. You could be a saint for someone who needs one.

In the name of the Father, and of the Son, and of the Holy Spirit, Amen.

Week Forty-three: *Finding Nemo*
Luke 15

As many of you know, my middle son has been driving me crazy lately. I've been asking people if they are interested in adopting him. So a couple of weeks ago, we had a bounce house on our lawn for the block party. We didn't really think through the logistics of having JP near a bounce house. He couldn't stay away, but there is only so much bounce house adults can take, and when we tried to drag him inside, he became a whiny mess. Eventually, we just told Diana to keep an eye on him while they were jumping, and we went inside.

God bless her, she tried. But Lou, a six-year-old from the block, and Michael, who's seven, came over, and Diana got distracted. When Dan came outside, he saw no children in the bounce house. He found Di. "Where's JP?" He asked. "He was right here," she said, bewildered. And he ran inside. "Mar, JP is lost." We went running up and down the block, calling for him, looking everywhere. I had visions in my head of him getting hit by a car. I was just about to call the police, when one of the neighbors said, "he's right here!" for JP had found something even better than a bounce house: our neighbor's trampoline.

The panic I felt in that moment, that my child, the same one who's been driving me crazy, the one who I joke about getting rid of—if my beloved little boy, the dear child of my heart, were gone? Could God punish me for thinking those terrible thoughts, joking those terrible jokes? The ultimate be careful what you wish for? It was one of the scariest moments of my life.

What this passage tells us is that deep distress, that searing pain, that's the way God feels all the time. Do you know the panic of losing something important? Maybe not a child—but a report due the next day? The keys to your car? God forbid, your cell phone? Jesus describes the familiar experience of distress at losing something precious.

Luke 15:8, "Or suppose a woman has ten silver coins and loses one. Won't she light a lamp and sweep the entire house and search carefully until she finds it?" Luke's gospel focuses on women and children, on ordinary, humble people. And here Jesus likens God to an ordinary woman, and her search to find something of value to her.

In the same way, Jesus likens God to a shepherd who goes off in search of a lost sheep: Luke 15:4, "If a man has a hundred sheep and one of them gets lost, what will he do? Won't he leave the ninety-nine others in the wilderness and go to search for the one that is lost until he finds it?"

These parables are the first two in a set of three, the lost sheep, the lost coin, and the third parable being the most famous of all, the parable of the lost son. And he tells them to explain why it is that he spends time with sinners.

Luke 15:1-2, "Tax collectors and other notorious sinners often came to listen to Jesus teach. This made the Pharisees and teachers of religious law complain that he was associating with such sinful people—even eating with them!"

In Jesus's day, eating with sinners made a person ritually unclean; it wasn't done. Not only were tax collectors known for being dishonest and corrupt, but they were also politically extremely unpopular, because they collaborated with the hated Roman occupiers. Think about if IRS agent, Russian mafia boss, and terrorist collaborator were all rolled into one person, and you've got tax collector. And sinners—we don't know what these sinners did in particular, but they were people society viewed as sinners. Who do you view as sinners? Do you automatically think of sexual sin, or addiction? Violent criminals? Or liars? Or do you think of the more insidious sins, like economic sin, envy and greed?

Jesus chose to spend time, not with the particularly holy people, but with people who society viewed as sinners. He hung out with those who were on the margins of society, the political, religious, and social outcasts. The lost.

How much time do Christians today spend with the lost? How much time do we spend seeking out people in nightclubs, bars, casinos, shopping malls, football stadiums, looking to share the good news of Christ? Or are we pigeonholed in our churches, keeping to ourselves, putting our light under a bushel? Jesus said we are the salt of the earth. Are we staying in the salt shaker, or are we bringing flavor to the world? We get distressed over the loss of a cell phone—but shouldn't we be more distressed about the loss of sinners God cares about? Because God does care about them. In these parables, Jesus gives examples of people losing things of real value to them; in the parable of the lost coin, Jesus recognizes that what we value is money.

It's as though Jesus recognizes that we humans are obsessed with this money stuff. He says, imagine losing a really big check—ten percent of your wealth. Wouldn't you turn over the garbage cans and rip apart the couch cushions—wouldn't you shine a light on all the dark, icky places of your house, trying to find it? That's what God is willing to do—shine a light on all the dark icky places we go in our sinfulness, in order to find us.

And the sheep—the sheep takes it to a place of relationship, but not a relationship between people in the parable of the lost sheep, Jesus is saying, ok, I know this work stuff is really important to you guys. Imagine dropping a big responsibility, a big project at work, you were supposed to take care of. That's how God feels about losing you. You would drop everything and try to find the thing you had lost. You would leave the ninety-nine sheep and look for the one who ran away. Jesus gives us these examples, the coin and the sheep, to show us that we have real value to God.

The parables of the lost sheep, the lost coin, and the lost son tells us that God is deeply distressed over the loss of his children. Why should this be? How did the lost get lost? After all, doesn't God know where his children are all the time? God can't really lose anything, can he?

What is it to be lost? It is to be out of contact, to be out of relationship with something. If you know where your keys are, they aren't lost, even if you aren't holding them in that particular moment. Looking at the three examples, the coin didn't decide to get lost. But the sheep chose to wander away, and the son made a conscious decision to leave. The lost coin, the lost sheep, and the lost son all became out of contact with the one who needed them. And it's true with the lost people as well. Some simply fell away; others wandered; and still others made a conscious decision to leave the church, to leave their faith. And God allows us that choice. Why? Because love allows independence. Love allows free choice. If I hold a gun to Dan's head and say, "you're going to the chapel, and we're going to get married" is that love? Of course not. Love has to allow the possibility of rejection. Love has to allow freedom.

Willa Cather wrote, there are only two or three great stories, and they go on repeating themselves as urgently as though they had never been told before. The story of the lost son was retold in a film that had echoes of Pinocchio and Jonah. Fathers and sons, trying to find one another. Can you think of what it was?

The story was, of course, Finding Nemo. It begins when the little fish Nemo, in defiance of his father, swims away and is caught by a scuba diver. Nemo's father, Marlin, undertakes a long journey to find his lost son, in the course of events getting caught in a whale—just like Geppetto, just like Jonah. And it's in the belly of the whale that the father learns that he has to allow his son to be independent, to grow up, to choose to swim away, and trust that he will come back. In order to find his son, he had to love him enough to let him go.

And this is the true meaning of love—God will go to great lengths to find us, but God loves us enough to let us go. God allows himself to go through that great pain of being estranged from His beloved child. That's what God did in order to find us—he lost his son. Remember back to the feeling I had losing JP? The terrible thought that I might have to witness his death? God did. God lost his son.

Matthew 27: 46, "About three in the afternoon Jesus cried out in a loud voice, *'Eli, Eli, lema sabachthani?'* (which means "My God, my God, why have you forsaken me?")

God lost his son for us. God went through that horrible pain because it was the only way to find us again. When Christ took on our lost state on the cross, God knew what it was to be estranged from His only son. And God did it for our sakes. God went all the way to the cross in order to find us. Like the woman who lit a lamp, God shed light on all the dark, horrible places, all the painful places—God shone a light on death itself, in order to find us.

Did you know that when God found you, there was a big, big party in heaven? All three stories end with rejoicing. What God wants, what God is ultimately looking for, is that joyful moment of reunion.

When we watch *Finding Nemo*, we rejoice because we want to see the father find his son. But do you realize that this world is a story, and God wants us to rejoice, not over the reunion of a computer-animated fish on a screen, but over the reunion of lost children with their father in heaven? God wants us to join the party—God wants us to join the story—God wants us to go out and shine a light on the dark places of the world, to turn over the trash cans of society, to eat with the sinners and the tax collectors and go to great, great lengths to find us. So don't hide your light under a bushel. Instead, use it to find what God has lost.

That moment, when you find your cell phone in a hidden crevice in the front seat of your car, when you find that thousand-dollar check in the deep recesses of your purse, when you find your son, jumping on the neighbor's trampoline, at that moment, all is right with the world. Help God make more of those moments. Jesus was a friend of sinners. Are you?

In the name of the Father, and of the Son, and of the Holy Spirit, Amen.

Week Forty-four: Born Again
John 3

Who is Jesus? A great speaker? A rabbi? A teacher? A holy person? One way to encounter the divine? Or is he God in human flesh? God-in-a-bod?

The Gospel of John begins with this truth: John 1:1, "In the beginning was the Word, and the Word was with God, and the Word was God." Jesus is God in human flesh, says the Gospel of John.

John 14:6, "I am the Way, the Truth, and the Life; no one comes to the Father except through me." Believing in Jesus is life, truth, and wholeness; to believe is to be born again, to have your whole life changed through Christ. The end of the Gospel tells us its purpose:

John 20:31, "These things are written so that you might believe and might have life in His name." The Gospel of John is a study in contrasts; darkness and light, blindness and sight, life and death. To believe in Christ is sight, light, life; to reject Christ is darkness, blindness, and death. Jesus is God in human flesh. In himself, he unites humanity with God. In accepting him, we are united with his death and resurrection, so that we, too, can be at peace with God the Father. It's not a matter of what we do that saves us; it's what we believe. It's who we believe in.

That's what Martin Luther and the Protestant reformers were all about—sola fide, by faith alone. Martin Luther was an Augustinian monk who had come, through his study of the Scriptures, to believe in salvation by grace through faith alone. Then he heard of the church's program of indulgences. Indulgences were being sold as a way to get your loved ones out of purgatory and into heaven. They paid, by the way, for the Sistine Chapel.

There was a marketing genius, Johann Tetzel, living near Luther who came up with slogans for the capital campaign like, "As soon as the coin in the coffer rings, the soul from purgatory springs." You could buy your loved ones' way into heaven, essentially. The ninety-five these, written in 1517, were the response of Augustinian monk Marin Luther to the indulgences. The first two theses are:

Thesis 1. When our Lord and Master Jesus Christ said, ``Repent" (Mt 4:17), he willed the entire life of believers to be one of repentance.

Thesis 2. This word cannot be understood as referring to the sacrament of penance, that is, confession and satisfaction, as administered by the clergy.

God gives grace to the sinner because he repents from his sin, not because the priest tells him he is forgiven. The rest of the theses go on to question the idea of purgatory; Luther believes that purgatory, of the purging of sin from the soul, is something that could happen at the moment of death, rather than a place where sinners have to wait for years before they can go to heaven. Luther also lays out how he believes that the pope cannot pardon all sin, just that which he has personally heard confessed to him. Luther details how the sale of indulgences hurts the faith of believers, and how it encourages believers to pay money just so they can keep sinning.

Thesis 36: Any truly repentant Christian has a right to full remission of penalty and guilt, even without indulgence letters.

Martin Luther did not, at the time of the 95 Theses, want to start a new church. He just wanted the church to stop preaching what he considered heresy. He wanted to give the Pope the benefit of the doubt:

Thesis 50: Christians are to be taught that if the pope knew the exactions of the indulgence preachers, he would rather that the basilica of St. Peter was burned to ashes than built up with the skin, flesh, and bones of his sheep.

Yet in the days after Luther posted his theses on the doors of local churches, he ignited a firestorm that ended in the Protestant Reformation and the creation of new churches, among them the Presbyterian Church. Our church was founded on the belief in the three essentials: faith alone, grace alone, Scripture alone. And I believe we would do well to return to those fundamental beliefs. They are the same essentials preached in the Gospel of John. Luther believed that the Gospels, not beautiful chapels, were the true treasure of the church:

Thesis 62: The true treasure of the church is the most holy gospel of the glory and grace of God.

And this treasure is what is laid out for us in John chapter 3. John 3 is the story of Nicodemus, who thinks he knows about being one with God. A Pharisee, he believes in good works, in following the law—much like, at the time of Luther, the good people of the church believed that giving the church money, and performing good works, could bring salvation. Nicodemus came to Jesus at night:

John 3:2, "After dark, one evening, he came to speak with Jesus."

He was in the dark, both literally and symbolically. He didn't want the other Pharisees to know he was talking to Jesus. He didn't understand what Jesus's teaching was about. When Jesus tells him, John 3:3, "Unless you are born again, you cannot see the Kingdom of God."

Nicodemus doesn't understand. He asks, how can I enter into my mother's womb? In so asking, Nicodemus is thinking about the flesh and not about the Spirit. But the point of John's Gospel is that Christ unites the Spirit of God with human flesh; that Jesus is God incarnate. It's not about just the Spirit, and it's not about just the flesh. It's about having your whole self-reborn, your whole life made new, by faith in Jesus Christ.

Jesus says, John 3:12, "But if you don't believe me when I tell you about earthly things, how can you possibly believe if I tell you about heavenly things?" He tries to explain to Nicodemus how God wants to accomplish the work of salvation. He does so by referring back to a passage of Scripture Nicodemus would have heard about several times by now—the serpent Moses lifted on a pole, which gave life to all who saw it. Remember how that same serpent became an idol in the time of the kings? It became an idol because the snake was never meant to be worshiped in and of itself; it was a symbol for Christ.

John 3:14-15, "As Moses lifted up; the bronze snake on a pole in the wilderness, so the Son of Man must be lifted up, so that everyone who believes in him will have eternal life." Seeing Christ and believing in him brings life; turning away brings death. Jesus goes on to explain, in the most famous verse of all Scripture: John 3:16, "For God so loved the world that He gave his only Son, so that whoever believes in him may not perish, but may have eternal life."

It's about believing in Jesus, entering into the light and life he offers, being born anew and living as a new person because of Christ. And the question before Nicodemus is the question before us today: Do you believe? Who is Jesus to you? Is he a nice teacher? A good man? Or is he your Lord and Savior? God in human flesh? The ruler of your heart and of your life?

Have you been born again, reborn in Christ? In our society, born-again Christians has a political meaning. But this passage is not about voting Republican or Democrat. It's about being a whole new person. A person who drips faith, truth, and love from her lips. A person who turns away from sin and death-dealing ways not out of guilt, but simply because those other things aren't as wonderful as following Jesus. A person who doesn't worry about money or health, doesn't worry about international terrorism or global warming because he believes all things are in God's hands. Not worrying is not the same as not caring; the point is to care without forgetting that we are cared for. Because God so loved the world.

The Greek word for world is cosmos; in Greek philosophy, the *cosmos* was the physical world, totally opposed to the spiritual. So one possible translation of John 3:16 would be, for God so loved the God-hating world, that He gave his only son. God loves the world even more than we do. So to be a believer is to place the world in God's hands.

If you and I were to truly do this, truly live in new, more faithful, more hopeful ways, people would flock to us because they would see the light and life and love in our faces, hear God speak through our voices, see the evidence of what God can do in our lives. So do you believe that Jesus is the Son of God, and even more, God himself? If so, does your whole life bear witness to that truth? Are you, like Luther, ready to nail God's truth to the church house door, proclaim it in the streets, knowing you could die for it? Or are you like Nicodemus—a believer in the dark? A half-believer? The Gospel lays it out clearly:

John 3:19-21, "And the judgment is based on this fact: God's light came into the world, but people loved the darkness more than the light, for their actions were evil. All who do evil hate the light and refuse to go near it for fear their sins will be exposed. But those who do what is right come to the light so others can see that they are doing what God wants." If you are born again, born into Christ, your whole life will change. Or as Luther put it:

Thesis 3: inner repentance is worthless unless it produces various outward mortification of the flesh.

Biblical scholar Karoline Lewis wrote that Jesus became God incarnate so that we could have an incarnational faith. In other words, Jesus became God in a bod so that we could honor God with our bods. So, Nicodemus is right, in a way, to be thinking about how to be physically born again, because that's what God seeks; a total transformation. To walk in the light, to have our lives be an open witness to who God is and what God does.

I look at true stories of people who gave all, who gave everything because of the Gospel.

In the 1990s, Soviet Russia was just beginning to allow free Christian worship. A Russian millionaire businessman rediscovered his faith, gave his friends the keys to his clothing factory, and went on a walk. "I felt a terrible need to get close to God," Yevgeny Pushenko said. "It was a spur-of-the-moment decision. If I had thought about it, I wouldn't have dared do it. Great decisions are made in the heat of the moment. I took with me two pairs of shoes, a few clothes and very little money. I walked through Siberia under very difficult conditions, walking through snow and mud. So as not to get lost, I followed the highway. I had to walk 2,000 kilometers through ravines and forests, walking on the Trans-Siberian express train lines, when there was no highway," he relates.

He said he slept anywhere, in caves, abandoned houses, churches. He ate fruit, vegetables, roots, and was sometimes fed by people in villages he passed. Pushenko not only had to confront the terrible weather conditions and the exhaustion but the suspicion of the authorities who at best regarded him as quaint or crazy and, at worst, as a spy. "I was often dragged off to police stations for questioning, since no one could comprehend why I would want to walk all the way to Jerusalem," he said.

When we asked him why he didn't retire to a monastery in Russia or attend a church back home to pray instead of taking such a dangerous journey, he explained: "I wanted to be purified, God led me like a little dog out of the mire of my sins."

Yevgeny Pushenko walked all the way to the Holy Land and in 1996 arrived at a place called Mt. Athos, where he has lived as the monk Athanassios ever since. And why would he do such a thing? Because once you see the light, once you are born again, you can never be the same. Jesus is either liar, lunatic, or Lord. And if he is Lord, that changes everything.

If He is Lord, it is the truth worth proclaiming in the streets, worth nailing to the church house door, worth dying for, and worth living for: that God so loved the world, that he gave His only Son, so that everyone who believes in him, may not perish, but may have eternal life. And that life can begin right now, today; by letting go of all that is pulling you away from Christ and living into faith in every moment of every day God gives you and me.

When we look at some people's lives, at the life of Martin Luther, or the life of Yevgeny Pushenko, we can say, unequivocally, here was a man who was born again. Will people say that of you? What needs to come into the light in your life? How do you need to be reborn today?

In the name of the Father, and of the Son, and of the Holy Spirit, Amen.

Week Forty-five: Church Potluck
Acts 2

In 2005, the results of a study by the Lilly Endowment were published, *Soul Searching: The Religious and Spiritual Lives of American Teenagers*, by Christian Smith and Melinda Lundquist. They described the beliefs of American teenagers as moral therapeutic deism. Basically, most American teenagers believe that God exists—that's deism, that God wants them to be good—that's the moralistic part, and that God will help them when they are in trouble—that's the term therapeutic.

Why do they believe this? The study suggested they believe this because it's exactly what their parents believe. If you hear nothing else from my sermon today, hear this: moralistic therapeutic deism is not what Jesus died for. Moralistic therapeutic deism is praying before a test. Moralistic therapeutic deism is coming to church when it is convenient. Moralistic therapeutic deism is giving whatever low bill happens to be in our wallet at the time. Moralistic therapeutic deism is like a child's Halloween costume of Jesus. It's fake. It's not the real thing. Perhaps it's being a falsification of faith makes it even more dangerous.

If you want your faith to be founded on thin air, if you want a meaningless life, if you want to give nothing to Jesus and receive nothing from him in return, then I suggest moralistic therapeutic deism.

Are we Christians, or are we moralistic therapeutic deists? I invite you to take out a pen or a pencil, and find an empty corner in your order of worship, and write down, honestly, what is the number one priority in your life? Is it your children? Is it your spouse? Is it yourself? Is it your health, your comfort, your own pleasure? Is it God? And if so, which God? Is it the God you know in your Lord and Savior, Jesus Christ?

Take a minute to write it down, and tear off that little section of paper, and hold it somewhere. For the earliest Christians, their number one priority was Jesus Christ. Our reading today is about the very first Christians. We read of them: Acts 2:42, "All who believed were together and had all things in common; they would sell their possessions and goods and distribute the proceeds to all, as any had need."

These very first Christians were a tiny minority in an unbelieving world. Roman religion was a bit like moral therapeutic deism in that it asked very little of people except that from time to time, they offer prayers to the emperor. Other than that, people were free to do as they liked. And people did, following a variety of different gods and goddesses according to whom seemed to be blessing them with health and wealth at the time. The Scripture says that Peter preached, "Save yourselves from this corrupt generation." And a corrupt generation it was.

Against this background, the twelve apostles began to preach to whoever would listen, the simple message of Jesus, "Come, follow me." And people did. They gave everything. They gave up their homes. They gave up their families. They gave up their wealth. They gave up their lives. All to follow Jesus. All so that he could be their Lord and their Savior. Their number one priority. Why would they ever do such a thing? Why follow this powerless, childless, penniless, homeless man who died the death of a slave, suffocating shamefully with his legs broken and his life bleeding out his side, with only a handful of women left weeping beside his cross?

Because these were people who had seen the risen Jesus. Because they believed—no, they *knew*—he was alive. Because they had touched his hands and his side. Because they walked with him on the road. Because they looked into his empty tomb. Because they saw the angels. Because he lives, I can face tomorrow. Because he lives, all fear is gone.

We who have seen Jesus, we who know he is risen, we can never be the same. We are transformed, from backwater fishermen to bold apostles, from prostitutes to prophetesses, from the castoffs of our culture to a revolution that will reshape the world. We will live for him. We will die for him. We will give anything for him. We celebrate because we know the truth. We know there is more to life than life. We know there is a world beyond the world. We know that Jesus has risen, and we celebrate.

When you read this chapter of Acts it sounds like one big worship-service-slash-party. These people had seen, themselves, a person risen from the dead. And so they no longer worried about trivialities like what is mine and what is yours. I mean, how would you respond if you had seen a dead person come back to life? We go to church on Easter and we proclaim, he is risen indeed. And then we go back to the parking lot and return to life as usual on Monday. But if we really believed it was true, how would we live?

How did they live? Well, their lives were one big church potluck. As I have studied this passage, I have come to believe that the church potluck, that unofficial sacrament of Protestantism, is a spiritual discipline. Of sharing what we have. Could you imagine what our world would be like if everyone could just share their own bounty? Like a giant potluck of everything? People who had too much fat would be able to share it with supermodels. People with a lot of hair could give some of it to people who have none. No one would be hungry. No one would be thirsty. No one would be lonely.

Imagine what it would be like if we as a church functioned like a church potluck. There would be no rich and no poor. The early Christians knew that this should be so. That's why Paul took up a collection for the poor church in Jerusalem. Is that how you see the church? Do you come ready to lay down your gifts before the Lord so that others may benefit? Or do you see church as kind of like a spiritual Walmart where you can come in, get what you need, and go on your way? Do you come to be a servant, or do you come to be served?

Rob Bell asked this question: "If someone were to look at your life, would they believe that Jesus had risen from the dead?" If someone were to look at your gifts of finances, time, and prayer, would they say, that person has been raised from the dead? When I look at Brother Yun's life the only possible conclusion, I can reach is that Jesus rose from the dead.

Brother Yun gave way more than ten percent. Brother Yun was imprisoned three times by the Chinese government for illegally pastoring a Christian church. During that time, he was beaten until his legs were broken. He was struck with electric batons. He was hit with whips and chains. He was stuck with needles under his fingernails one at a time. He was urinated upon by his fellow cellmates. He was tortured to confess the names of fellow Christians. In 1984, in order to withstand torture and because the Lord directed him, Brother Yun fasted from food, water, and speech for seventy-four days. This is believed to be medically impossible. His fast ended only when he saw his family and shared communion with them. At that time, he weighed sixty-six pounds. He came back to his prison cell and his first words were the good news of the Gospel. All of the fellow cellmates who had urinated on him and ridiculed him became Christians because of his witness. The prisoners wrote all over the cell walls the Bible verses Brother Yun had memorized since he had no Bible. Brother Yun gave his whole life to the church. He went into his kitchen and brought everything he had to the church potluck. Why? Because he had seen the risen Lord. If someone were to look at your life, would the only possible conclusion they could reach be that Jesus had risen from the dead? You have in your hand a piece of paper. What is written on it tells—what is the single most important thing in your life?

Maybe you wrote your wife or your husband. Well, Jesus has a spouse too. That bride is the church which means everything to him. The church is not another charity that does good things to be added to your benevolences. The church is the bride of Jesus, the very body of Jesus here on earth to proclaim his name and to do his will.

Maybe you wrote your child—I can understand that. Well God had his own child. God had an only son whom he loved even more than you love your precious one. And God watched him bleed and die for your sake. Because he loved you even more.

Maybe you wrote "myself" on that piece of paper. Thank you for being honest. God agrees with you.

Do you know what God wrote on God's little piece of paper? God would have written your name. God loves you more than anything else in the world. That is why God gave everything so that you could have new life in his name. Won't you do the very best thing you can do for yourself by giving your whole life to Jesus?

If you wrote that God is the most important thing in your life, does your every waking minute bear witness to that truth? If someone were to look at your life, would they believe that Jesus had risen from the dead? I know that he lives.

Many of you may know that I do a lot of work with suicide prevention. You may not know why. My cousin, Nick, died by suicide at the age of 22. In the midst of all that suffering, we saw the hand of God. Living next door to my uncle was an Episcopal priest, and my uncle was raised Episcopalian. But this Episcopalian priest was perhaps the one person in the world who could say to my uncle, I know what you're going through, because Father Tony lost his own child at about the same age, and he experienced suicide firsthand. Father Tony was the person perhaps best in all the world to stand with my uncle in this tragedy, and Father Tony happened to be living next door to my uncle, and he came to the hospital every day. He was able to baptize my cousin in the hospital, and to stand beside my uncle. And for or the first time in his adult life, my uncle joined a church. I look at life coming out of death in this way, and I believe with all my heart in the God who raised Jesus from the dead.

Whenever I've been to a church potluck, by the grace of God we have just the right number of casseroles, (The casserole being a central doctrine of Protestant faith,) just enough salads, and just enough desserts. Yes, some of them come from Wal-Mart, but some of us are honest enough to know that Wal-Mart can do a better job than we can!

At our potluck, no one goes away hungry. So when we give to our church, let's pull out the best from our kitchens. Let's each bring a specialty. Let's make a dish with love.

Let's give God our best, not our leftovers. And then let's all enjoy a feast. A feast of a church that is thriving and growing and sharing good news. A feast we can all enjoy—A feast of the Spirit, a feast that's a foretaste of that great heavenly banquet, where most delicious meal of all time will be laid out for us to enjoy, where we will feast and celebrate together with all the saints, and the deepest hungers of our souls will be fulfilled.

Are you coming? What are you bringing?

In the name of the Father, and of the Son, and of the Holy Spirit, Amen.

Week Forty-six: Have it Your Way
Acts 17

When you were young, did you ever walk around in a gas station or a trinket shop and see a rack of those personalized magnets? Rows and rows of names, pink for girls and blue for boys, the names arranged more or less alphabetically.

If your name was Mary Ann spelled M-A-R-Y-SPACE-A-N-N, you'd be pretty likely to find your name on a magnet and you could feel special.

Personalization has come a long way from there, as marketers realize more and more that the concept sells. Everything is marketed as made to order just for you. No one orders a cup of coffee anymore. People order a decaf vanilla soy milk latte with whip.

Just about anything you want can have your name printed right on it. You can go online and imagine the car you want.

We can choose the colors on our electronic gadgets now, and somehow deciding you want pink plastic on your cell phone is supposed to proclaim to the whole world who you are. Like Goldilocks finding the chair that's not too big not too small just right and the soup that's not to hot not to cold just right. Even Burger King cashed in, with its slogan of 40 years, "Have It Your Way", As though it's revolutionary to decide whether you want cheese or mustard on your hamburger. And it works. It works! because nobody wants to be boxed in. We don't want to be a number we don't want to be one of the millions, we want to be one in a million. I want to choose whether my hair is extra fine, fine, normal, color treated, or dry. I want to have permission to think outside the bun. I want to find my name on that rack—spelled my way!

If we, tiny and limited as we are, don't appreciate being boxed in, don't want to be defined by outsiders, but want to be allowed to define ourselves, how do you think God feels?

When Paul walks through the city of Athens, Verse 16, "While Paul was waiting for them in Athens, he was deeply distressed to see that the city was full of idols." The translation doesn't quite capture it. The Greek says that Paul was distressed in the spirit within him, in his inner spiritual and emotional being, Paul was troubled just by being around these sculptures and artifacts that claimed to represent God.

The learned people of Athens saw these as beautiful and historic works of art, but Paul could not get over the basic truth. That to him these works in gold, silver, and stone, came from the art and imagination of humans trying to define God. Attempting to box God in. Now we all do this.

We all try to stick God into the comforting images, and the acceptable places, and the familiar actions we want from our God. I am conscious that even in the act of preaching, while I try to stick to what God has revealed about Godself in Scripture. Nonetheless by the words I use and the images I use, and the passages of Scripture I use and do not use, I am sure that I do not do justice to the fullness, the awesomeness of God. Any language about God at all is in the end human language. And institutions about God, institutions of religion, are human institutions.

And over the years, religion has been relentlessly guilty of trying to box in God. Of saying, we know all there is to know about God and you don't. Of acting like God lives here and only here, and God has no business at your school or at your volunteer organization or at your temple.

A Sunday school teacher handed out week calendars to all her students and asked them to write in all their activities this week. School, soccer practice, birthday parties, family dinner, TV time and then asked them to write in time for God. The students obediently blocked off Sunday morning, and those involved in church activities wrote in the times of those. But doesn't God show up at school? I heard once that as long as there are tests, there will be prayer in school. And doesn't God show up at soccer practice? How would a person play soccer with the awareness that God was there? Is there any reason we can't thank God who gave us our birth, at our birthday parties? And isn't God sitting in at family dinner? Is it even possible that, whether you want God there or not, God shows up when you're watching TMZ on TV?

Look at what is going on in this story in Acts, Verse 19, "So they took him and brought him to the Areopagus and asked him, "May we know what this new teaching is that you are presenting?"" Here is Paul in the Areopagus, literally, the word Areopagus means Mars Hill.

The place where Paul is preaching is dedicated to and actually named after an idol. This hill is a public place of defense where people defend their actions before a council of the city's elders, of judges. Paul defends his God in this place, this place steeped in Greek culture and religion, and he defends his God using that tradition. Verse 23, "For as I went through the city and looked carefully at the objects of your worship, I found among them an altar with the inscription, 'To an unknown god.' What therefore you worship as unknown, this I proclaim to you." Paul sees an altar that says, "to an unknown God".

Scholars have looked into why an altar that said this might have existed. The Greek historian Epimenides recorded that during a famine in Athens, people walked around with sheep and wherever a sheep lay down, they would build an altar to try to appease the gods and stop the famine. Sometimes a sheep would lie down near a temple dedicated to Zeus, or a statue dedicated to Athena. So they knew to which god the altar should be dedicated. But sometimes a sheep would lie down, and they didn't know which god laid claim to that particular space, so they dedicated it to an unknown God. Paul seizes on this altar, on this tradition and says hey Athenians, you realize you don't know everything about God, Let me tell you what I know. And then Paul takes from Greek philosophy. Stoics were in the audience, so he quotes from Stoic philosophers. Paul's listeners would have known the quote "in him we live and move and have our being" and recognized its Stoic authority.

Verse 28, "For 'In him we live and move and have our being'; as even some of your own poets have said, 'For we too are his offspring.'" Clement of Alexandria identified the quote "we are God's offspring" as having come from the Stoic philosopher Aratus. Look at what Paul is doing here; what Paul is saying is mirrored by how he is saying it. Paul is saying that God is trying to reach the Athenians where they are, and Paul is looking at their culture quoting from their culture, standing in their culture to try to reach them. God is using their culture to try to reach them. God is saying, "Have it your way." God is speaking to them in their language, using their religion and philosophy to reach their hearts, because God wants each of us to have it our way. God comes to us in ways to which we can relate. It's the truth at the heart of the incarnation of God in Christ. God desires so deeply to reach us, that God comes to us wherever we are.

Like many people who notice such things, at one point in my life I was very angry whenever I saw an image of a white Jesus. I made passionate arguments that historically, Jesus was a Mediterranean Jew and should always be depicted with dark skin and hair and Semitic features.

Then I went to a Chinese church and saw on the walls images of Jesus and Mary and all the disciples with Chinese features to their skin, eyes, and hair. I realized then that there really is no description in the Gospels of what Jesus really looked like. And maybe there's a reason, maybe God loves us enough to let us picture Jesus in a way that each one of us can relate to. Because after all, the point is not that God was a Mediterranean Jew. That wasn't the important part. The point is that God was one of us. The point is that God wants to reach you and me and will go to any length to be personal to us.

In the world of products and marketing there's a limit. There's the moment when you can't find that perfect shade of green for your car, or Burger King doesn't quite get your particular brand of medium rare, or there's no magnet on the rack with Marianne spelled M-A-R-I-A-N-N-E but God doesn't have that limit. God loves us way too much to be anything less than perfectly personal. God will go anywhere and do anything to reach you, just you. God is big enough for you and me and everybody who desires a relationship with him. You can't box God in, our God is too big. Our God thinks outside the box. Egyptians tried to box God in, they said, what kind of God would come after these slaves? And God thought outside the box and parted that Red Sea. Job's friends tried to box God in. They said, if you're suffering Job, you must have done something to deserve it. God thought outside the box showed up and told those so-called friends what's what. The philosophies of the ages tried to Box God in. They said, the almighty God would never stoop to come down from heaven, to live the life of an ordinary man, would never eat breakfast and go to parties and suffer like us. God thought outside the box and did just that, all of that. Death finally tried to box God in, and guess what? God thought outside of that coffin, of that box, too.

God will break out of all our boxes. God has a way of just showing up where God doesn't belong. At school and soccer practice, at football and family dinner, at bowling and birthday parties, even on TV. In him we live and move and have our being. Everywhere and every time you are, God wants to be loving you, communicating with you, and giving you outside the box opportunities to serve him in the world. Because God won't be boxed into Sunday. God shows up on Monday, Tuesday, Wednesday, Thursday, Friday and Saturday. What I'm saying is that God loves you and me enough, and God is big enough to come to us wherever we are. To speak to us in whatever language we hear. We in the church today, just like the church of Acts, need to learn to speak new languages. That is what our Evangelism Team is doing, and that's what the Gideon Society is doing. We need to speak the language of skateboarding.

The First United Presbyterian Church was a small, aging congregation. They were troubled with these skateboarders hanging out at odd hours in the church parking lot, skateboarding and messing around and looking rather scruffy. The church had to decide what to do about the skateboarders. But instead of pushing them away, the church reached out, welcoming strangers into their midst. Eventually this group of scruffy teens began to look more like a youth group. And in time, eleven young people were baptized into the church. One of those young people, shortly afterward, found herself pregnant. And rather than push her away, again the church wrapped its arms around her. She said, "Without this church, I don't know where I would be today." God has a way of just showing up where God doesn't belong with the skateboarders beating up the church parking lot. At school and soccer practice, at football and family dinner, at bowling and birthday parties…everywhere and every time you are, God wants to be; loving you, communicating with you, and giving you outside-the-box opportunities to serve him in the world. So have Him your way. Among the many and diverse ministries of the church, God has a place just for your personality and your gifts. God a message and a mission with your name on it—spelled just right.

In the name of the Father, and of the Son, and of the Holy Spirit, Amen.

Week Forty-seven: Attitude of Gratitude
Romans 5

I just love Paul. There are some Christians who struggle with what Paul said about the social issues of his time. But to reduce Paul to those passages is to miss the forest for the trees. And Paul's forest is Paul's focus, and indeed Paul's fortress: and that is grace. Grace is the focus, the center of his message; and grace is his fortress, because grace strengthens Paul against everything.

I've been thinking about why God chose Paul, and it's truly amazing when you think about it. First, Paul understood the law. He had been a Pharisee, someone who had tried to observe the over six hundred laws of Moses. Paul loved the law and understood its moral focus. God wanted someone who would appreciate the beauty and fullness of the law so that he could appreciate the greater beauty and fullness of grace. And Paul knew grace. God hand-picked someone who had participated in murdering Christians. Now, when you think about it, it's amazing that God chose, for his apostle to the Gentiles and for the author of most of the New Testament, someone who had never met Jesus during his earthly life. But there were two reasons, I believe, that Paul's later conversion was within God's plan: first, God wanted someone who had persecuted the church, so the church had to be already existing. Paul's persecution of the church allowed him to recognize, in the most amazing conversion story perhaps in all of Scripture, in the greatest "what have I done?" moment, that he had been involved in killing God's chosen apostles, that in his zeal for the law he had become, actually, an enemy of God. Paul understood grace, and so he fought for the inclusion of Gentiles into the church. He is adamant in Romans that: 3:23 "All have sinned and fallen short of the glory of God."

The second reason why it makes so much sense that Paul was a later convert was because Paul believed without seeing. Paul never encountered Christ in his earthly life. Instead, Paul encountered the risen Jesus. I believe God chose an apostle who had never known Jesus in life because God knew that most Christians would never have that opportunity, and so he wanted someone to speak to us who knew what it meant to have faith through the words of others. Paul did encounter the risen Christ, but he needed other believers to tell him the stories of the Gospels; Paul had to hear the stories of Matthew, Mark, Luke, and John, just as we do, because he had never been there. Paul was also a member of the Jewish faith, and culturally and ethnically a Jew, but by God's design, he was also a Roman citizen, with the travel and access privileges that allowed, and he had some familiarity with Greco-Roman philosophy and culture. Finally, God chose Paul because he was human.

Paul dealt with weaknesses in his body—we don't know what they were, but they made Paul humbler. They made him real! Paul is someone we can relate to. We know that he was a physically smaller guy, and not much to look at, by his own account. But he was very human, he was very us, and so he is the perfect person to share with us the truth of God's grace.

Each of Paul's letters expand upon what grace means. Chronologically, we see that:

Galatians—first journey

1 and 2 Thessalonians—second journey

Romans—third journey

Each of these expositions of the faith becomes fuller as Paul goes deeper in his understanding of grace and law, deeper in his relationship with the Father, Son, and Holy Spirit, and Romans is Paul's theological masterpiece, the fullest explanation of what it means to be justified by grace through faith.

And here is the outline of what Romans says:

Introduction (1:1-17)

Our failure to live up to God's law (1:18—3:27),

The free gift of justification (3:28—4:25),

The joy of life in Christ (5:1—8:39),

What about God's chosen people? (9:1—11:36),

How should we then live? (12:1—15:13),

Conclusion (15:14—16:27)

Romans is a full blueprint of what it means to be a Christian, and it would be a great book for the new believer to study. It's also beautifully written; God worked through a poetic gift in Paul. Passages like this one:

Romans 8:39, "nor height, nor depth, nor anything else in all creation, will be able to separate us from the love of God in Christ Jesus our Lord."

How can you not rejoice when you read that? But today we dive deeper into Romans 5, in which Paul rejoices in the amazing gift of grace, and the joy of the new life in Christ. Paul proclaims that:

Romans 5:1, "Therefore, since we are justified by faith, we have peace with God through our Lord Jesus Christ,"

Since we have been justified by faith, that is, since we have been made right with God, not because of what we have done, but what God has done for us—which is the core message of grace, by the way—that's going to change everything. And the first thing that it changes is our minds. Why does Paul begin by talking about the changes in our thoughts?

Joyce Meyers translates Proverbs 23:7: Where the mind goes, the man follows. Your thoughts will lead your behavior. So for Paul, the first thing that God transforms is our minds. God brings us peace. Why do we go through this ritual every week, of sharing the peace with our neighbors? IT's so ritualistic, it might feel, dare I say it, kind of Catholic, and it's not entirely hygenic. We share the peace because of Romans 5:1, among other passages: when we are made right with God, we are at peace, in our minds, in our hearts, in our world. We have this assurance that flows from being made righteous with God. We know our ultimate destiny in Christ.

Ann Jervis compared the experience of being justified to two people thrown into an Olympic-size pool. One person is a swimmer, one is not. The swimmer knows that she's got a way to go, she might not like it, it's going to be a journey, but she's going to make it. That's what it means to be justified, to be saved. Paul doesn't sugar-coat the life of faith. Just because you're a believe doesn't mean you won't suffer.

Romans 5:3-5, "And not only that, but we also boast in our sufferings, knowing that suffering produces endurance, and endurance produces character, and character produces hope, and hope does not disappoint us, because God's love has been poured into our hearts through the Holy Spirit that has been given to us."

The point is not whether you will suffer, but how you deal with it. Someone this week said to me, I can't be happy, because I don't have this, this, and this. That person compared his life to me to a fitted sheet on a bed. Have you ever made a bed, and you're putting on that darn fitted sheet, and you get one corner on, like the relationship corner, but then another corner comes off, like the career corner, or the health corner. Well, when you live deeply in faith, it's like you get a bigger sheet. You have peace in your heart, you trust in God, and so you find it easier for everything to get into place. Your bed, ok, your set of stuff to handle hasn't gotten any smaller, but your capacity to handle it is greater.

Suffering produces endurance, endurance produces character, character produces hope. That last one has always been interesting for me. How does character produce hope? Isn't character about being a good person, doing the right thing, making good choices? Well, hope is a choice. I've been thinking about hope, and John Piper points out that hope in the worldly sense is different from hope in the biblical sense. In the worldly sense, you can say "I hope it won't rain today" and that almost means you think it's going to rain, but you hold out a little bit of desire for a sunny day anyway. That's not what biblical hope is. When we hope biblically, we actually believe and have faith that something will happen, even despite all the evidence that it will not. But the something is not immediate good. Biblical hope is not hope for a fatter paycheck, or that the Lions will win on Thanksgiving. Biblical hope is the long-term eschatological belief that good will ultimately triumph over evil. Here's my definition of biblical hope:

Biblical hope = expecting that God will be God.

And that's what Paul is talking about. It's a choice! Will you and your family be all right? Will you see God after you die? Will this world be redeemed? Choose to expect God will be God. And our suffering increases our capacity to make that choice, because when we keep choosing to trust God in difficult experiences, our faith gets bigger. Our sheet gets bigger. God strengthens our character and we become better able to choose hope. Like Paul in prison, knowing that he would eventually die for his faith; he was full of joy anyway! That's hope.

Endurance is a capacity that increases as we challenge ourselves. This year, as we have for the past ten years or so, Dan and I will run the Turkey Trot. It's kind of an odd tradition for rainy, cruddy Thanksgiving weather; but the more you think about it, the more it makes sense. First, from a physical standpoint, you gotta burn some calories before you sit down to a two thousand calorie meal. Second, a hot shower feels seriously awesome after a run in the cold. And then, you get dressed up and eat your pumpkin pie guilt free. Third, Thanksgiving is a day for an attitude of gratitude. And running will adjust your attitude. I strongly believe that no one actually likes running. For me, someone who has run, to one extent or another, my whole adult life, I still get out there, start running, and immediately want to stop. We run the race that's set before us not because it's fun, but because endurance produces character. It increases our capacity; it expands the sheet.

As Christians, we have a renewed mindset because of the greatest story ever told, the story of Christ's death and resurrection. And it changes everything. We have an attitude of gratitude. Paul's joy in this passage of Romans is overwhelming. He is clearly overcome by the awesomeness of what Christ did.

Romans 5:8, "But God proves his love for us in that while we still were sinners Christ died for us."

Paul points out that our attitude towards others changes fundamentally because of what Christ did. For many of us, Thanksgiving fills us with a sense of dread, because we have to deal with family that are not easy. But remember that when we were still sinners, Christ died for us. At Thanksgiving, we are called to have an attitude adjustment towards others, not because life is so easy, but because God is so good. If Paul can give thanks awaiting imprisonment, beating, and death, you and I can take a moment to give thanks amid the less than perfect circumstances of our own lives. We are called to think higher thoughts, to the renewing of our minds, to set our hearts on godly things, to allow suffering to produce character, and character endurance, and endurance, hope; we are called to an attitude of gratitude this Thanksgiving.

When I look at Paul, I see how God planned and ordered the gospel to be preached in such an amazing way by this apostle to the Gentiles, including you and me. And I know and I trust that God has so much more in store for me as well. He is lining everything up now in my life so that I can glorify him in the fullest way possible.

And I have to wonder, why do I ever waste energy doubting God? Each experience of my life has been like another Turkey Trot, another race—and just like in the annual Thanksgiving run, sometimes I do better, sometimes I do worse. But what matters is not the time I finish, or the place I come in. What matters is that I finish. What matters is that I keep letting God expand my endurance, build my character, develop my attitude of gratitude, increase my capacity for hope.

That is what the Christian life is all about; creating an attitude of gratitude in each of us, no matter the circumstances of this life. We hope for what we have not seen, giving thanks with patient endurance; and hope will not disappoint.

In the name of the Father, and of the Son, and of the Holy Spirit, Amen.

Week Forty-eight: Harmony in The Church
1 Corinthians 12

Today, we are changing lightbulbs in the sanctuary. So I would begin by asking: How many Baptists does it take to change a light bulb? Nine: seven to form a committee on the changing of the bulb, one to call an electrician, and one to make a casserole.

How many Episcopalians does it take to change a lightbulb? Why. my grandmother gave me that lightbulb!!!!

How many Pentecostals does it take to change a light bulb? Ten. One to change the bulb and nine to pray against the spirit of darkness.

How many Catholics does it take to change a light bulb? I hear they use candles.

How many Calvinists does it take to change a light bulb? None. God has predestined when the light will be on. Calvinists do not change light bulbs. They simply read the instructions and pray the light bulb will be one that has been chosen to be changed.

How many Unitarian Universalists does it take to change a light bulb? "We neither affirm nor reject the use of a lightbulb. If you have found a lightbulb helpful in your journey, that is good. If one would wish, they could submit an original poem or interpretive dance about their lightbulb, for the annual lightbulb celebration, where a variety of light bulb traditions will be explored, including long-life, incandescent, three-way, and tinted, all of which are valid paths to luminescence."

And how many Presbyterians does it take to change a lightbulb? Ten—one to change the bulb, and nine to sit around and talk about why the old one was better.

The lightbulb jokes exist because the church is a flawed and deeply divided institution. It's no wonder we know so many people who claim to be spiritual, but not interested in "organized religion." Organized religion means religious community. And if your Thanksgiving was anything like mine, it was wonderful; and it was also a good reminder that community is as rewarding as it is challenging.

The key is to live in harmony with one another. Harmony is what happens when different notes on the scale complement one another. Every note has a fundamental number of vibrations, and the harmonic noted how many multipliers of the fundamental creates a harmonic sound. Nature loves harmony; barn owls, for instance, were played the Blue Danube Waltz, and their brains filled in the missing notes! But it appears we are hard wired for harmony—brain images demonstrate that the brain is actually more activated when hearing harmonic and chords than dissonant ones. Are you living in harmony with others? We are meant to get along, even though we are different; you can't have harmony without difference.

This passage in 1 Corinthians celebrates our differences, our diversity. Paul is writing to a church in Corinth that is deeply divided. Some people in the church have these amazing spiritual gifts. They can heal illness, they can cast out demons, they can speak in unknown tongues. And those with these miraculous gifts are wondering whether those without them are really filled with the Holy Spirit.

To this church, Paul writes of baptism. He reminds them that "we have all been baptized into one body by one Spirit, and we all share the same Spirit." It seems that in the early church, when a person was baptized, the church leader would say "You are no longer Jew or Greek, slave or free, male or female. You have been clothed with Christ." Galatians 3:28, "There is no longer Jew or Greek, there is no longer slave or free, there is no longer male and female; for all of you are one in Christ Jesus."

At that moment, all divisions were erased. At that moment, that believer became part of the one body of Jesus here on earth. Now the amazing thing is that to create harmony, we need one note to take the lead, and the others simply harmonize with it. For example, a C chord wraps around the C note. I sing soprano when I sing with a choir, because singing the harmony is more difficult; it's harder to find the notes. But without the alto, there is no harmony; you need both.

And it's the same in the church.

Verse 22-23, "In fact, some parts of the body that seem weakest and least important are actually the most necessary. And the parts we regard as less honorable are those we clothe with the greatest care."

We need one another. And those that seem the least value, we are called to lift up the highest. Is this the way we really live in the church? Do we lift up the altos? For example, Shirley folds the bulletins every Sunday. Thank you,

Shirley, for being Christ's hands in this church. And Norm comes in every Saturday night to turn up the heat. Thank you for being Christ's feet in the church. Cindy stays late every Sunday to count the money. Thank you, Cindy, for being part of the body of Christ. And Kristen watches over our building and keeps it clean and orderly. Thank you, Kristen, for being part of the body of Christ.

We don't honor the altos enough. We don't lift up the feet or the ears or the tired hands of the church as much as we should. We call the elders to the front of the church; the liturgists and the pastor and even the band certainly get their moments to be recognized. But there are so many people who are never recognized and lifted up the way that God commands us in his Word. And perhaps that's one of the reasons people are disillusioned with the church; we operate the way the world does, giving greater honor to the sopranos, failing to live in harmony.

Verse 25, "This makes for harmony among the members, so that all the members care for each other. If one part suffers, all the parts suffer with it, and if one part is honored, all the parts are glad." We need one another, even the people who challenge us, even the people who we tend to forget or dismiss, we need them all the more. I think of the wolves. Wolves are scary, difficult creatures; they are predators, and humans nearly drove them out of North America. But recently, environmentalists convinced the national parks to reintroduce wolves to Yellowstone. And something amazing happened. This is from Sustainable Human:

"Before the wolves turned up - they'd been absent for 70 years - the numbers of deer (because there had been nothing to hunt them) had built up and built up in the Yellowstone Park and despite efforts by humans to control them they'd managed to reduce much the vegetation there to almost nothing. They had just grazed it away. But as soon as the wolves arrived, even though they were few in number, they started to have the most remarkable effects. First, of course, they killed some of the deer, but that wasn't the major thing. Much more significantly, they radically changed the behavior of the deer. The deer started avoiding certain parts of the park - the places where they could be trapped most easily - particularly the valleys and the gorges and immediately those places started to regenerate.

In some areas, the height of the trees quintupled in just six years. And as soon as that happened, the birds started moving in. The number of beavers started to increase because beavers like to eat the trees. And the dams they built in the rivers provided habitats for otters and muskrats and ducks and fish and reptiles and amphibians. The wolves killed coyotes and as a result of that, the number of rabbits and mice began to rise, which meant more hawks, more weasels, more foxes, more badgers. Ravens and bald eagles came down to feed on the carrion that the wolves had left. Bears fed on it, too. And their population began to rise as well partly also because there were more berries growing on the regenerating shrubs. And the bears reinforced the impact of the wolves.

But here's where it gets really interesting. The wolves changed the behavior of the rivers. They began to meander less. There was less erosion. The channels narrowed. More pools formed. More riffle sections. All of which were great for wildlife habitats. The rivers changed in response to the wolves. So the wolves, small in number, transformed not just the ecosystem of the Yellowstone National Park - this huge area of land...but also, its physical geography."

We need the wolves. We need everyone. We need everyone to be here. If we are missing a note, we are missing our harmony. So I ask, who is missing? Who is missing from our sound? Do we need to bring in the wolves? I see young men are missing, children are missing, black and brown faces are missing, and we need them. We need the harmony.

So if you are a soprano, if you are a leader, if you are one of the pillars of the church, and sometimes it frustrates you when we call forward the children, or invite in the homeless, or people with mental challenges, or if you simply have trouble getting along with someone else in the church, remember that we are all needed. Remember that we are called to honor the altos, the neglected ears and noses and feet of the church. Remember that we need the wolves. Remember that we need everyone, every single person here, and a great many people out there, to create the beautiful music God is composing here. And do not forget that you too are part of that harmony.

I have a privilege every week in that I can look out and see all of you, staring back at me.

And when I look at all of you, it is a beautiful sight. Because I see on your faces your faith, and your hope, and your love. When I look at you, I see something more than ordinary people. I look at you and I see the face of Christ. The Holy Spirit is living in you. Remember that you are the holy body of Christ and be thankful.

In the name of the Father, and the Son, and the Holy Spirit, Amen.

Week Forty-nine: Garbage
Philippians 4

There's something each of us does every week that can feel like an annoying obligation, but we know we have to do it, so we do. Can you think what it is? No! It's not going to church! It's taking out the garbage.

Taking out the garbage at my house is especially un-fun because we have two children in diapers. Now, I've managed to get out of the task for almost three of the past eight years, and all I had to do was get pregnant so I can't do the cat litter. Come to think of it, that may be why we have three children.

If no one took out the trash, do you know what would happen to our homes? They'd get flooded with trash. No one wakes up in the morning and says, I'd like to make ten gallons of trash today. But we just do. Trash happens.

When Ari Derfel goes to a restaurant and receives a drink, the first thing he thinks about is where he's going to put the plastic straw when he goes home. This man collected his garbage for an entire year, just to see how much trash one person created—and it was 96 cubic feet. We make a lot of trash. And I think it's the same with our thoughts. Trash, junk, just accumulates in there. We collect it, all day long, without thinking about it or planning for it. News stories, celebrity gossip, regular gossip, advertising—we spend ridiculous amounts of time thinking about negative things. Even the junk we listen to in the car—a lot of it, if we're honest, is just plain garbage.

What happens if we don't take the garbage out of our minds? There's a saying: garbage in, garbage out. The Bible puts it this way, in Proverbs 23:7: For as he thinks in his heart, so *is* he. Where the mind goes, the man follows, says Joyce Meyer.

Paul, writing from prison, says "Always be full of joy in the Lord." Philippians 4:4.

Now, we wonder, Paul can't really mean this, can he? Aren't there times in our lives when we are grieving, or hurting, and it's natural not to be full of joy?

The reason we can always be full of joy is that biblical joy is not the same as worldly happiness. Worldly happiness is grounded in circumstances, but biblical joy is grounded in certain hope. You can be sad because your husband or your wife has just died, but be joyful at the same time, because you trust in a truth greater than death. For instance, we call the day Jesus died Good

Friday. That's not because we believe that it was a happy day, but we are joyful when we think that through death, God brought us new life.

Why should Christians always be full of joy?

Paul explains:

Philippians 4:5, "Let everyone see that you are considerate in all you do. Remember, the Lord is coming soon."

How is this tied to being joyful? For one thing, if we are joyful, we can't help but be kinder to others. If our life is grounded in the ultimate reality of Christ, suddenly in makes a big difference how we treat the waitress at our table, or the cashier at the grocery store, or our family and coworkers. I met a woman once who always answered the phone, not with her name, but with "praise the Lord." Now, I think when you answer the phone with "praise the Lord," it affects how you would treat people over the phone. When our hearts are set on good and holy things, when we are aware that Christ is near at hand, we become kinder to others.

Now the worst of the garbage that can stink up our minds is worry. Worry is the opposite of faith. Paul says:

Philippians 4:6-7, "Don't worry about anything; instead, pray about everything. Tell God what you need and thank him for all he has done. Then you will experience God's peace, which exceeds anything we can understand. His peace will guard your hearts and minds as you live in Christ Jesus."

In Greek, the word "worry" is *peripateo*, and it means "to walk around in circles." And that's what we do when we worry: we walk around in circles, and we don't get anywhere. The big lie that worry tells us is that by thinking about something, we can control it. Some of you are still worrying about things that happened years ago, as though you can change the past. You can't change the past, and you can't determine the future. Here's something a wise person taught me: outcomes are not my job. You and I are called to do our part in the present moment and leave the outcome up to God. Why? Because you and I aren't the best judge of what the outcome should be! So don't let worry be the stinky, moldy cheese in the garbage pail of your mind. Take it out.

How do you take out the garbage of your mind? Well, it's a little different from taking out the garbage from your home. The best way to get garbage out is actually to put something better in, so that it takes up all the space and there's no room left for junk. The good news is, if you know how to worry, you know how to pray. Every time you feel that worry coming in, turn it to a prayer. Say, God, I entrust the outcome to You. Paul tells us how to keep the garbage out:

Philippians 4:8-9, "And now, dear brothers and sisters, one final thing. Fix your thoughts on what is true, and honorable, and right, and pure, and lovely, and admirable. Think about things that are excellent and worthy of praise. Keep putting into practice all you learned and received from me—everything you heard from me and saw me doing. Then the God of peace will be with you."

The best way to keep garbage out is to let God in. To think of the whatever is true, and honorable, whatever is right, and pure, and lovely and admirable, the things that are excellent and worthy of praise. This isn't just about the power of positive thinking. This is about making room for the things of God in our minds, giving space for God to speak to us. Recently Dan and Diana were watching together the movie *Field of Dreams*. It's a story about heaven and baseball and a man who builds a baseball diamond in a cornfield. It's also a movie that demonstrates the eternal truth that when you have something important to say, you should have James Earl Jones say it. This man Ray hears thoughts in his head telling him to build this baseball field, and one of the thoughts is: if you build it, he will come. In that case, it was making a space for his father to come back from heaven and play ball with Ray. But the basic thought is true: if you build it, He will come. If you make space for holy things in your thoughts, God will fill it with joy.

One way we can do this is by memorizing Scripture. I've provided you with a memory verse this week, as with every week this year, having no idea if anyone has actually taken the time to memorize these verses, but the more we fill our mind with Scripture, the more we will have to fall back on in those moments when we need encouragement. Here are just a few thoughts from the Word:

Memory Verse ~ Zephaniah 3:17: "The LORD your God is with you, He is mighty to save. He will take great delight in you, He will quiet you with his love, He will rejoice over you with singing."

"Nothing is impossible with God." Luke 1:37

2 Corinthians 12:9 "My grace is sufficient for you, for My power is made perfect in weakness."

1 Samuel 16:7 "For the Lord does not see as mortals see; they look on the outward appearance, but the Lord looks on the heart."

When we decorate for Christmas, it creates a great joy in my heart. The day after Thanksgiving, we start a fire in the fireplace, turn on the Christmas music, and trim every blessed needle, every nook and cranny of our home. For once, our house is clean, neat, and tidy, and yes, the garbage is taken out; and there is light, and beauty, and the joy of the season.

What if we were to do the same with our thoughts? What if we were to take out the garbage, and make room for joy and light and love, for something beautiful this season? Perhaps if we did, we'd discover a bit of the joy to the world that God wants to give us this season; perhaps if we did, we wouldn't just say "peace on earth and goodwill to men," we'd experience it, even for a moment, in our hearts.

In the name of the Father, and of the Son, and of the Holy Spirit, Amen.

Week Fifty: A Man of Business
2 Timothy 2

Many people come to me in a day with, "now I know you're busy." Busyness, I would like to contend, is a problem for Christians; I'd even go so far as to call it a sin. Ebeneezer Scrooge, for example, is the epitome of busyness:

"At this festive season of the year, Mr. Scrooge," said the gentleman, taking up a pen, "it is more than usually desirable that we should make some slight provision for the Poor and destitute, who suffer greatly at the present time. Many thousands are in want of common necessaries; hundreds of thousands are in want of common comforts, sir."

"Are there no prisons?" asked Scrooge.

"Plenty of prisons," said the gentleman, laying down the pen again.

"And the Union workhouses?" demanded Scrooge. "Are they still in operation?"

"They are. Still," returned the gentleman, "I wish I could say they were not."

"The Treadmill and the Poor Law are in full vigor, then?" said Scrooge.

"Both very busy, sir."

"Oh! I was afraid, from what you said at first, that something had occurred to stop them in their useful course," said Scrooge. "I'm very glad to hear it."

"Under the impression that they scarcely furnish Christian cheer of mind or body to the multitude," returned the gentleman, "a few of us are endeavoring to raise a fund to buy the Poor some meat and drink and means of warmth. We choose this time, because it is a time, of all others, when Want is keenly felt, and Abundance rejoices. What shall I put you down for?"

"Nothing!" Scrooge replied.

"You wish to be anonymous?"

"I wish to be left alone," said Scrooge. "Since you ask me what I wish, gentlemen, that is my answer. I don't make merry myself at Christmas and I can't afford to make idle people merry. I help to support the establishments I have mentioned—they cost enough; and those who are badly off must go there."

"Many can't go there; and many would rather die."

"If they would rather die," said Scrooge, "they had better do it, and decrease the surplus population. Besides—excuse me—I don't know that."

"But you might know it," observed the gentleman.

"It's not my business," Scrooge returned. "It's enough for a man to understand his own business, and not to interfere with other people's. Mine occupies me constantly. Good afternoon, gentlemen!"

Charles Dickens reminds us that Scrooge always was a good man of business. Scrooge says, "My business occupies me constantly." And so, being too busy, he ignores the most important thing he can do with his day: helping others in need.

What is business, really, but busy-ness? What is business, if not taking up our schedules with work that makes us busy? Ultimately, I submit to you, busy-ness is sinful, because it distracts us from Jesus Christ. I am reminded of the story of Mary and Martha.

In Luke 10: "But Martha was distracted by the big dinner she was preparing. She came to Jesus and said, 'Lord, doesn't it seem unfair to you that my sister just sits here while I do all the work? Tell her to come and help me.' But the Lord said to her, 'My dear Martha, you are worried and upset over all these details! There is only one thing worth being concerned about. Mary has discovered it, and it will not be taken away from her.'"

Now, at Christmastime, which are you: Mary or Martha? Are you distracted by busy-ness? Or are you looking to the one thing that matters, sitting at the feet of Christ? I admit that this is a great struggle for me. My tendency is to live by what I heard described as the tyranny of the urgent. Whatever most needs to be accomplished—whether it be a sick parishioner or the sermon that needs to be preached on Sunday or the crying baby—that's what I take care of, and I don't tend to read a lot of books, or take time for exercise, or spend as much time in quiet reflection like I really need to do. That's why I'm so thankful that God forces me to sit down, once a week, and reflect on Scripture; to sit at the feet of Jesus.

Sitting at the feet of Jesus is paramount for preachers. Today, we contemplate Paul's pastoral letter to Timothy, who was the bishop of Ephesus. Ephesus was a notoriously sinful city, the home of the temple of Artemis, and the place where Paul got into a huge conflict with the silversmiths, and later fought with animals. It was a place where magical thinking and superstition reigned. So Timothy, as its bishop, had an uphill battle. Does that sound something like the world we are living in today, in which people are engaged in every kind of idol worship, and the silversmiths are in charge? Because of the uphill battle Timothy faces, it is of primary importance that Timothy keeps Christ, and nothing else, at the center of his life and worship.

Paul describes the life Timothy must live: 2 Tim 2:3-4: "Endure suffering along with me, as a good soldier of Christ Jesus. Soldiers don't get tied up in the affairs of civilian life, for then they cannot please the officer who enlisted them."

This fall I studied the law of armed conflict, and the distinction between a soldier and a civilian is central to that law. Once you are a soldier, your status as a person changes. You no longer stand for yourself, but as a representative or agent of the force that deployed you. Soldiers can be targeted; civilians can't. Thinking about this from a spiritual perspective, once you become a Christian, you are now a target of the enemy. Furthermore, one thing in the law of armed conflict that differentiates an army from a band of rebels is the degree of structure of the armed forces. In a military, you expect a command structure. That's what Paul says here as well; your job is to please the officer who enlisted you, in this case, Christ. For that reason, you cannot live as a civilian any longer. You must not be tied up in your own business. A soldier's time is not his own. You must instead, as a good soldier, face every day thinking about your mission; to glorify Christ in all you do.

The second example Paul uses is the example of the athlete. 2 Tim 2:5: "And athletes cannot win the prize unless they follow the rules." Athletes' time is not their own, and they are not in charge of the structure of the contest. Rather, they must train and prepare for the contest according to the rules of the game. Clocks and timing are very important in sports; there's always the game clock, the play clock, to be thinking about. You can't get distracted and forget your object; sometimes, you have to take the shot, make the snap, get the play going. The same way, we as Christians can't get distracted by other business; instead, we have to remain focused on the contest at hand.

The third example Paul uses is the example of the farmer. 2 Tim 2:6: "And hardworking farmers should be the first to enjoy the fruit of their labor."

Farmers understand time, because their work is determined by the seasons of the year. They understand patience and living based on God's time rather than their own. Farmers cannot get distracted by the business of life; when it's harvest time, they must hurry up and get the crops in immediately. However, farmers also get to enjoy the fruit of their labor. Here, Paul means that Timothy must enjoy Christ, and spend time himself deepening his relationship with Christ, so that he can enjoy the fruit of new life.

Paul gives the Gospel in one sentence: 2 Tim 2:8: "Always remember that Jesus Christ, a descendant of King David, was raised from the dead. This is the Good News I preach."

The resurrection of Jesus from the dead is the truth that all of Scripture leads up to. As God was working through the Torah, through the prophets and kings, all of it is crowned with the resurrection of Jesus Christ. We must never forget the joy and beauty of God's amazing message that love and life triumph over sin and death. This is the eternal truth we proclaim; none of the rest matters. In Timothy's community, a lot of people had been distracted by theological arguments. 2 Tim 2:14: "Remind everyone about these things, and command them in God's presence to stop fighting over words. Such arguments are useless, and they can ruin those who hear them."

It can be interesting to talk about whether, in Communion, Christ is spiritually or physically present; or the tension between predestination, free will, and foreknowledge; or how if God is really all-powerful, can he make a rock so big he himself can't lift it? I have my own answers to these and other questions, and you have yours, but that's not really important. We're fighting a war here. We're running a race. We're reaping a harvest. We can't afford to get distracted, to get too involved in theological arguments. It just becomes another form of busy-ness.

Instead, we must stay at the feet of Christ. We must preach Christ, we must proclaim Christ, we must worship Christ, we must imitate Christ.

Paul writes, 2 Timothy 2:19: "But God's truth stands firm like a foundation stone with this inscription: 'The Lord knows those who are his,' and 'All who belong to the Lord must turn away from evil.'

Paul also, in verse 11-13, quotes an early Christian hymn to remind Timothy that it's all about living in Christ. These words remind me of the simple hymn: "On Christ the solid Rock I stand, all other ground is sinking sand, all other ground is sinking sand."

My faith is not based on dogma or doctrine, on theology or philosophy; it's based only in the Gospel of Jesus Christ. That God came to us, God died for us, God rose for us in the person of Jesus of Nazareth. That's the truth that captivated me as a child, the one true, great story, the Word of God made flesh, and He is the reason for everything that I do. It's not Jesus plus political stance, or Jesus plus your view on homosexuality, or Jesus plus your denomination's statements. What saves us, what gives us hope, the truth worth living for and dying for is Jesus Christ alone.

New Testament scholar John Frederick writes, "For the weary soul struggling with depression, the single parent, the oppressed, the outsider, the forgotten, the lonely, the rejected, and all who carry the burdens of this sinful world, we do not first and foremost offer revisions of dogmas, or defenses of dogmas, or systems of theological facts consisting of an interconnected set of dogmas -- we offer them Jesus."

In this Christmas season, let us not be Scrooges, too worried about matters of business to see the human beings in our midst, too concerned with our busy schedules to make room for Christ, to sit at the feet of Jesus. Instead, today, let us take to heart the words of Timothy—not just the words of 2 Timothy, but also the words of another Tim; who said, quite simply, the same truth, the one at the heart of the Gospel, the truth we proclaim today: "God bless us, everyone." So may it be, and so may we proclaim this Christmas.

In the name of the Father, and of the Son, and of the Holy Spirit, Amen.

Week Fifty-one: Entertaining Angels
Hebrews 12

In my previous congregation, we had a kitchen installed shortly after I came. It was a beautiful kitchen, with new countertops, a high-speed dishwasher that cleaned the coffee cups in five minutes, and an amazing industrial coffee maker that never needed to be filled with water. But when it was installed, there was great resistance to one concept: putting labels on the cabinets. They were so beautiful, everyone said. Can't we put the labels on the inside of the cabinets? But we all recognized that would not really work. Because a church kitchen can never stay that pretty.

That's the thing with churches; they're communal places. When you put something down somewhere, it's liable to be gone when you go to look for it again. Especially if it's edible. Churches are places where things tend to move; where things tend to get broken; churches are places where nothing stays nice. Or at least, they should be. Because God calls us to show hospitality to others; to create places of community that serve those in need. The church is not really our home, it's God's home. And what God wants is to share His home with others.

Hebrews 13:1-2, "Keep on loving each other as brothers and sisters. Don't forget to show hospitality to strangers, for some who have done this have entertained angels without realizing it!"

The preacher of Hebrews calls us to love one another as brothers and sisters. That means that the church is an extended family, and our church building is to be a place of love for all. Have you ever asked what God wants to do with your home? Your personal, family home? When we decorate, design our kitchens, update our bathrooms, we don't necessarily think about what God wants. We think about what we want, what's comfortable, what's trendy—as though we were all going to be featured in *Better Homes and Gardens*. We don't tend to think about what's most hospitable to others, or what's most helpful to the community, or what best honors God. Yet Hebrews 13:2 says to show hospitality not to members of our church, not to members of our family, not to friends of the family or even acquaintances, but to strangers.

This is a very challenging proposition. But you may say to me, this is from a different time, when people had to travel long distances by foot or by camel, and they had to stop and rest. They depended on hospitality. It was a different world; there was less crime. This is also the Bible, God's Word, the sharp sword that cuts into our hearts; show hospitality to strangers, for some who have done this have entertained angels unawares. The preacher of Hebrews is recalling Genesis 18, when Abraham and Sarah entertained the three angels at the Oaks of Mamre, who brought them good news of the coming of Isaac. This preacher is saying that when we allow strangers into our homes, we could be entertaining God in disguise.

That also means that when we refuse to make room for the stranger, we could be refusing a place for God in our lives. After all, when the innkeepers of Bethlehem turned away a young couple on a busy night, they had no idea that they were denying hospitality to the Holy One himself. As for the notion that there was less crime in the ancient world, I think those of us who have read through Judges can recognize that the ancient world was not always a friendly place for travelers. For the early Christian audience of Hebrews, it was a particularly scary thing to welcome a stranger, for as Christians they were practicing an illegal religion, and you never know who could report you to the Roman authorities.

Another way in which we open our homes to Christ is through the way we treat families.

Hebrews 13:4, "Give honor to marriage, and remain faithful to one another in marriage. God will surely judge people who are immoral and those who commit adultery." Have you ever heard someone describe marriage as just a piece of paper? The Word of God calls us as Christians, whether we are married or not, to honor marriage rather than to dismiss it. Marriage has become counter-cultural these days, and fidelity to one person for life has become an outdated concept in the eyes of the world. However, God's design of marriage is a beautiful one, in which people give themselves entirely to one another for life in every way. It's the opposite of the appeasing of selfish lusts in sexuality, it's the giving over of oneself entirely to another person. And it's not easy. If you are married, part of giving your home to God's design is working on your marriage. And if you aren't married, it's honoring marriage and supporting others who are married, and it's also treating the members of your household and family with love and respect.

Hebrews 13:5-6, "Don't love money; be satisfied with what you have. For God has said, 'I will never fail you. I will never abandon you.' So, we can say with confidence, 'The Lord is my helper, so I will have no fear. What can mere people do to me?'"

When we think about our homes, if you are like me, you are thinking about money. About the plumbing that needs to be fixed, the bathroom you'd like to redo, the wallpaper or floors that "need" updating. Recently I went to a dinner at the home of one of Diana's classmates who was very excited to show off her renovations. Their home was very modern and beautiful, the kind of thing you can only do when your kids are old enough that they won't destroy it. We got home and our house felt kind of shabby and old-fashioned, the bathroom with its 1940s peach tile, the furnishings cobbled together from family donations and garage sales. "Be satisfied with what you have," the Bible says. When we think of our space as God's space, the beauty is important only insofar as our space is inviting to others. "Keeping up with the Joneses" in terms of our homes is really based in the love of money. And God doesn't want us to get caught up in money, loving it or worrying about it. So, we don't need to get caught up in keeping up with the Joneses or trying to get on HGTV. We don't have to worry about impressing anyone. What can mere mortals do to us anyway?

Summing up all these commands, what we are called to do as Christians is quite simply to treat others the way you would want to be treated. That's what making space for God in our homes looks like. This is the great calling to you and to me: to open our hearts and doors and lives to others, to show kindness and mercy to others the way God has shown kindness and mercy to us.

And I think it is a stronger call at this time of year. Recently, a homeless couple came by the church. They were here because, like many persons without a home, we allow them to use this church's address to receive mail, and he was looking for a state ID. As they were leaving, the woman began to look at the mitten tree where we are collecting warm clothes for those in need, and I allowed her to take a hat—she said she didn't have one. You know, among all the things I did that day, perhaps the most important was just being at the church so that someone in need could get a hat.

When we open our homes to others, when we open our hearts to others, it feels right. It feels like the best thing we can do with our time, our money, our homes. Especially at Christmastime. And why is that? Perhaps it's because God opened Himself to us. When God came down from heaven, and was born in a stable, making his bed in a feeding trough, He made Himself accessible to us. It was an act of divine hospitality. He made his home among mortals, and in so doing, he made earth just a little bit like heaven. The divine became man at Christmas, and so perhaps at Christmas, every man becomes just a little more divine. Open yourself to the divine. Open your home. Open the doors of your life this Christmas. May there always be room in the inn of your home, and the inn of your heart.

In the name of the Father, and of the Son, and of the Holy Spirit, Amen.

Week Fifty-two: Wrapped
Revelation 22

Are you ready for Christmas? When it comes to Christmas, I am a great procrastinator in one area: wrapping. I will be wrapping my last Christmas gifts sometime tomorrow afternoon. But I've heard it said that you never get ready for Christmas, it just arrives, and whatever has gotten done has gotten done.

If it's this hard to prepare for Christ when we have a date on the calendar to work with, how can we be prepared to meet him eternally, when we do not know the day or the hour?

This week we are reading Revelations as we complete the Year of the Bible. I'm myself a couple of weeks behind, but I'm in the December readings, which I think is pretty good for a person who had a baby in 2017. Revelations is the hardest book of the Bible for many people. I have trouble keeping track of—are we in seals or lampstands? How much of the earth is destroyed at this time? Who exactly are Gog and Magog?

Revelations is not, I believe, a book we can read looking to understand everything in it. Rather, the message of Revelations is very simple: God wins. Revelation was written at a time much like ours in one way: the church was not in charge. The church was being persecuted by the Roman authorities, and Revelation is the response: Rome will fall, Jesus will return, and God wins.

If you are ready to meet Jesus, this is good news. If you aren't ready, this is bad news. Because Jesus is coming, and although we are closer today than we ever have been, and the reestablishment of the State of Israel might mean that Christ's coming is close at hand, and I hope so, we do not know the day nor the hour, and it becomes idle to speculate. Our job is not to speculate. Our job is to be ready for Christ to come. And if we are ready, He will spare us from the pain of the destruction of the earth. That's what the Rapture teachings really have at their heart: the belief that Christ will spare the faithful from the pain of the end times. So we want Christ to come. We long for Him to come. We long for the age in which peace, and justice, and goodness are restored; when the lion will lie down with the lamb, and a little child will lead them. We long for God to win. Which is why the last words of the Bible are, Amen! Come Lord Jesus.

Revelation 22:17: The Spirit and the bride say, "Come." Let anyone who hears this say, "Come." Let anyone who is thirsty come. Let anyone who desires drink freely from the water of life.

Like all of Revelation, this verse is ambiguous, that is, it has two meanings. First, the Spirit and the bride say, Come. This is a call for Christ to come. The Spirit is, of course, the Holy Spirit, and the bride is the bride of Christ, the church, waiting for him as a bride waits for her groom on the wedding day. It is our deep desire, the cry of our hearts: Come, Lord Jesus!

We desire union with Christ. I speak to many people who want to be in heaven today, who are ready to go and meet Christ, who even long for death. It's a strange thing that for people with strong faith, death is a friend. If you have a deep faith, death is not a fearful proposition, because you trust that the One who loved you into life will love you in the great beyond. As Dumbledore said in Harry Potter, death is the last great adventure.

But the problem comes in for Christians when we are living so focused on death, or so focused on Christ's return, that we aren't seeing the present need. And that is why there is a second meaning to this verse. The other meaning is a call for those who are in need to come to us and know Christ. The Spirit and the bride say, come. Let anyone who hears this say, come, let anyone who desires drink freely from the water of life. Until the day we meet Christ, we are called to provide the water of life to all who are thirsty: to care for the needy in body and the needy in spirit, by offering them the love of Christ. We are called to invite others to greater life. Perhaps, over the holidays, you will have an opportunity to lovingly say to another person: come and drink freely from the water of life. Maybe by sharing your own faith journey; maybe by offering to pray with someone; maybe by simply offering a glass of water to a guest in your home.

Revelation 22:18-19: "And I solemnly declare to everyone who hears the words of prophecy written in this book: If anyone adds anything to what is written here, God will add to that person the plagues described in this book. And if anyone removes any of the words from this book of prophecy, God will remove that person's share in the tree of life and in the holy city that are described in this book."

As much of Revelation does, this passage contains strong language of God's condemnation. Which is the double-edged sword of Revelation: Revelation, like the Gospel, is meant to comfort the afflicted and afflict the comfortable. This verse is a reminder that we have to take the Word of God seriously, and not try to add to it or detract from it. The Word of God is enough on its own. We do not need any more holy books. I'm sure for those of us who have been reading the Bible all year, we can confidently say there is enough there, when you study it and take it to heart, to give you spiritual guidance in every way for life. There's nothing to add, and nothing to take away. If we read it, and follow what the Word of God says, we can be prepared for the trials and tribulations of this life, and we can be ready for the life to come. We can be ready to meet Jesus. Revelation 22:21: "He who is the faithful witness to all these things says, 'Yes, I am coming soon! 'Amen! Come, Lord Jesus!"

The world was not ready to receive Christ when he came to Bethlehem, but he came all the same. The great longing of the world was fulfilled that Christmas night. In the next few weeks, should Christ delay his return, we will be studying how the prophecy of the Old Testament is fulfilled. And we see that the great longings of God's people were fulfilled in Christ. All that longing you felt for Jesus, in the depths of the description of the Temple in Exodus, in the doom and gloom of Jeremiah, it was fulfilled when God came down to earth in a manger bed at Christmas. And if he came then, if he answered our longing on that day, we must have faith that he can, and he will do it again. It's hard to wait. It tests our faith that Christ's return has been delayed. But think of it this way: in God's time, two thousand years is just the blink of an eye. Perhaps he's waiting for you and me to offer the water of life to one more person, one last person who needs to know Christ before he comes. Let us trust that the one who came when we needed him most, will come again to make all things new. And let us join that great prayer of the church, Amen! Come Lord Jesus.

We come now to the final words of Scripture: Revelation 22:22: "May the grace of the Lord Jesus be with God's holy people."

God's final word is a word of grace. God's final word is the trusting prayer that even if we are not entirely ready, God is ready to forgive and to cover us with His love. I invite you to watch "Christmas with the Kranks". This is a heartwarming little film about a couple who decides to skip Christmas and go on a cruise instead. The entire subdivision gets really angry, unrealistically angry, that this couple is not decorating, not giving to charities, not participating in the Christmas project. Then the couple learns their daughter is coming home with her fiancé, and she's expecting a big family Christmas. The entire neighborhood ends up helping the Kranks to get ready, and the story turns into one of grace and redemption, not only for the Kranks, but for the neighbors who turn out to be good people after all.

The last word is always one of grace. So let mine be one of grace. That reading the Bible in a year is a good project, but if you didn't finish, or if you didn't finish on time, God takes your halfway and accepts it. If you aren't ready for Christmas, if your presents don't even get wrapped, your loved ones will accept them, nonetheless. And so it is with God. Even our imperfect offerings are received as perfect in His sight, for the sake of His Son. That's the beauty of the story of Jesus: God didn't meet us in palaces, or temples, or when everything was perfect and shiny and new. God met us in the dirt and the smells and the imperfect welcome of the stable. We failed to make room for Christ, but Christ came in nonetheless, into our dirt and mess and clutter, to redeem it with His love. Let him come into your mess, and clutter, and dirt this Christmas; into your imperfect welcome; into your unwrapped gift. Let him come into your stable. Whether you think you are ready, or you are not, Christ is coming. Let him in.

Let him wrap our imperfect gifts with His grace.

In the name of the Father, and of the Son, and of the Holy Spirit, Amen.

In Gratitude

I give thanks to my husband, Dan, and my children, Diana, JP, and Charlie, who appear more than once within these pages, as they are the primary channels by which I learn of the power, grace, and love of God.

I would also like to think Kristen Reinhardt for her many hours of compiling and editing this manuscript, without which it would never have been completed, which work she did as a gift to me; and Keith Wissman and Cindy Eastman, for reading the manuscript and adding their comments. Finally, thank you David Russell Tullock, for the opportunity to work on this project.

To God alone be the glory.

Bible Reading Schedule

January	
1-Jan	Genesis 1-2
2-Jan	Genesis 3-5
3-Jan	Genesis 6-9
4-Jan	Genesis 10-11
January 5/6	Genesis 12-14
7-Jan	Genesis 15-17
8-Jan	Genesis 18-20
9-Jan	Genesis 21-24
10-Jan	Genesis 25-26
11-Jan	Genesis 27-31
January 12/13	Genesis 32-36
14-Jan	Genesis 37-40
15-Jan	Genesis 41-44
16-Jan	Genesis 45-47
17-Jan	Genesis 48-50
18-Jan	Exodus 1-2
January 19/20	Exodus 3-6
21-Jan	Exodus 7-10
22-Jan	Exodus 11-12
23-Jan	Exodus 13-15
24-Jan	Exodus 16-18
25-Jan	Exodus 19-20

January 26/27	Exodus 21-24
28-Jan	Exodus 25-27
29-Jan	Exodus 28-31
30-Jan	Exodus 32-34
31-Jan	Exodus 35-40
February	
1-Feb	Leviticus 1-3
February 2/3	Leviticus 4-7
4-Feb	Leviticus 8-10
5-Feb	Leviticus 11-15
6-Feb	Leviticus 16-17
7-Feb	Leviticus 18-20
8-Feb	Leviticus 21-23
February 9/10	Leviticus 24-27
11-Feb	Numbers 1-4
12-Feb	Numbers 5-8
13-Feb	Numbers 9-12
14-Feb	Numbers 13-16
15-Feb	Numbers 17-20
February 16/17	Numbers 21-25
18-Feb	Numbers 26-30
19-Feb	Numbers 31-33
20-Feb	Numbers 34-36

21-Feb	Deuteronomy 1-4		19-Mar	1 Samuel 13-15
22-Feb	Deuteronomy 5-7		20-Mar	1 Samuel 16-19
23-Feb	Deuteronomy 8-11		21-Mar	1 Samuel 20-23
24-Feb	Deuteronomy 12-16		22-Mar	1 Samuel 24-26
25-Feb	Deuteronomy 17-20		March 23/24	1 Samuel 27-31
26-Feb	Deuteronomy 21-26		25-Mar	2 Samuel 1-4
27-Feb	Deuteronomy 27-30		26-Mar	2 Samuel 5-7
28-Feb	Deuteronomy 31-34		27-Mar	2 Samuel 8-10
March			28-Mar	2 Samuel 11-14
1-Mar	Joshua 1-5		29-Mar	2 Samuel 15-18
March 2/3	Joshua 6-8		30-Mar	2 Samuel 19-20
4-Mar	Joshua 9-12		31-Mar	2 Samuel 21-24
5-Mar	Joshua 13-17		**April**	
6-Mar	Joshua 18-21		1-Apr	1 Kings 1-4
7-Mar	Joshua 22-24		2-Apr	1 Kings 5-8
8-Mar	Judges 1-5		3-Apr	1 Kings 9-11
March 9/10	Judges 6-8		4-Apr	1 Kings 12-16
11-Mar	Judges 9-12		5-Apr	1 Kings 17-19
12-Mar	Judges 13-16		April 6/7	1 Kings 20-22
13-Mar	Judges 17-21		8-Apr	2 Kings 1-3
14-Mar	Ruth 1-4		9-Apr	2 Kings 4-8
15-Mar	1 Samuel 1-3		10-Apr	2 Kings 9-12
March 16/17	1 Samuel 4-8		11-Apr	2 Kings 13-17
18-Mar	1 Samuel 9-12		12-Apr	2 Kings 18-21

April 13/14	2 Kings 22-25	10-May	Nehemiah 11-13
15-Apr	1 Chronicles 1-9	May 11/12	Esther 1-2
16-Apr	1 Chronicles 10-16	13-May	Esther 3-4
17-Apr	1 Chronicles 17-21	14-May	Esther 5-7
18-Apr	1 Chronicles 22-27	15-May	Esther 8-10
19-Apr	1 Chronicles 28-29	16-May	Job 1-3
April 20/21	2 Chronicles 1-5	17-May	Job 4-7
22-Apr	2 Chronicles 6-9	May 18/19	Job 8-10
23-Apr	2 Chronicles 10-12	20-May	Job 11-14
24-Apr	2 Chronicles 13-16	21-May	Job 15-17
25-Apr	2 Chronicles 17-20	22-May	Job 18-19
26-Apr	2 Chronicles 21-25	23-May	Job 20-21
April 27/28	2 Chronicles 26-28	24-May	Job 22-24
29-Apr	2 Chronicles 29-32	May 25/26	Job 25-28
30-Apr	2 Chronicles 33-36	27-May	Job 29-31
May		28-May	Job 32-34
1-May	Ezra 1-3	29-May	Job 35-37
2-May	Ezra 4-6	30-May	Job 38-39
3-May	Ezra 7-8	31-May	Job 40-42
May 4/5	Ezra 9-10	**June**	
6-May	Nehemiah 1-2	June 1/2	Psalms 1-6
7-May	Nehemiah 3-4	3-Jun	Psalms 7-12
8-May	Nehemiah 5-7	4-Jun	Psalms 13-18
9-May	Nehemiah 8-10	5-Jun	Psalms 19-24

6-Jun	Psalms 25-30
7-Jun	Psalms 31-36
June 8/9	Psalms 37-41
10-Jun	Psalms 42-49
11-Jun	Psalms 50-54
12-Jun	Psalms 55-59
13-Jun	Psalms 60-66
14-Jun	Psalms 67-72
June 15/16	Psalms 73-77
17-Jun	Psalms 78-83
18-Jun	Psalms 84-89
19-Jun	Psalms 90-97
20-Jun	Psalms 98-103
21-Jun	Psalms 104-106
June 22/23	Psalms 107-110
24-Jun	Psalms 111-118
25-Jun	Psalm 119
26-Jun	Psalms 120-127
27-Jun	Psalms 128-134
28-Jun	Psalms 135-139
29-Jun	Psalms 140-145
30-Jun	Psalms 146-150

July

1-Jul	Proverbs 1-4
2-Jul	Proverbs 5-9
3-Jul	Proverbs 10-13
4-Jul	Proverbs 14-17
5-Jul	Proverbs 18-21
July 6/7	Proverbs 22-24
8-Jul	Proverbs 25-29
9-Jul	Proverbs 30-31
10-Jul	Ecclesiastes 1-6
11-Jul	Ecclesiastes 7-12
12-Jul	Song of Songs 1-8
July 13/14	Isaiah 1-4
15-Jul	Isaiah 5-7
16-Jul	Isaiah 8-12
17-Jul	Isaiah 13-16
18-Jul	Isaiah 17-20
19-Jul	Isaiah 21-23
July 20/21	Isaiah 24-27
22-Jul	Isaiah 28-30
23-Jul	Isaiah 31-35
24-Jul	Isaiah 36-39
25-Jul	Isaiah 40-43
26-Jul	Isaiah 44-48
July 27/28	Isaiah 49-51
29-Jul	Isaiah 52-57
30-Jul	Isaiah 58-62

31-Jul	Isaiah 63-66	26-Aug	Ezekiel 40-43
August		27-Aug	Ezekiel 44-48
1-Aug	Jeremiah 1-6	28-Aug	Daniel 1-3
2-Aug	Jeremiah 7-10	29-Aug	Daniel 4-6
August 3/4	Jeremiah 11-15	30-Aug	Daniel 7-9
5-Aug	Jeremiah 16-20	31-Aug	Daniel 10-12
6-Aug	Jeremiah 21-25	**September**	
7-Aug	Jeremiah 26-29	1-Sep	Hosea 1-3
8-Aug	Jeremiah 30-33	2-Sep	Hosea 4-6
9-Aug	Jeremiah 34-36	3-Sep	Hosea 7-8
August 10/11	Jeremiah 37-39	4-Sep	Hosea 9-11
12-Aug	Jeremiah 40-45	5-Sep	Hosea 12-14
13-Aug	Jeremiah 46-52	6-Sep	Joel 1-3
14-Aug	Lamentations 1-5	September 7/8	Amos 1-2
15-Aug	Ezekiel 1-6	9-Sep	Amos 3-5
16-Aug	Ezekiel 7-11	10-Sep	Amos 6-7
August 17/18	Ezekiel 12-15	11-Sep	Amos 8-9
19-Aug	Ezekiel 16-19	12-Sep	Obadiah
20-Aug	Ezekiel 20-24	13-Sep	Jonah 1-4
21-Aug	Ezekiel 25-28	September 14/15	Micah 1-2
22-Aug	Ezekiel 29-32	16-Sep	Micah 3-5
23-Aug	Ezekiel 33-36	17-Sep	Micah 6-7
August 24/25	Ezekiel 37-39	18-Sep	Nahum 1-3
		19-Sep	Habakkuk 1-3

20-Sep	Zephaniah 1-3	16-Oct	Luke 1-2
September 21/22	Haggai 1-2	17-Oct	Luke 3-6
23-Sep	Zechariah 1-2	18-Oct	Luke 7-9
24-Sep	Zechariah 3-4	October 19/20	Luke 10-12
25-Sep	Zechariah 5-6	21-Oct	Luke 13-15
26-Sep	Zechariah 7-8	22-Oct	Luke 16-18
27-Sep	Zechariah 9-11	23-Oct	Luke 19-21
September 28/29	Zechariah 12-14	24-Oct	Luke 22-24
30-Sep	Malachi 1-4	25-Oct	John 1-2
October		October 26/27	John 3-5
1-Oct	Matthew 1-4	28-Oct	John 6-8
2-Oct	Matthew 5-7	29-Oct	John 9-12
3-Oct	Matthew 8-11	30-Oct	John 13-17
4-Oct	Matthew 12-15	31-Oct	John 18-21
October 5/6	Matthew 16-19	**November**	
7-Oct	Matthew 20-23	1-Nov	Acts 1-4
8-Oct	Matthew 24-25	November 2/3	Acts 5-7
9-Oct	Matthew 26-28	4-Nov	Acts 8-9
10-Oct	Mark 1-3	5-Nov	Acts 10-12
11-Oct	Mark 4-7	6-Nov	Acts 13-15
October 12/13	Mark 8-10	7-Nov	Acts 16-18
14-Oct	Mark 11-13	8-Nov	Acts 19-20
15-Oct	Mark 14-16	November 9/10	Acts 21-23

11-Nov	Acts 24-26	6-Dec	Titus 1-3
12-Nov	Acts 27-28	December 7/8	Philemon
13-Nov	Romans 1-3	9-Dec	Hebrews 1-2
14-Nov	Romans 4-5	10-Dec	Hebrews 3-4
15-Nov	Romans 6-8	11-Dec	Hebrews 5-7
November 16/17	Romans 9-11	12-Dec	Hebrews 8-10
18-Nov	Romans 12-16	13-Dec	Hebrews 11-13
19-Nov	1 Corinthians 1-6	December 14/15	James 1-5
20-Nov	1 Corinthians 7-10	16-Dec	1 Peter 1-5
21-Nov	1 Corinthians 11-14	17-Dec	2 Peter 1-3
22-Nov	1 Corinthians 15-16	18-Dec	1 John 1-5
November 23/24	2 Corinthians 1-5	19-Dec	2 John
25-Nov	2 Corinthians 6-9	20-Dec	3 John
26-Nov	2 Corinthians 10-13	December 21/22	Jude
27-Nov	Galatians 1-6	23-Dec	Revelation 1-3
28-Nov	Ephesians 1-6	24-Dec	Revelation 4-6
29-Nov	Philippians 1-4	25-Dec	Revelation 7-9
30-Nov	Colossians 1-4	26-Dec	Revelation 10-13
December		27-Dec	Revelation 14-16
1-Dec	1 Thessalonians 1-5	December 28/29	Revelation 17-19
2-Dec	2 Thessalonians 1-3	December 30/31	Revelation 20-22
3-Dec	1 Timothy 1-3		
4-Dec	1 Timothy 4-6		
5-Dec	2 Timothy 1-4		

CPSIA information can be obtained
at www.ICGtesting.com
Printed in the USA
BVHW061609021219
565404BV00013B/1712/P

9 781949 888706